A

SCRIPTURAL EXPOSITION

OF THE

BAPTIST CATECHISM

A

SCRIPTURAL EXPOSITION

OF THE

BAPTIST CATECHISM

BENJAMIN BEDDOME

SOLID GROUND CHRISTIAN BOOKS
Birmingham, Alabama USA

Solid Ground Christian Books
2090 Columbiana Rd, Suite 2000
Birmingham, AL 35216
205-443-0311
sgcb@charter.net
solid-ground-books.com

A SCRIPTURAL EXPOSITION OF THE BAPTIST CATECHISM
By Way of Question and Answer

Benjamin Beddome (1717-1795)

Solid Ground Classic Reprints

First printing of new edition January 2006

Taken from second edition corrected by W. Pine, Bristol, UK , 1776

Cover work by Borgo Design, Tuscaloosa, AL
Contact them at nelbrown@comcast.net

Cover image is of Bourton-on-the-Water where Beddome spent most of his ministerial life. Image is used by permission of Ric Ergenbright, whose outstanding work is seen at ricergenbright.com.

SPECIAL THANKS TO:

Dr. James Renihan for his suggestion to reprint this volume, for writing the Introduction, and especially for providing us with digital photographs of each page taken by him.

Dr. Michael Haykin for his enthusiastic support of this project, and for writing the Biographical Sketch of Beddome.

Mr. Frederick "Pete" Nuckols, my brother-in-law, who labored over every one of the digital images as he re-typed the entire document for SGCB. This was a labor of love indeed!

ISBN: 1-59925-052-7

A

SCRIPTURAL EXPOSITION

OF THE

BAPTIST CATECHISM

BY WAY OF

QUESTION and ANSWER

By BENJAMIN BEDDOME, M.A.

SECOND EDITION, corrected

Περί ὧν κατηχήθης. Luke i. 4.

Κοινωνείτω δὲ ὁ κατηχούμενος τὸν λόγον τῷ κατηχοῦντι ἐν πᾶσιν ἀγαθοῖς. Gal. vi. 6.

BRISTOL

Printed by W. PINE, 1776

TABLE OF CONTENTS

Biographical Sketch of Beddome   i

Introduction to this New Edition   xi

The Author's Preface   xv

Introductory Questions 1 – 6   1

Questions on *What We Are to Believe*   13

Questions on *What Duty God Requires*   87

Textual Index   198

BENJAMIN BEDDOME (1717-1795)

OF BOURTON-ON-THE-WATER

A GODLY BACKGROUND

John Beddome (1674-1757), the father of the subject of this biographical sketch, was the Baptist minister of Alcester Baptist Church, Warwickshire, at the time of his son's birth. John Beddome had come to this church in 1697 from the Baptist congregation that met in Horselydown, Southwark, London, where the pastor was the renowned Benjamin Keach (1640-1704), one of the seventeenth-century fathers of the Calvinistic Baptist denomination.

In an important move, the Alcester church took on Bernard Foskett (1685-1758) as co-pastor to the elder Beddome in 1711. Foskett would later became the first principal of Bristol Baptist Academy, the oldest Baptist seminary in the world and in the eighteenth century a force for much spiritual blessing among the Calvinistic Baptists. The younger Beddome would study at this seminary in the 1730s.

In 1714 John Beddome married Rachel Brandon, a wealthy heiress and a descendant of Charles Brandon, the first Duke of Suffolk and brother-in-law to Henry VIII. Benjamin, the first of five children to survive infancy, was born three years later. When Beddome was seven years of age, his father left the Midlands to accept a call to pastor the Pithay Church, Bristol. At the time there were two Calvinistic Baptist congregations in the city: Broadmead, where John Beddome's life-long friend Bernard Foskett had become pastor in 1720, and the larger Pithay Church, which contained 500 or so members in the early 1720s. Possibly acting on the advice of Foskett, the Pithay church approached the elder Beddome about assuming the pastorate. His acceptance in 1724 necessitated the removal of his family to Bristol in the summer of that year.

CONVERSION

Although he regularly sat under his father's preaching in the Pithay as he was growing up, Benjamin showed little interest in the things of Christ, and understandably his parents were deeply concerned about his state. In fact, not until he was twenty years of age did God's Word strike home to his heart, and his parents see the fruit of many years of prayer for their son's conversion.

On August 7, 1737, a visiting preacher to the Pithay by the name of Ware spoke on Luke 15:7 ['I tell you that in the same way there will be more rejoicing in heaven over one sinner who repents than over ninety-nine righteous persons who do not need to repent," KJV]. So deeply was Beddome affected by the sermon that for some time afterwards he would be in tears while his father preached, and he would hide himself in one of the galleries so that his weeping would not be widely observed.

CALLED TO THE MINISTRY

Soon after his conversion Beddome was led to consider pastoral ministry. He spent a couple of years in theological training under the tutelage of Bernard Foskett. Then, in 1739, he moved to London to continue his studies at the Fund Academy in Tenter Alley, Moorfields, where a John Eames (d.1744) was the theological tutor.

It was during this sojourn in London that Beddome became a member of Prescot Street Baptist Church in October, 1739. Early the following year the London church took steps to formally recognize God's hand on Benjamin's life for pastoral ministry and to set him apart for that work.

REVIVAL AT BOURTON-ON-THE-WATER

Beddome visited Bourton-on-the-Water, Gloucestershire, in the spring of 1740. Here he would minister in this picturesque village, dubbed by some "the Venice of the Cotswolds," till his death fifty-two years later. The origins of the church that he pastored lay in the halcyon days of Calvinistic Baptist advance during the period of the Commonwealth, when England was ruled by that quintessential Puritan, Oliver Cromwell (1598-1658). But in the days immediately before Beddome's coming the church was not in a flourishing state.

From 1740 to 1743 Beddome laboured with great success in the Bourton church. Significant for the shape of his future ministry was a local revival that took place under his ministry in the early months of 1741. Around forty individuals were converted, including John Collett Ryland (1723-1791), a leading Baptist minister in the latter half of the eighteenth century now chiefly remembered for a stinging rebuke he gave to young William Carey (1761-1834).

It may well have been this taste of revival that made Beddome a cordial friend to those who were involved in the evangelical revivals of the mid-eighteenth century, men like George Whitefield and the Mohegan Indian preacher Samson Occom (1723-1792), and that gave him an ongoing hunger to read of revival throughout British society on both sides of the Atlantic. Within a year of the Bourton awakening, for instance, Beddome had purchased a copy of Jonathan Edwards' *The Distinguishing Marks of a Work of the Spirit of God* (1741), which would have given him a marvellous foundation for thinking about and labouring for revival.

In July, 1743, the Bourton church extended an invitation to Beddome to become what they called their "teaching elder." Readily acceding to their request, he was ordained on September 23 of that year.

EARLY YEARS OF MINISTRY

The early years of Benjamin Beddome's ministry at Bourton-on-the-Water saw great numerical growth in the membership of the church. Between 1740 and 1750 the church membership more than doubled. By 1751 it stood at 180. Describing the state of the church members in 1750, Beddome could thus declare: "my labours have been, and are still, in a measure, blest unto them, above a hundred having been added since my first coming amongst them."

A Gloucestershire local historian, Derrick Holmes, has noted that the success of Beddome's ministry during his first ten years at Bourton is probably due to a number of factors. There were a number of good men active as deacons and in the leadership of the church during this period, including Beddome's father-in-law, Richard Boswell. Then, Beddome had developed the ability to preach in a manner fully comprehensible to his village congregation. Robert Hall, Jr. (1764-1831), himself no mean preacher, noted that as a speaker Beddome was "universally admired for the piety and unction of his sentiments, the felicity of his arrangements [of sermons], and the purity, force, and simplicity of his language."

CATECHIZING

Also Beddome was thoroughly convinced that vital Christianity was a matter of both heart and head. And like others in the Reformed tradition of which his denomination was a part, Beddome found the method of catechizing helpful in matching head knowledge to heart-felt faith. In fact, when Beddome's obituary was written in 1795, it was observed that "one considerable instrument" of his success at Bourton during the 1740s had been his use of catechetical instruction.

During the early years of his ministry Beddome used Benjamin Keach's *The Baptist Catechism* extensively, but clearly felt that the questions and answers of this catechism needed to be supplemented by further material. So he composed what was printed in 1752 as *A Scriptural Exposition of the Baptist Catechism by Way of Question and Answer*, which basically reproduced the wording and substance of the catechism drawn up by Keach, but added various sub-questions and answers to each of the main questions. It is this catechism that is reproduced below.

The *Scriptural Exposition* proved to be fairly popular. There were two editions during Beddome's lifetime, the second of which was widely used at the Bristol Baptist Academy, the sole British Baptist seminary for much of the eighteenth century. In the nineteenth century it was reprinted once in the British Isles and twice in the United States, the last printing being in 1849.

NUMBERS IN THE CHURCH

During the 1750s and the first half of the 1760s the numerical growth of the church began to slow. In 1751 the total number of members stood at 180. Between 1752 and 1754 none were added to the church and fifteen members were lost through death. In 1755, though, there were twenty-two individuals who came into the membership of the church by baptism. Another year which saw a large accession to the church was 1764, when twenty-eight new members were added. But a good number must have died since the mid-1750s, for in that year the membership stood at 183.

The next thirty years of Beddome's ministry, though, actually saw decline in the church membership. Between

1765 and 1795, 53 new members were added by conversion and baptism. But in this same period 105 of the members died, 12 were dismissed to other Baptist works and 2 were excluded. Thus, by 1795, the year that Beddome died, the church had 123 on the membership roll, sixty less than in 1764.

It is quite clear from letters that Beddome wrote on behalf of the church to the local Baptist association during the last three decades of his ministry that he lamented this lack of growth. The size of the congregation maintained its own, probably around five or six hundred, to the end of his life, but that vital step of believer's baptism leading to full church membership was taken by far fewer in the final three decades of his ministry than in the first two and a half.

A prayer written by Beddome in the church's 1786 letter to the local association well expresses his concern: "Come from the 4 winds O Breath & breathe upon these slain that they may live. Awake O Northwind & come thou South, blow upon our Garden that the Spices may flow out."

Nevertheless, there is no hint that Beddome ever thought of abandoning his post.

EARTHLY TRIALS

These decades were also fraught with earthly trials. In 1762 he wrestled with what a fellow Baptist pastor, Daniel Turner (1710-1798), termed "a nervous disorder, attended with spiritual darkness and distress." Three years later his eldest son, John, died at the age of fifteen. A second son, Benjamin, died in 1778 of what Rippon calls "a putrid fever." It is notable that the very day on which the younger Benjamin died, his father, little suspecting the news he would receive the next morning, wrote the following hymn to be sung at the close of the morning service that day.

My times of sorrow, and of joy,
Great God, are in thy hand;
My choicest comforts come from Thee,
And go at thy command.

If thou should'st take them all away,
Yet would I not repine;
Before they were possess'd by me,
They were entirely thine.

Nor would I drop a murmuring word,
Tho' the whole world were gone,
But seek enduring happiness
In Thee, and Thee alone.

What is the world with all it's store?
'Tis but a bitter-sweet;
When I attempt to pluck the rose
A pricking thorn I meet.

Here perfect bliss can ne'er be found,
The honey's mix'd with gall;
Midst changing scenes and dying friends,
Be thou my all in all.

Six years later a third son, Foskett, drowned in the Thames at Deptford. His dear wife had died earlier that year.

From the mid-1770s on he began to suffer from gout and experience tremendous difficulty in walking. Eventually it got to the point that he had to be carried to the church, and he would preach to his congregation seated. Despite his physical infirmities, though, Beddome simply refused to give up preaching.

At the heart of this refusal lay a deeply-held conviction about the vital importance of preaching. What historian Michael Walker has said of the nineteenth-century British Baptist community is equally true of Beddome and many of his fellow Calvinistic Baptists in the eighteenth century: they regarded the pulpit as "a place of nurture, of fire and light, from which words gave wings to the religious apsirations of the hearers, bringing them...to the gates of heaven."

BEDDOME'S HYMNS

At the time of Beddome's death in 1795, almost his sole publication was his *Scriptural Exposition.* In the years that followed, though, a good number of his sermons were published, as was a volume of 830 hymns. It is noteworthy that close to one hundred of these hymns were still appearing in hymnals at the end of the nineteenth century, though today, only a handful are still being sung. Robert Hall, Jr. spoke for many of his fellow Baptists when he said of Beddome's gifts as a writer of hymns: "Mr. Beddome was on many accounts an extraordinary person. ...Though he spent the principal part of a long life in a village retirement, he was eminent for his colloquial powers...as a religious poet, his excellence has long been known and acknowledged in dissenting congregations."

Beddome did not write his hymns with the intention of ever getting them published. He was in the habit of preparing a hymn to be sung at the close of the morning worship service, which would pick up the theme of his sermon, a practice that prompted Horton Davies to describe Beddome as an "indefatigable sermon summarizer in verse." However, he did allow thirteen of his hymns to be published in a hymnal edited by fellow Baptists John Ash (1724-1779) and Caleb Evans (1737-1791) in 1769, *A Collection of Hymns Adapted to Public Worship.* Twenty or so years later, thirty-six of them appeared in the first edition of John Rippon's *A Selection of Hymns from the Best Authors* (1787). It was more than twenty years after his death that Robert Hall, Jr. supervised the publication of the entire collection of 822 hymns and 8 doxologies.

A CONCLUDING WORD

Beddome's ministry was very much a ministry between the times—those times of Baptist advance in the seventeenth century and those of revival in the final couple of decades of the eighteenth century. Nevertheless, his life and ministry are an eloquent example of the truth of those concluding lines in George Eliot's *Middlemarch*: "That things are not so ill with you and me as they might have been, is half owing to the number who lived faithfully a hidden life, and rest in unvisited tombs."

Dr. Michael A.G. Haykin
Toronto Baptist Theological Seminary

FURTHER READING

Anonymous, "Memoir" in Sermons printed from the manuscripts of the late Rev. Benjamin Beddome (London: William Ball, 1835), ix-xxviii.

Thomas Brooks, Pictures of the Past: The History of the Baptist Church, Bourton-on-the-Water (London: Judd & Glass, 1861).

Kenneth Dix, "Thy Will Be Done": A Study in the Life of Benjamin Beddome", The Bulletin of the Strict Baptist Historical Society, 9 (1972) [this article occupies the bulk of the Bulletin and is lacking pagination].

Robert Hall, "Recommendatory Preface to a Volume of Hymns" in The Works of the Rev. Robert Hall, A.M. (New York: Harper & Brothers, 1852), II, 456-457.

G. Hester, "Baptist Worthies—Benjamin Beddome", The Baptist Magazine, 57 (1865), 441-446.

Derrick Holmes, "The Early Years (1655-1740) of Bourton-on-the-Water Dissenters who later constituted the Baptist Church, with special reference to the Ministry of the Reverend Benjamin Beddome A.M. 1740-1795" (Unpublished Certificate in Education Dissertation, St Paul's College, Cheltenham, 1969).

John Rippon: "Rev. Benjamin Beddome, A.M. Bourton-on-the-Water, Gloucesteshire", Baptist Annual Register, 2 (1794-1797), 314-326.

Introduction to this New Edition

At the 1693 London General Assembly of Particular Baptist churches of England and Wales the following was among the matters decided: *'That a Catechism be drawn up, containing the substance of the Christian religion, for the instruction of children and servants, and that brother William Collins be desired to draw it up.'* Collins, a pastor of the Petty France church in London, seems to have quickly completed his task for by 1695 the fifth edition of *A Brief Instruction in the Principles of Christian Religion: Agreeable to the Confession of Faith, put forth by the Elders and Brethren of many Congregations of Christians, (baptized upon Profession of their Faith) in London and the Country; owning the Doctrine of Personal Election, and Final Perseverance* had been published.[1]

On the title page, this *'Advertisement to the reader'* is found:

> Having a desire to shew our near Agreement with many other Christians, of whom we have great Esteem; we some Years since put forth a Confession of our Faith, almost in all Points the same with the *Assembly*, and *Savoy*, which was subscribed by the Elders and Messengers of many Churches baptized

---

[1] Since the 1695 edition was the *'fifth,'* it is obvious that earlier editions had been published. I have not, however, been able to find any bibliographic evidence for them beyond this mention. It is also important to note that this Catechism is sometimes popularly known as *Keach's Catechism.* The reason for this is unclear, though it is probable that Benjamin Keach played some part, perhaps in revising the Catechism done by Collins. Certainly, Keach's name was more recognizable than his colleague in London. When one compares later editions of the Catechism, minor differences—perhaps revisions—are evident. Beddome makes no mention of the name of an author.

on profession of their Faith; and do now put forth a short Account of *Christian Principles*, for the Instruction of our Families, in most things agreeing with the *Shorter Catechism* of the *Assembly*. And this we were the rather induced to, because we have commonly made use of that *Catechism* in our Families: And the Difference being not much, it will be more easily committed to Memory.

In 1677, the Baptist churches published a Confession demonstrating their commitment to Reformed theology based on the great confessions of the Presbyterians and Congregationalists. This allowed them to assert their close agreement with their fellow dissenting and persecuted brethren. Now in response to the request of the General Assembly, Collins published (anonymously) a catechism employing the same methodology. The well-known and highly esteemed *Westminster Shorter Catechism* served as the familiar basis for the Baptist work.

In his *Preface*, Benjamin Beddome indicates that similar circumstances led to the production of his *Exposition*. A perceived need, combined with appeals from many others based on their high esteem for his wisdom and abilities moved Beddome to take up this work. He desired to help remedy at least two needs. On the one hand, there was the lack of an exposition suited to Baptist doctrine and polity. Many useful Paedobaptist works were readily available, but there was nothing to reflect specifically Baptist views. On the other hand, knowledge of the truth, and the godliness that attends it, were at low ebb in many of the Baptist churches. Beddome knew that if fathers were supplied with a concise resource to assist them in instructing their families in the truth, the cause of the gospel among the churches would be greatly strengthened. As you read through his *Exposition*, you will see just how successful he was. Beddome's tool is just as useful for the 21st century as it was for his own.

The *Baptist Catechism* is, as we have said, based on the familiar *Westminster Shorter Catechism*. Certainly there have been revisions, especially at the beginning and in the questions on the sacraments, but in the main the structure and contents are identical. Beginning with several foundational and introductory questions about God, Man and the Scriptures, the *Catechism* proceeds to question six "*What things are chiefly contained in the Holy Scriptures?,*" and the answer provides the structure for most of the rest of the document: "*The Holy Scriptures chiefly contain what man ought to believe concerning God, and what duty God requireth of man.*" Questions 7 through 43 tell us what we are to believe about God, and questions 44-114 describe the duty that God requires of man. In this way, the *Catechism* provides a very helpful and simple summary of these two great matters. The one who masters the content of each part will be a wise and practical Christian!

Beddome's *Exposition* is really very simple. His goal is to bring the reader to an understanding of the truth of each question and answer by means of thorough exposure to the Scriptures. As each question is presented, Beddome contemplates a wide variety of related issues, addressing each one by way of further question and answer, and supported by a wide range of references to the text of the Bible. In reality, his *Exposition* is more a simple summary of the teaching of the Word of God than anything else. The *Catechism,* as a document faithful to Scripture, is merely the vehicle by which the reader is presented with the abundant resources of the Holy Book. Beddome has collated a wide variety of texts in support of the doctrine presented in each question and answer.

While his exposition is simple, it is also profound. It is a distillation of the Word of Life. The reader will, over and over again, marvel and worship at the profundity of Christian Doctrine. Its beauty and majesty, its internal coherence, its heavenly nature are repeatedly evident throughout this work. Though the stated purpose of the *Exposition* is to assist those who are uninstructed, even those who are advanced in the faith will profit from meditation on its sublime themes. If we are to learn about the things of God, and our duty to him, how can we possibly think that these truths are anything but deep? Not everyone will agree with all of his citations. There are times when Beddome uses texts in ways that we might not—but these are few and far between. None of us would agree with every citation we find in any book. If you disagree with his use of a particular text, work hard to find another more suitable text to support the doctrine expounded. Whenever this book sends you back to the Scripture, give thanks to God for another useful benefit to your soul—and to others. You will rejoice as you traverse the broad expanse of the Bible with Benjamin Beddome as your guide. I am sure that you will be thrilled at how this book brings you to know Scripture better.

Fathers and Teachers who use this material will do well to emphasize two things—its structure, and the Scripture upon which it is based. This is really the genius of Beddome's work. After carefully working through all of his information, one is able to see that the system of doctrine so carefully unfolded in the *Catechism* is indeed the same as that found in the Word of God. In this way, as the learner grows in understanding of who God is, and what He requires of us, he will be convinced that he is indeed fulfilling the mandate of Scripture.

It really is a great pleasure to see this important work brought back into print. In Christian homes in England and America it has been of enormous usefulness. Our prayer is that it will again be recognized for its great profitability, and serve the cause of the same Lord Jesus loved by William Collins, Benjamin Keach, Benjamin Beddome, and the host of those who have loved our Savior before. May His Name be praised forever!

Dr. James Renihan
Institute for Reformed Baptist Studies
Escondido, California

THE

AUTHOR'S

PREFACE

The Paedobaptist churches having been long furnished with many useful and instructive expositions of their catechisms, and something of the same nature being greatly wanted amongst those of the Baptist persuasion; I was at length induced, by the pressing solicitations of many of my friends, to compose the following, in imitation of Mr. Matthew Henry's, which was published with great acceptance several years ago.

When we consider the melancholy state of those churches and families, where catechizing is entirely thrown aside, how much many of them have degenerated from the faith, and others from the practice of the gospel; little need to be said in vindication of this exercise to those, in whom a zeal for both still remains, and I hope will be ever increasing.

May the great God smile upon this faint attempt for his glory, and may that church especially, to which I stand related, accept it as a small acknowledgement of their many favors, and a token of the sincerest gratitude and affection from

> *Their willing, tho' unworthy servant in the gospel of our* Lord Jesus.

BENJAMIN BEDDOME

Bourton upon the Water,
FEB. 27, 1752.

A

SCRIPTURAL EXPOSITION

Question 1. Who is the first and chiefest Being?
Answer. God is the first and chiefest Being.

Is God the first of all beings? Yes. *'I am the first,'* Isaiah 44:6. Is he the first cause of all beings? Yes. *Of whom are all things,* 1 Corinthians 8:6. Are all other causes subordinate to the first cause? Yes. *O Assyrian, the rod of mine anger and the staff in their hands is mine indignation,* Isaiah 10:5. Is God the first in creation? Yes. *He spake and it was done,* Psalm 33:9. Is he the first in providence? Yes. *For in him we live, and move, and have our being,* Acts 17:28. Is he the first in government? Yes. *Thy throne is established of old,* Psalm 93:2. Is he the first in the world of grace? Yes. *All things are of God, who hath reconciled us to himself,* 2 Corinthians 5:18. Is he first in the displays of his love? Yes. *We love him because he first loved us,* 1 John 4:19. Can we be beforehand with God? No. *Who hath first given unto him, and it shall be recompensed unto him again,* Romans 11:35.

Should God then be first in our thoughts? Yes. *When I awake I am still with thee*, Psalm 139:18. And first in our esteem? Yes. *Whom have I in heaven but thee*, Psalm 73:25. Should we first give ourselves unto him? Yes. *But first gave their own-selves unto the Lord*, 2 Corinthians 8:5. And should he have the first fruits? Yes. *My soul desireth the first ripe fruits*, Micah 7:1.

Is God the chiefest being? Yes. *Who is like unto thee, O Lord?* Exodus 15:11. Is he above all pretenders? Yes. *He is a great King, above all gods*, Psalm 95:3. Is he chief in heaven? Yes. *Who in heaven can be compared unto the Lord*, Psalm 89:6. Is he chief on earth? Yes. *Thou Lord art high above all the earth.* Palm 97:9. Is he only one of the chief? No. *For he is the Most High*, Psalm 56:2. And will he ever retain his pre-eminency? Yes. *For he is the Most High for evermore*, Psalm 92:8.

Should God then be chiefly loved? Yes. *Thou shalt love the Lord thy God with all thine heart*, Luke 10:27. And chiefly feared? Yes. *Rather fear him who is able to destroy both soul and body in hell*, Matthew 10:28. And are those happy who are interested in him? Yes. *Happy is that people whose God is the Lord*, Psalm 144:15

Q 2. Ought every one to believe there is a God?
A. Everyone ought to believe there is a God; and it is their great sin and folly who do not.

Are there any that disbelieve the being of a God? Yes. They say in their *heart there is no God*, Psalm 14:1. And does this open a door to all immoralities? Yes. *They are corrupt, they have done abominable works*, ibid. Is the being of God then a necessary article of the Christian faith? Yes. *He that cometh to God must believe that he is*, Hebrews 11:6. And is it the foundation of all practical religion? Yes. *How shall they call on him in whom they have not believed*, Romans 10:14. Is God's existence a comfortable thought to the saint? Yes. *Verily, there is a God that judgeth in the earth*, Psalm 58:11. And an awful thought to the wicked? Yes. *Fear ye not me saith the Lord*, Jeremiah 5:22.

Did the first man believe there was a God? Yes. For he *heard his voice and was afraid*, Genesis 3:10. Did other men in the first ages of the world believe it? Yes. For they called *upon his name*, Genesis 4:26. Have not all nations believed it? Yes. *They knew God, though they glorified him not as God*, Romans 1:21. Do holy spirits above believe there is a God? Yes. *They rest not day and night, saying, 'holy, holy, holy, Lord God Almighty,'* Revelation 4:8. Do the devils believe it? Yes. *The devils believe and tremble*, James 2:19. Do we do well then to believe it? Yes. *Thou believest that there is one God, thou dost well*, ibid.

Is ignorance of God a folly? Yes. *My people are foolish, they have not known me*, Jeremiah 4:22. And a shame? Yes. *Some have not the knowledge of God, I speak it to your shame*, 1 Corinthians 15:34. And a sin? Yes. *They have perverted their way, and forgotten the Lord their God*, Jeremiah 3:21. Is it an inexcusable sin? Yes. *They are without excuse*, Romans 1:20. And a destructive sin? Yes. *He shall be driven from light unto darkness, this is the place of him that knoweth not God*, Job 18:21.

Q 3. How may we know there is a God?

A. The light of nature in man and the works of God plainly declare there is a God; but his word and Spirit only do it fully and effectually for the salvation of sinners.

Is there a light in man? Yes. *The Spirit of man is the candle of the Lord*, Proverbs 20:27. Is this light obscured by the fall? Yes. *Having the understanding darkened*, Ephesians 4:18. Is it sufficient then to teach us any thing? Yes. *Doth not even nature itself teach you*, 1 Corinthians 11:14. Doth it instruct us in the being of a God? Yes. *Because that which may be known of God is manifest in them, for God hath shewed it to them*, Romans 1:19. But is that knowledge which it affords attended with many doubts and uncertainties? Yes. Thus the *Athenians* are said *to seek the Lord, if haply they might feel after him and find him*, Acts 17:27. And are there many things concerning God, which it neither doth nor can discover? Yes. *For the natural man receiveth not the things of the Spirit of God, because they are spiritually discerned*, 1 Corinthians 2:14.

May God be known by his works of creation? Yes. *For the invisible things of him from the creation are clearly seen, being understood by the things that are made*, Romans 1:20. Do the heavenly bodies prove the Being of a God? Yes. *The heavens declare the glory of God*, Psalm 19:1. And our own bodies? Yes. *I am fearfully and wonderfully made*, Psalm 139:14. And may we learn this from every creature? Yes. *Ask now the beasts, and they shall teach thee*, Job 12:7.

Is God known by his works of providence? Yes. *Who knoweth not in all these, that the hand of the Lord hath wrought this,* Job 12:9. Is he known by his works of terror? Yes. *The Lord is known by the judgment he executeth,* Psalm 9:16. And by his works of mercy? Yes. *He hath not left himself without witness in that he did good,* Acts 14:17. Is God known by the accomplishment of prophecies? Yes. *I am God, and there is none else declaring the end from the beginning,* Isaiah 46:9,10. Do miracles declare the existence of God? Yes. *This is the finger of God,* Exodus 8:10. But have men by these means attained to a sufficient knowledge of God? No. For *the world by wisdom knew not God,* 1 Corinthians 1:21.

Is God known by his word? Yes. For *it is profitable for doctrine,* 2 Timothy 3:16. Were men in the dark without the word? Yes. For it is a *light that shineth in a dark place,* 2 Peter 1:19. Should we then have recourse to the word for the knowledge of God? Yes. *To the law and to the testimony,* Isaiah 8:20. And are those to blame who indulge unscriptural notions concerning him? Yes. *Intruding into the things they have not seen,* Colossians 2:18.

Is the word sufficient to afford us the saving knowledge of God? No. For some *hear and understand not,* Isaiah 6:9. Is this then only to be attained by the Spirit? Yes. For *the letter killeth, but the Spirit giveth life,* 2 Corinthians 3:6. And is the Spirit promised for this purpose to all that sincerely ask it? Yes. *Your heavenly Father shall give the holy Spirit to them that ask him,* Luke 11:13.

Q 4. What is the word of God?
A. The Holy Scriptures of the Old and New Testament are the word of God, and the only certain rule of faith and obedience.

Are the Scriptures of the Old and New Testament the word of God? Yes. *All Scripture is given by inspiration of God,* 2 Timothy 3:16. Might not this revelation be imposed upon us by evil spirits? No. *For if Satan be divided against himself how shall his kingdom stand,* Matthew 12:26. Might it not be intruded upon us by wicked and designing men? No. *Do men gather grapes off thorns, or figs off thistles,* Matthew 7:16. Might it not be the fruit of pious craft in good men? No. *I say the truth in Christ, I lie not,* Romans 9:1.

Were holy men then moved to speak what they did? Yes. *Holy men of God spake as they were moved by the Holy Ghost,* 2 Peter 1:21. Were they moved to write what they spoke? Yes. *The Lord said, 'write the vision, make it plain upon tables',* Habakkuk 2:2. Does God own what men have thus written as his? Yes. *I have written to him the great things of my law,* Hosea 8:12. Were the writings of the Old Testament inspired? Yes. *For the prophecy came not of old time by the will of man,* 2 Peter 1:21. And may the same be affirmed of those of the new? Yes. *The revelation of Jesus Christ, which God sent by his angel to his servant John,* Revelation 1:1.

Were the penmen of the sacred Scriptures satisfied of their own inspiration? Yes. *The God of Israel said, the rock of Israel spake to me,* 2 Samuel 23:3. But might they not be deceived? No. *We have not followed cunningly devised fables,* 2 Peter 1:16. Did they write what they knew? Yes. *That which we have seen and heard declare we unto you,* 1 John 1:3. And what others who were their contemporaries knew? Yes. *For this thing was not done in a corner,* Acts 26:26. Did they take any undue methods to gain credit? No. *My speech and my preaching was not with enticing words of man's wisdom,* 1 Corinthians 2:4. Had they no secular aims? No. *For wherefore we both labor and suffer reproach,* 1 Timothy 4:10.

Were the divine writings confirmed by miracles? Yes. *God also bearing them witness with signs and wonders,* Hebrews 2:4. Did the gospel gain early credit? Yes. *Their sound went out into all the earth, and their words unto the ends of the world,* Romans 10:18. Have many confirmed and sealed it with their blood? Yes. *They were slain for the word of God,* Revelation 6:9. And hath it a witness to the heart of every true Christian? Yes. For *he that believeth hath the witness in himself,* 1 John 5:10.

Is the word of God a rule? Yes. It is *a lamp to our feet, and a light to our path,* Psalm 119:105. Do we need such a rule? Yes. For *we all like sheep have gone astray,* Isaiah 53:6. Is the word of God a sufficient rule? Yes. *The law of the Lord is perfect,* Psalm 19:7. Is it a plain rule? Yes. *The words of his mouth are all plain to him that understandeth,* Proverbs 8:8,9. Is it an extensive rule? Yes. *The commandment is exceeding broad,* Psalm 119:96. Is it an abiding rule? Yes. *The word of the Lord endureth for ever,* 1 Peter 1:23. And is it the only rule? Yes. *For if any man shall add to these things, God will add to him the plagues written in this book,* Revelation 22:18.

Are not unwritten traditions a rule? No. *Ye have made the commandment of God of none effect by your traditions,* Matthew 15:6. Is the Authority of the church a rule? No. For our *faith should not stand in the wisdom of men,* 1 Corinthians 2:5. Are the sentiments of great men a rule? No. *The prophet and the priest have erred*, Isaiah 28:7. Is the light of nature a sufficient rule? No. For it is said of those that were guided by it, *The way of peace they have not known*, Romans 3:17. Is the light within a certain rule? No. *The way of a man is not in himself*, Jeremiah 10:23. Are not the examples of many a rule? No. *Thou shalt not follow a multitude to do evil*, Exodus 23:2. Are not the examples of the good a sufficient rule? No. We must *be followers of* them *only as they are of Christ*, 1 Corinthians 11:1. May not what angels say be depended upon as a certain rule? No. *Though an angel from heaven preach any other gospel to you, let him be accursed*, Galatians 1:8. Or a voice from heaven? No. For *we have a more sure word of prophecy*, 2 Peter 1:19.

Is it necessary then that the Scriptures should be translated? Yes. For *if I come unto you speaking with tongues, what shall I profit you*, 1 Corinthians 14:6. Should we readily receive and embrace them? Yes. *They received the word with all readiness of mind*, Acts 17:11. And should we make them our rule? Yes. *Let us walk by the same rule*, Philippians 3:16.

Q 5. May all men make use of the Holy Scriptures?
A. All men are not only permitted, but commanded and exhorted to read, hear, and understand the Holy Scriptures.

Should the Scriptures be read? Yes. *Seek ye out of the book of the Lord and read*, Isaiah 34:16. Should we read them to ourselves? Yes. *The eunuch returning and sitting in his chariot read Esaisas the prophet*, Acts 8:28. Should we read them to others? Yes. *Thou shalt read this law before all Israel*,

Deuteronomy 31:11. And should we cause others to read them? Yes. *Cause that this epistle be read also in the church of the Laodiceans,* Colossians 4:16.

Should the Scriptures be read attentively? Yes. *What is written in the law, how readest thou,* Luke 10:26. Should they be read diligently? Yes. *Search the Scriptures,* John 5:39. Should we persevere in reading of them? Yes. *He shall read therein all the days of his life,* Deuteronomy 17:19. Should we do this particularly on the Sabbath-day? Yes. For they were *read every Sabbath-day,* Acts 13:27. And should we prefer them to all other writings? Yes. *For what is the chaff to the wheat,* Jeremiah 23:28.

Was reading the Scriptures an ancient custom? Yes. *For Moses of old time was read in the synagogues,* Acts 15:21. Was it the practice of Christ? Yes. *As his custom was, he went up into the synagogue and stood up for to read,* Luke 4:16. Is the matter contained in the Scripture worthy of our attention? Yes. *In them ye think ye have eternal life,* John 5:39. Does the neglect hereof lead to ignorance and error? Yes. *Ye do err, not knowing the Scriptures,* Matthew 22:29. And is a blessing promised to the diligent performance of it? Yes. *Blessed is he that readeth, and they that hear the words of this prophecy,* Revelation 1:3.

Should the word of God be heard? Yes. *He that is of God, heareth God's word,* John 8:47. Should all God's word be heard? Yes. *We are here present to hear all things that are commanded thee of God,* Acts 10:33. Should we hear God's word with holy reverence? Yes. *The Lord looketh to him that trembleth at his word,* Isaiah 66:2. And with delight? Yes. *The common people heard Christ gladly*, Mark 12:37. And in faith? Yes. *Believe his prophets, so shall you prosper*, 2 Chronicles 20:20. And with meekness? Yes. *With meekness receive the ingrafted word*, James 1:21. And with settled resolutions of obedience? Yes. We must *observe to do*, Deuteronomy 32:46. Should we desire to hear the word again and again? Yes. *They besought that these words might be preached to them the next Sabbath-day*, Acts 13:42.

Do all thus hear the word? No. Some *put the word of God from* them, Acts 13:46. Is this an instance of their folly? Yes. *Lo, they have rejected the word of the Lord, and what wisdom is in them*, Jeremiah 8:9. And will it be to their prejudice? Yes. *Whoso despiseth the word shall be destroyed*, Proverbs 13:13.

Should we be careful to understand the Scriptures? Yes. *Whosoever readeth let him understand*, Matthew 24:15. Are there some things in Scripture difficult to be understood? Yes. *In which are some things hard to be understood*, 2 Peter 3:16. Does this call for diligence? Yes. *If thou seekest her as silver, and searchest for her as for hid treasure, then shalt thou understand the fear of the Lord*, Proverbs 2:4,5. And for prayer? Yes. *Open thou mine eyes that I may behold wondrous things, out of thy law*, Psalm 119:18.

Have all an understanding of the Scriptures? No. Some are *without understanding*, Romans 1:31. Is this owing in some to willful negligence? Yes. *They know not, neither will they understand*, Psalm 82:5. And in others to judicial blindness? Yes. *Make the heart of this people fat, and their ears heavy, and shut their eyes, lest they see with their eyes, and hear with their ears, and understand*, Isaiah 6:10. Is the Scripture like to be wrested by those that do not understand it? Yes. *Which they that are unlearned and unstable wrest,* 2 Peter 3:16. And is the case of such deplorable? Yes. *If our gospel be hid, it is hid to them that are lost,* 2 Corinthians 4:3.

Are we not only permitted but commanded and exhorted to make use of the Holy Scriptures? Yes. *Let him that hath an ear to hear, hear what the Spirit saith unto the churches,* Revelation 2:29. Is this the duty of all? Yes. *Give ear O heavens and I will speak, and hear O earth the words of my mouth,* Deuteronomy 32:1. Is it the duty of ministers as well as people? Yes. *Give attendance unto reading,* 1 Timothy 4:13. And of young as well as old? Yes. *From a child thou hast known the holy Scriptures,* 2 Timothy 3:15.

Q 6. What things are chiefly contained in the Holy Scriptures?
A. The Holy Scriptures chiefly contain what man ought to believe concerning God, and what duty God requireth of man.

Are men by nature ignorant of God? Yes. *'And they know not me,' saith the Lord,* Jeremiah 9:3. And of duty? Yes. *They know not to do right,* Amos 3:10. Does ignorance lead to sin? Yes. *I did it ignorantly,* 1 Timothy 1:13. But is it an excuse for sin? No. *Pour out thy fury upon the Heathen, that know thee not,* Jeremiah 10:25. And are the Scriptures appointed for our instruction? Yes. *The entrance of thy words giveth light,* Psalm 119:130.

Are all things profitable and necessary contained in the Holy Scriptures? Yes. *They are able to make us wise unto salvation,* 2 Timothy 3:15. Do the Scriptures teach plainly? Yes. *We use great plainness of speech,* 2 Corinthians 3:12. Do they teach powerfully? Yes. *For the word of God is quick and powerful,* Hebrews 4:12.   Do they teach sinners? Yes. *O ye simple understand wisdom, O ye fools be of an understanding heart,* Proverbs 8:5. Do they teach saints? Yes. *I speak as to wise men,* 1 Corinthians 10:15.

Is it necessary that men should know God?   Yes. *Acquaint now thyself with him,* Job 22:21.   Does grace and peace come to the soul in this way? Yes. *Grace and peace be multiplied to you through the knowledge of God,* 2 Peter 1:2.   And is ignorance of God a great reproach? Yes. *The ox knoweth his owner, and the ass his master's crib, but Israel doth not know,* Isaiah 1:3.   Can men know God aright without his word? No. *Remember that at that time ye were without God in the world,* Ephesians 2:12. May all that may be known of God without the word, be better known in and by the word? Yes. *Through faith we understand that the worlds were framed by the word of God,* Hebrews 11:3.   Should we therefore have recourse to the Scriptures for the knowledge of God? Yes. *For if we receive his words, then shall we find the knowledge of God,* Proverbs 2:1,5.

Is obedience to God a due debt?   Yes. *Therefore brethren we are debtors,* Romans 8:12.   Is it a debt due from all?   Yes. *The commandment of God is made known unto all nations for the obedience of faith,* Romans 16:26.   But especially from the saints?   Yes. *They which have believed in God, must be careful to maintain good works,* Titus 3:8. And are the duties of obedience best learned from the divine word?   Yes. For the *Scripture is profitable for instruction in righteousness,* 2 Timothy 3:16.

Do the Scriptures teach us to obey without hesitating?   Yes. *Immediately I conferred not with flesh and blood,* Galatians 1:16.   And without reserve or exception? Yes. *Ye shall not turn aside to the right hand or the left,* Deuteronomy 5:32. And without reluctance? Yes. *I delight to do they will, O my God,* Psalm 40:8. And without assuming? Yes. *When ye have done all these things, say we are unprofitable servants,* Luke 17:10.   And without fainting? Yes. *Let us not be weary in well doing,* Galatians 6:9.   And will other methods be ineffectual for instruction where the written word fails? Yes. *If they hear not Moses and the prophets, neither will they be persuaded though one rose from the dead,* Luke 16:31.

Q 7. What is God?

A. God is a Spirit, infinite, eternal, and unchangeable in his being, wisdom, power, holiness, justice, goodness, and truth.

Is God a Spirit? Yes. *God is a Spirit,* John 4:24. Is he incorporeal and invisible? Yes. *Ye have not heard his voice at any time, nor seen his shape,* John 5:37. Is he a perfect spirit? Yes. *He is light, and in him is no darkness,* 1 John 1:5. Is he an active spirit? Yes. *My Father worketh hitherto,* John 5:17. Is he a self-sufficient and independent spirit? Yes. His name is *I am that I am,* Exodus 3:14. Is he an immortal spirit? Yes. *Who only hath immortality,* 1 Timothy 6:16. Is he above all other spirits? Yes. *He is the Father of spirits,* Hebrews 12:9.

Can we then form any adequate conception of the divine Being? No. *What likeness can you compare unto him,* Isaiah 40:18. Are the organs of sense improperly ascribed unto him? Yes. *Hast thou eyes of flesh, or seest thou as man seeth,* Job 10:4. Can he be gratified with carnal things? No. *I will take no bullock out of thy house, nor he goats out of thy fold,* Psalm 50:9. Should he be worshipped in a spiritual manner? Yes. *Whom I serve with my spirit,* Romans 1:9. May we expect spiritual blessings from him? Yes. *Who hath blessed us with all spiritual blessings,* Ephesians 1:3. And is he the only suitable portion for our spirits? Yes. *The Lord is my portion saith my soul,* Lamentations 3:24.

Is God infinite and omnipresent? Yes. *Whither shall I flee from thy presence,* Psalm 139:7. Is he in heaven? Yes. *If I ascend up into heaven thou art there,* Psalm 139:8. But is he confined to heaven? No. *The heaven of heavens cannot contain thee,* 2 Chronicles 2:6. Is his essence diffused through the whole universe of things? Yes. *He is above all and through all and in all,* Ephesians 4:6. Is he then near to every one of us? Yes. *He is not far from every one of us,* Acts 17:27. Should this be a support to the saints under their burden? Yes. *Be strong for I am with you, saith the Lord,* Haggai 2:4. And a spur to holy actions? Yes. *Walk before me, and be thou perfect,* Genesis 17:1.

Is God eternal? Yes. *The eternal God is thy refuge,* Deuteronomy 33:27. Was he from everlasting? Yes. *Art thou not from everlasting, O Lord my God,* Habakkuk 1:12. Will he be to everlasting? Yes. *From everlasting to everlasting, thou art God,* Psalm 90:2. Is he only eternal? Yes. *I am the first, and I am the last, and besides me there is no God,* Isaiah 44:6. Should he therefore be feared? Yes. *He is the living God, and an everlasting King, at his wrath, the earth shall tremble,* Jeremiah 10:10. And be trusted? Yes. *Trust ye in the Lord for ever, for in the Lord Jehovah is everlasting strength,* Isaiah 26:4. Is this perfection of God humbling to man? Yes.

Where wast thou when I laid the foundation of the earth, Job 38:4.   And glorious to himself?   Yes. *Now to the King eternal, immortal, invisible, be honor and glory for ever and ever,* 1 Timothy 1:17.

Is God unchangeable?   Yes.   *Thou art the same,* Psalm 102:27.   Is he absolutely so?   Yes.   *With him there is no shadow of turning,* James 1:17.   Is he so in his own nature and perfections?   Yes.   *I am the Lord, I change not,* Malachi 3:6.   And in his will? Yes.   *His counsel shall stand,* Isaiah 46:10.   And in his love?   Yes.   *I have loved thee with an everlasting love,* Jeremiah 31:3.   And in his special favors? Yes.   *The gifts and calling of God are without repentance,* Romans 11:29.   May not God change through some unforeseen accident?   No.   For *known unto God are all his works from the beginning of the world,* Acts 15:18.   Or through want of power to effect what he has determined?   No.   For he is *the Almighty God,* Genesis 17:1.   Is it well for us that God is unchangeable?   Yes.   *Therefore the Sons of Jacob are not consumed,* Malachi 3:6.

Is God wise?   Yes.   *Counsel is mine and sound wisdom,* Proverbs 8:14.   Doth his wisdom appear in creation and providence?   Yes.   *He is wonderful in counsel, and excellent in working,* Isaiah 28:29.   And in redemption?   Yes.   *Herein he hath abounded towards us in all wisdom and prudence,* Ephesians 1:8.   Is he infinitely wise?   Yes.   *His understanding is infinite,* Psalm 147:5.   Is he originally so?   Yes. *With whom took he counsel, and who instructed him,* Isaiah 40:14.   Is he perfectly so?   Yes.   *The foolishness of God is wiser than man,* 1 Corinthians 1:25.   And is he incomprehensibly so?   Yes.   *O the depth of the riches, both of the wisdom and knowledge of God,* Romans 11:33.   Is there any counterworking his wisdom? No. *There is no wisdom nor understanding nor counsel against the Lord*, Proverbs 21:30. Doth all wisdom proceed from him? Yes. *He giveth wisdom unto the wise*, Daniel 2:21. Should we therefore seek it at his hands? Yes. *If any man lack wisdom, let him ask it of God*, James 1:5.

Is God powerful? Yes. *Power belongeth unto God*, Psalm 62:11. Can he do all things? Yes. *Is there any thing too hard for me*, Jeremiah 32:27. Can he do all things with the greatest ease? Yes. *He taketh up the isles as a very little thing*, Isaiah 40:15. Can he do all things in the most perfect manner? Yes. *He is a rock, his work is perfect*, Deuteronomy 32:4. Is God's power necessary to give a sanction to his laws? Yes. *There is one Lawgiver, who is both able to save and destroy*, James 4:12. Is it irresistible? Yes. *None can stay his hand*, Daniel 4:35. Is it subject to decay? No. *The Lord's hand is not shortened, that it cannot save*, Isaiah 59:1. Does it extend to evil spirits and wicked men? Yes. *The deceiver and deceived are his*, Job 12:16. Is it then a great folly to sin against such a God? Yes. *Do we provoke the Lord to jealousy, are we stronger than he*, 1 Corinthians 10:22.

Is God holy? Yes. He is *the holy one of Israel*, Isaiah 41:21. Is he supremely holy? Yes. *There is none holy as the Lord*, 1 Samuel 2:2. Does the holiness of God particularly appear in the work of redemption? Yes. *Zion shall be redeemed with judgment and her converts with righteousness*, Isaiah 1:27. Have the Heathen by the light of nature acknowledged the holiness of God? Yes. *I know that the spirit of the holy Gods is in thee*, Daniel 4:9. And do spirits above make it the matter of their praise? Yes. *They continually say, Holy, holy, holy, Lord God Almighty,* Revelation 4:8. And should we imitate them herein? Yes. *Bless his holy name,* Psalm 103:1.

Is God just? Yes. *The Lord is righteous,* Psalm 129:4. Is he absolutely and perfectly so? Yes. *Is there any unrighteousness with God, God forbid,* Romans 9:14. Is he just in inflicting temporal judgments? Yes. *O Lord, righteousness belongeth unto thee, but unto us confusion of face,* Daniel 9:7. And eternal vengeance? Yes. *Is God unrighteous, who taketh vengeance?* Romans 3:5. Does the justice of god eminently appear in the undertaking and sufferings of Christ? Yes. *Whom God hath set forth to be a propitiation through faith in his blood to declare his righteousness,* Romans 3:25. Should we then acknowledge the justice of God? Yes. *Howbeit thou art just,* Nehemiah 9:33. And seek to avoid the direful effects of it? Yes. *Escape for thy life, lest thou be consumed,* Genesis 19:17.

Is God good? Yes. *Thou Lord art good,* Psalm 86:5. May his goodness excite our wonder? Yes. *How great is his goodness,* Zechariah 9:17. And should it excite our gratitude? Yes. *O give thanks unto the Lord for he is good,* Psalm 106:1. Is God universally good? Yes. *He is good to all,* Psalm 145:9. Is he good to sinners? Yes. *He sendeth rain on the just and on the unjust,* Matthew 5:45. Is he in an especial manner good to his own people? Yes. *That I may see the good of thy chosen,* Psalm 106:5. Doth God take the contempt of his goodness heinously? Yes. *Or despisest thou the riches of his goodness,* Romans 2:4.

Is God a God of truth? Yes. *These things saith he that is true,* Revelation 3:7. Is he true to his promises? Yes. *Thou wilt perform the truth to Jacob,* Micah 7:20. And to his threatenings? Yes. *But my words did not they take hold of your fathers,* Zechariah 1:6. And to Christ? Yes. *Once have I sworn by my holiness that I will not lie unto David,* Psalm 89:35. Is God unchangeable in his truth? Yes. *The truth of the Lord endureth for ever,* Psalm 117:2. Should we therefore believe God? Yes. We should judge *him faithful who hath promised,* Hebrews 11:11. And that rather than man? Yes. *Let God be true, but every man a liar,* Romans 3:4. But though we believe not, does God continue faithful? Yes. *For what if some did not believe? shall their unbelief make the faith of God without effect?* Romans 3:3.

Q 8. Are there more gods than one?
A. There is but one only, the living and true God.

Is God the living God? Yes. *He is the living God,* Daniel 6:26. Hath he life in himself? Yes. *The Father hath life in himself,* John 5:26. Doth he give life to others? Yes. *He quickeneth all things,* 1 Timothy 6:13. Should living men therefore seek to the living God? Yes. *Should not a people seek unto their God? For the living to the dead?* Isaiah 8:19.

Is God the true God? Yes. *This is the true God,* 1 John 5:20. Is he the only true God? Yes. *This is life eternal to know thee the only true God,* John 17:3. And are all other gods false gods? Yes. *They are vanity and the work of errors,* Jeremiah 10:15.

Is that God whom we serve, this only living and true God? Yes. *The Lord, he is the true God, he is the living God, and an everlasting King,* Jeremiah 10:10.

And is he but one? Yes. *Hear, O Israel, the Lord our God is one Lord*, Deuteronomy 6:4. Does God assume this prerogative to himself? Yes. *Is there a God besides me, yea, there is no God, I know not any*, Isaiah 44:8. And have his people always ascribed it to him? Yes. *Unto us there is but one God*, 1 Corinthians 8:6. But do not those who assert the deity of Christ destroy the unity of the godhead? No. For he says, *I and my Father are one*, John 10:30.

Are there many Gods in name? Yes. *There are gods many, and lords many*, 1 Corinthians 8:5. But are these gods by nature? No. *When ye knew not God, ye did service to them which by nature are no gods*, Galatians 4:8. Are they then to be reputed of? No. *We know that an idol is nothing in the world*, 1 Corinthians 8:4. Are those guilty of the greatest absurdity who worship them? Yes. *Those that make them are like unto them, and so is every one that trusteth in them*, Psalm 115:8. Do we well therefore not to imitate them? Yes. *Little children keep yourselves from idols*, 1 John 5:21.

Q 9. How many persons are there in the Godhead?
A. There are three persons in the Godhead, the Father, the Son, and the Holy Spirit; and these three are one God, the same in essence, equal in power and glory.

Is there a plurality in the godhead? Yes. *For God said, 'Let us make man,'* Genesis 1:26. Does the godhead consist of three persons? Yes. *There are three that bear record in heaven*, 1 John 5:7. Is the Father a distinct person from the Son and Spirit? Yes. *My Father which gave them me is greater than all*, John 10:29. Is the Son a distinct person from the Father and Spirit? Yes. *The Lord* (i.e., the Father) *said unto my Lord* (i.e, the Son) *sit thou at my right hand,* Psalm 110:1. And is the Spirit a distinct person, both from the Father and the Son? Yes. *The Comforter, which is the Holy Ghost, whom the Father will send in my name, he shall teach you all things,* John 14:26. Are these the same in essence, affection, and operation? Yes. *These three are one,* 1 John 5:7. May it with any propriety then be said, that there are three Gods? No. *For the Lord is one, and his name is one,* Zechariah 14:9.

Is the Son called God? Yes. *Who is over all God blessed for evermore,* Romans 9:5. Is the Spirit called God? Yes. *Why hath Satan filled thine heart to lie to the Holy Ghost, thou hast not lied unto man but unto God,* Acts 5:3,4. Is the Son called Jehovah? Yes. He is *the Lord* (Heb. Jehovah) *our righteousness,* Jeremiah 23:6. Is the Spirit called Jehovah? Yes. *They tempted the Lord* (Heb. Jehovah) Exodus 17:7, compared with Isaiah 63:10. *They vexed his Holy Spirit* – Is this name given to any but God? No. *The most high over all the earth, is he whose name alone is Jehovah,* Psalm 83:18.

Is the Son eternal as well as the Father? Yes. *Before Abraham was, I am,* John 8:58. Is the Spirit eternal? Yes. *He is called the eternal Spirit,* Hebrews 9:14. Is the Son omnipresent? Yes. *Where two or three are gathered together in my name there am I,* Matthew 18:20. Is the Spirit so too? Yes. *Whither shall I go from thy Spirit,* Psalm 139:7. Is the Son omniscient? Yes. *Thou knowest all things,* John 21:17. And is the Spirit so? Yes. *He searcheth all things,* 1 Corinthians 2:10. Is the work of creation ascribed to the Son? Yes. *All things were made by him,* John 1:3. Is it also ascribed to the Spirit? Yes. *The Spirit of God hath made me*, Job 33:4. And is creation a work peculiar to God? Yes. *He that built all things is God*, Hebrews 3:4.

Is the Father the object of prayer? Yes. *Pray to thy Father which is in secret*, Matthew 6:6. Is the Son also the object of prayer? Yes. *Lord Jesus receive my spirit*, Acts 7:59. And the Spirit? Yes. *Grace and peace be unto you from the seven spirits which are before the throne,*[2] Revelation 1:4. Are we baptized in the name of all the three persons in the Trinity? Yes. *Baptizing them in the name of the Father, and the Son, and of the Holy Ghost*, Matthew 28:19. And is religious worship a prerogative of deity? Yes. *Worship God*, Revelation 19:10; 22:9.

Are divine blessings derived from all three persons in the godhead? Yes. *The grace of the Lord Jesus Christ, and the love of God, and the communion of the Holy Ghost, be with you all*, 2 Corinthians 13:14. Have each of these their distinct province in the affair of man's salvation? Yes. *Through him we both have access by one Spirit unto the Father*, Ephesians 2:18. Is the unity in the godhead a motive to unity among the saints? Yes. *That they all may be one as thou Father art in me and I in thee, that they also may be one in us*, John 17:21. Should we hold fast this doctrine? Yes. *Hold fast the form of sound words*, 2 Timothy 1:13.

---

[2] i.e., The one holy and eternal Spirit, who is so called either in allusion to the seven churches, or to show forth the variety and perfection of his gifts and graces. Daniel 9:19 seems to be an instance of prayer put up to all three persons.

Q 10. What are the decrees of God?

A. The decrees of God are his eternal purpose according to the counsel of his will, whereby, for his own glory, he hath fore-ordained whatsoever comes to pass.

Hath God pre-determined all future events? Yes. *He worketh all things according to the counsel of his own will,* Ephesians 1:11. Doth nothing then come by chance? No. *The lot is cast into the lap, but the whole disposal thereof is of the Lord,* Proverbs 16:33. Do God's decrees extend to the conduct of good men? Yes. *They are created unto good works, which God hath before ordained that they should walk in them,* Ephesians 2:10. And to their salvation? Yes. *They are vessels of mercy, which he hath afore prepared to glory,* Romans 9:23. Do God's decrees extend to the conduct of wicked men? Yes. *Him being delivered by the determinate counsel of God, ye by wicked hands have crucified and slain,* Acts 2:23. And to their destruction? Yes. *Who were of old ordained to their condemnation,* Jude ver. 4. Is it lawful for men to cavil at God's decrees? No. *Who art thou that repliest against God? Hath not the potter power over the clay, of the same lump, to make one vessel to honor, and another unto dishonor?* Romans 9:20.

Are God's decrees sovereign and free? Yes. They are *according to the good pleasure of his will,* Ephesians 1:6. Are they eternal? Yes. *For we are chosen in Christ before the foundation of the world,* Ephesians 1:4. Are they infinitely wise? Yes. We read of *the manifold wisdom of God according to his eternal purpose,* Ephesians 3:10,11. Are they most holy? Yes. *Thy councils of old are faithfulness and truth,* Isaiah 25:1. Are they impenetrable and unsearchable? Yes. *Who hath known the mind of the Lord,* Romans 11:34. Are they absolute and unchangeable? Yes. *He is of one mind and who can turn him,* Job 23:13. Are they calculated for his own glory? Yes. *He hath made all things for himself,* Proverbs 16:4.

Are all God's decrees accomplished? No. He declares *from ancient times the things that are not yet done,* Isaiah 46:10. But will they be all accomplished? Yes. *Surely as I have thought, so shall it come to pass,* Isaiah 14:24. And will any thing come to pass that God hath not decreed? No. For *who is he that saith, and it cometh to pass when the Lord commanded it not,* Lamentations 3:37.

Should we be curious to know the divine decrees? No. For *secret things belong to God,* Deuteronomy 29:29. Are God's precepts then, and not his decrees, the rule of our conduct? Yes. *Things which are revealed belong unto us and to our children,* Deuteronomy 29:29.

Q 11. How doth God execute his decrees?
A. God executeth his decrees in the works of creation and providence.

Doth God execute his own decrees? Yes. *My counsel shall stand, and I will do all my pleasure,* Isaiah 46:10. Doth God execute his decrees in the works of creation? Yes. *For thy pleasure they are and were created,* Revelation 4:11. Was creation the first external work wherein God began to execute his decrees? Yes. *In the beginning God created the heavens and the earth,* Genesis 1:1. Doth God also execute his decrees in the works of providence? Yes. *He doth according to his will in the armies of heaven, and among the inhabitants of the earth,* Daniel 4:35.

Doth God make use of good angels for the execution of his decrees? Yes. *They do his commandments,* Psalm 103:20. And of evil angels? Yes. *I will be a lying spirit in the mouth of all the prophets, and he said, go forth and do so,* 1 Kings 22:22. And of men? Yes. *That saith of Cyrus, he is my shepherd, and shall perform all my pleasure,* Isaiah 44:28. And of inferior creatures? Yes. *I will hiss, for the fly that is in the uttermost parts of the rivers of Egypt,* Isaiah 7:18. But does God sometimes work without instruments? Yes. *Mine own arm brought salvation,* Isaiah 63:5.

Are God's works inextricable? Yes. *For no man can find out the work that God makes from the beginning to the end,* Ecclesiastes 3:11. Can they be amended? No. *Whatsoever God doth – nothing can be put to it, nor any thing taken from it,* Ecclesiastes 3:14. Ought they to be studied? Yes. They are *sought out of them that have pleasure therein,* Psalm 111:2. And should we learn of God first to determine, and then to do? Yes. *Thou shalt also decree a thing, and it shall be established unto thee,* Job 22:28.

Q 12. What is the work of creation?
A. The work of creation is God's making all things of nothing, by the word of his power, in the space of six days, and all very good.

Did God create the world? Yes. *Thou Lord in the beginning hast laid the foundation of the earth, and the heavens are the works of thine hands,* Hebrews 1:10. And all things in it? Yes. *God made the world and all things therein,* Acts 17:24. Did he create the soul of man? Yes. *Who formeth the spirit of man within him,* Zechariah 12:1. And the body of man? Yes. *In thy book were all my members written,* Psalm

139:16. Did he create the highest angels? Yes. *By him were all things created, whether they be thrones,* etc. Colossian 1:16. And the meanest insects? Yes. *God made every thing that creepeth upon the earth after his kind,* Genesis 1:25. And what omnipotence wrought, did omniscience approve? Yes. *God saw every thing that he had made and behold it was very good,* Genesis 1:31.

Did God need any assistance in his work? No. *Who hath prevented me, that I should repay him,* Job 41:11. Did he make all things out of nothing? Yes. For *the things which are seen were not made of the things that do appear,* Hebrews 11:3. And by his word? Yes. *He said let there be light and there was light,* Genesis 1:3. And in six days? Yes. *In six days the Lord made heaven and earth,* Exodus 20:11. Did he appoint every creature its proper station and use? Yes. *Let there be lights in the firmament, and let them be for signs and for seasons, for days and for years,* Genesis 1:14. Does God go on to create? No. *On the seventh day God rested from all his works,* Genesis 2:2.

Q 13. How did God create man?
A. God created man, male and female, after his own image, in knowledge, righteousness, and holiness, with dominion over the creatures.

Were there any men before Adam? No. He was *the first man,* 1 Corinthians 15:45. Are all men then derived from Adam? Yes. *He hath made of one blood all nations of men,* Acts 17:26. And did Adam himself derive his being from God? Yes. *Who was the Son of God,* Luke 3:38.

Did God create man male and female? Yes. *Male and female, created he them,* Genesis 5:2. Was there a difference in the manner of their creation? Yes. *For the man is not of the woman, but the woman of the man,* 1 Corinthians 11:8. And in the order of their creation? Yes. *For Adam was first formed, and then Eve,* 1 Timothy 2:13. And in the end of their creation? Yes. *For the man was not created for the woman, but the woman for the man,* 1 Corinthians 11:9.

Was man made after the image of God? Yes. *God created man after his own image,* Genesis 1:27. Did that image consist in knowledge? Yes. For we are *renewed in knowledge after the image of him that created us,* Colossians 3:10. And in righteousness and holiness? Yes. For the *new man after God, is created in righteousness and true holiness,* Ephesians 4:24. And in authority and government? Yes. For *thou hast put all things under his feet,* Psalm 8:6. Was this state of man a very glorious one? Yes. *Thou hast crowned him with glory and honor,* Psalm 8:5. But was it an abiding one? No. For *man being in honor abideth not,* Psalm 49:12.

Q 14. What are God's works of providence?
A. God's works of providence are his most holy, wise, and powerful preserving and governing all his creatures, and all their actions.

Is God's providence universal? Yes. *His kingdom ruleth over all,* Psalm 103:19. Does it extend to all worlds? Yes. *Whatsoever the Lord pleased that did he in heaven and in earth,* Psalm 135:6. And to all creatures? Yes. *He upholdeth all things by the word of his power,* Hebrews 1:3. Does it extend to inanimate creatures? Yes. *He binds the sweet* influences of the Pleiades, and looses the bands of Orion, Job 38:31. And to the animal creation? Yes. The stork knoweth her appointed times, Jeremiah 8:7. Does it order all events relative to particular persons? Yes. Man's days are determined, the number of his months are with God, Job 14:5. And to kingdoms and societies of men? Yes. He changeth the times and the seasons, he removeth kings and setteth up kings, Daniel 2:21. Doth God exercise a special providence over some places? Yes. Thus Canaan was a land that God cared for, Deuteronomy 11:12. And over some persons? Yes. He is the Saviour of all men, but especially of them that believe, 1 Timothy 4:10. Is it a desirable thing to be interested in God's special providence? Yes. Remember me, O Lord, with the favor which thou bearest to thy people, Psalm 106:4.

Doth God's providence extend to all actions? Yes. A man's heart deviseth his way, but God directeth his steps, Proverbs 16:9. Doth it extend to all natural actions? Yes. In him we live and move, Acts 17:28. And to all fortuitous actions? Yes. Thus a certain man drew a bow at a venture and smote the King of Israel between the joints of the harness, 1 Kings 22:34. And to all good actions? Yes. The steps of a good man are ordered by the Lord, Psalm 37:23. And to evil actions? Yes. It was not you that sent me hither but God, Genesis 45:8. And can God bring good out of evil? Yes. You thought evil against me, but God meant it unto good, Genesis 50:20. Are God's providences mysterious? Yes. His judgments are a great deep, Psalm 36:6. But are they harmonious? Yes. They work together, Romans 8:28.

Is preservation an act of providence? Yes. *Which holdeth our soul in life*, Psalm 66:9. Did God preserve us in our infant state? Yes. *Thou art my God from my mother's belly*, Psalm 22:10. And will he preserve us in declining years? Yes. *To hoary hairs will I carry*, Isaiah 46:4. Doth he give us food? Yes. *He filleth our hearts with food and gladness*, Acts 14:17. And rest? Yes. *He giveth his beloved sleep*, Psalm 127:2. Doth he preserve us from threatening dangers? Yes. *He keepeth all our bones*, Psalm 34:20. And endow us with wisdom for our several trades? Yes. Bezaleel and Aholiab were *filled with the Spirit of God in all manner of workmanship*, Exodus 35:31. Does God's care extend to the meanest creatures? Yes. Not a sparrow *shall fall to the ground without your Father*, Matthew 10:29.

Is government also an act of providence? Yes. *God ruleth by his power for ever*, Psalm 66:7. Doth God maintain the laws and ordinances of nature? Yes. Thus we read of his *covenant of the day, and his covenant of the night*, Jeremiah 33:20. But doth he sometimes suspend and act contrary to them? Yes. *So the sun stood still in the midst of heaven, and hasted not to go down about a whole day*, Joshua 10:13. Doth he uphold all creatures in their operations? Yes. *The eagle mounteth up at his command, and maketh her nest on high*, Job 39:27. But can he also restrain those operations? Yes. He *shut the lions mouth*, Daniel 6:22. Doth he exercise a peculiar government over the church? Yes. *God ruleth in Jacob*, Psalm 59:13.

Is God's government supreme? Yes. *He is King of kings and Lord of lords*, Revelation 19:16. Is it just and rightful? Yes. *Thine is the kingdom, O Lord*, 1 Chronicles 29:11. Is it most wise? Yes. *How unsearchable are his judgments,* Romans 11:33. Is it holy? Yes. *The Lord is righteous in all his ways, and holy in all his works,* Psalm 145:17. Is it absolute and arbitrary? Yes. *Why dost thou strive against him for he giveth not account of any of his matters,* Job 33:13. Is it effectual and uncontrollable? Yes. *What his soul desireth that he doth,* Job 23:13.

Is God's providential government an argument for trust and confidence? Yes. *Commit thy way unto the Lord,* Psalm 37:5. And for silence and submission? Yes. *Be still, and know that I am God,* Psalm 46:10. And for praise and thanksgiving? Yes. *Allelujah, the Lord God omnipotent reigneth,* Revelation 19:6.

Q 15. What special act of providence did God exercise towards man in the estate wherein he was created?
A. When God had created man, he entered into a covenant of life with him upon condition of perfect obedience: forbidding him to eat of the tree of the knowledge of good and evil, upon pain of death.

Did God make man perfectly holy? Yes. *God made man upright,* Ecclesiastes 7:29. And perfectly happy? Yes. For he *blessed him,* Genesis 1:28. Did he give him a law? Yes. *The Lord God commanded the man,* Genesis 2:16. And was man as God's creature obliged to obey that law? Yes. *Remember, O Israel, for thou art my servant, I have formed thee,* Isaiah 44:21.

Was the covenant which God entered into with Adam, a covenant of life? Yes. *For the law is not of faith but the man that doth them shall live in them,* Galatians 3:12. Was there a special command given him by way of trial? Yes. *Of the tree of knowledge of good and evil thou shalt not eat,* Genesis 2:17.

And was death threatened in case of disobedience? Yes. *In the day thou eatest thou shalt surely die*, Genesis 2:17. Was he under any natural necessity to break this law? No. For *of every other tree of the garden* he had liberty to *eat*, Genesis 2:16.

Was this covenant made with Adam as a public head? Yes. For he was *the figure of him that was to come*, Romans 5:14. Was Eve included in it? Yes. For *God said unto the woman, what hast thou done*, Genesis 3:13. Was this law worthy of God? Yes. *Shall not the Judge of all the earth do right*, Genesis 8:25. Is the second covenant better than the first? Yes. *For Christ is the Mediator of a better covenant*, Hebrews 8:6.

Q 16. Did our first parents continue in the estate wherein they were created?
A. Our first parents being left to the freedom of their own will, fell from the estate wherein they were created, by sinning against God.

Did man fall from that estate in which he was created? Yes. *They have sought out many inventions*, Ecclesiastes 7:29. Did he fall from a state of knowledge? Yes. His *understanding* is *darkened*, Ephesians 4:18. Did he fall from a state of holiness? Yes. He is *alienated from the life of God*, ibid. And from a state of freedom? Yes. *He that committeth sin is the servant of sin*, John 8:34. And from a state of rest? Yes. *There is no peace saith my God unto the wicked*, Isaiah 57:21. And from a state of communion with God? Yes. For *Adam and his wife hid themselves from the presence of the Lord God*, Genesis 3:8. And from a state of happiness? Yes. *So he drove out the man*, Genesis 3:24. And do all mankind imitate the sin of their first parents? Yes. *They like Adam have transgressed the covenant,* Hosea 6:7.

Did God foresee Adam's sin? Yes. *I knew that thou wouldst deal very treacherously,* Isaiah 48:8. But was he the author of it? No. For he is a *God of truth and without iniquity, just and right* is *he,* Deuteronomy 32:4. Is man's ruin then from himself? Yes. *O Israel, thou hast destroyed thyself,* Hosea 13:9.

Should Adam's fall teach us to be watchful over ourselves? Yes. *Let him that thinketh he standeth take heed lest he fall,* 1 Corinthians 10:12. And to disclaim all confidence in the creature? Yes. For *surely men of low degree are vanity, and men of high degree are a lie,* Psalm 62:9.

Q 17. What is sin?
A. Sin is any want of conformity unto, or transgression of, the law of God.

Does sin suppose a law? Yes. *For where no law is there is no transgression,* Romans 4:15. Is sin the breach of a law? Yes. *For it is the transgression of the law,* 1 John 3:4. Is the omission of what the law requires sin? Yes. *They hearkened not unto my words nor to my law,* Jeremiah 6:19. And the commission of what it forbids? Yes. *They have trespassed against my law,* Hosea 8:1. Is sin then aggravated by a knowledge of God's law? Yes. *And knowest his will, being instructed out of the law,* Romans 2:18.

Doth the law of God extend to our thoughts? Yes. He that *looketh upon a woman to lust after her committeth adultery in his heart,* Matthew 5:28. And to our words? Yes. *Let no corrupt communication proceed out of your mouth,* Ephesians 4:29.

And to our actions? Yes. *O do not this abominable thing which I hate,* Jeremiah 44:4. And to the temper of our minds? Yes. *Thou shalt love the Lord thy God with all thine heart and with all thy soul and with all thy mind,* Matthew 22:37. And is every breach of the law sinful? Yes. *For all unrighteousness is sin,* 1 John 5:17.

Q 18. What was the sin whereby our first parents fell from the estate wherein they were created?
A. The sin whereby our first parents fell from the estate wherein they were created, was their eating the forbidden fruit.

Did our first parents sin? Yes. *Thy first father hath sinned,* Isaiah 43:27. Did they sin by eating the forbidden fruit? Yes. *For she took of the fruit and did eat, and gave also to her husband with her, and he did eat,* Genesis 3:6. Was there in this sin the lust of the flesh? Yes. *For she saw that the tree was good for food,* Genesis 3:6. And the lust of the eye? Yes. *For she saw that it was pleasant to the eyes,* Genesis 3:6. And the pride of life? Yes. *For she saw that it was a tree to be desired to make one wise,* ibid. Was it an instance of horrid rebellion against God? Yes. *Hast thou eaten of the tree whereof I commanded thee that thou shouldst not eat,* Genesis 3:11. And of amazing folly in man? Yes. *This their way* was *their folly,* Psalm 49:13.

Did our first parents fall without a tempter? No. For *the serpent said unto the woman, Yea hath God said,* Genesis 3:1. Was this serpent the devil? Yes. *The old serpent is the devil and Satan,* Revelation 20:2. But could he force their consent? No. *Resist the devil and he will fly from you,* James 4:7. Did he notwithstanding prevail? Yes. *The serpent beguiled me and I did eat,* Genesis 3:13. Did he in all this aim at their destruction? Yes. For he *is Abaddon,* (the destroyer) Revelation 9:11.

Did Satan act a subtle part in tempting? Yes. *The serpent beguiled Eve through his subtlety,* 2 Corinthians 11:3. Did he promise impunity? Yes. *Ye shall not surely die,* Genesis 3:4. Did he promise improvement? Yes. *Your eyes shall be opened,* Genesis 3:5. Did he feed them with high thoughts of themselves? Yes. *Ye shall be as gods,* ibid. Did he suggest to them hard thoughts of God? Yes. For he said, *God doth know this,* verse 5. Was it an instance of his policy first to assault the woman? Yes. For she *is the weaker vessel,* 1 Peter 3:7. And to assault her when alone? Yes. *For two are better than one—for if they fall, the one will lift up his fellow,* Ecclesiastes 4:9,10.

Q 19. Did all mankind fall in Adam's first transgression?
A. The covenant being made with Adam, not only for himself but for his posterity, all mankind descending from him by ordinary generation sinned in him, and fell with him in his first transgression.

Are all mankind descended from Adam and Eve? Yes. For *Adam called his wife's name Eve because she was the mother of all living,* Genesis 3:20. Are we all concerned in our first parent's disobedience? Yes. *By one man sin entered into the world,* Romans 5:12. Is our nature tainted with the filth of that sin? Yes. For *what is man that he should be clean, and he which is born of a woman that he should be righteous,* Job 15:14. Is the guilt of it imputed to us? Yes. For *by the offence of one, judgment came upon all men to condemnation,* Romans 5:18. Are we exposed to the dreadful consequences of it? Yes. *So death passed upon all men, for that all have sinned,* Romans 5:12. And have we no power of our own to prevent all this? No. For *whilst we were yet without strength Christ died for us,* Romans 5:6.

Was this the case of Adam's immediate descendants? Yes. For *he begat a son in his own likeness,* Genesis 5:3. Is it the case of all those who in future ages descend from him? Yes. *For we have all borne the image of the earthly,* 1 Corinthians 15:49. But was it the case of Christ? No. He was *that holy thing,* Luke 1:35. Was he therefore descended from Adam in a way of ordinary generation? No. *For his mother was found with child by the Holy Ghost,* Matthew 1:18. Should we be humbled for original sin? Yes. *Behold I was shapen in iniquity,* Psalm 51:5.

Q 20. Into what estate did the fall bring mankind?
A. The fall brought mankind into an estate of sin and misery.

Is all mankind in a state of sin? Yes. *For both Jews and Gentiles are all under sin,* Romans 3:9. Were they brought into this state by the fall? Yes. *In whom all have sinned,* Romans 5:12. Hath sin corrupted the whole man? Yes. *The whole head is sick, and the whole heart faint,* Isaiah 1:5. Doth an inclination to sin appear very early? Yes. *The wicked are estranged from the womb, they go astray as soon as they are born,* Psalm 58:3. And doth it continue even after grace is implanted? Yes. *For if we say that we have no sin, we deceive ourselves,* 1 John 1:8.

Is mankind in a state of misery? Yes. *Woe unto us that we have sinned,* Lamentations 5:16. Is the whole creation the worse for sin? Yes. *The creature is now made subject to vanity*, Romans 8:20. But do sinners above all others feel the sad effects of it? Yes. *Evil pursueth sinners*, Proverbs 13:21. Is it great misery that is consequent upon the fall? Yes. *The misery of man is great upon him*, Ecclesiastes 8:6. Is it intolerable? Yes. *My punishment is greater than I can bear*, Genesis 4:13. And is it abiding? Yes. *The wrath of God abideth on him*, John 3:36.

Are all men sensible of this? No. *For they say they shall have peace, though they walk in the imagination of their heart*, Deuteronomy 29:19. But should they be sensible of it? Yes. *Now consider this ye that forget God, lest I tear you in pieces*, Psalm 50:22. And shall they be sensible of it? Yes. *They shall see and be ashamed*, Isaiah 26:11. And are the saints sensible of it? Yes. *O wretched man that I am, who shall deliver me from the body of this death*, Romans 7:24.

Q 21. Wherein consists the sinfulness of that estate whereinto man fell?
A. The sinfulness of that estate whereinto man fell, consists in the guilt of Adam's first sin, the want of original righteousness, and the corruption of his whole nature, which is commonly called original sin; together with all actual transgressions which proceed from it.

Hath Adam's sin brought all mankind into a state of guilt? Yes. *By one man's disobedience many were made sinners*, Romans 5:19. Doth this appear in the case of those who never committed actual sin? Yes. *For death reigned from Adam unto Moses, even over them that had not sinned after the similitude of Adam's transgression*, Romans 5:14. Is it usual for God thus to impute the sins of the fathers to the children? Yes.

He visiteth the iniquity of the fathers upon the children, Exodus 20:5. And is he just in so doing? Yes. *There is no unrighteousness in him,* John 7:18.

Hath sin deprived us of our original righteousness? Yes. *We are far from righteousness,* Isaiah 46:12. Are there no remains of it? No. *In me, that is in my flesh, dwelleth no good thing,* Romans 7:18. Are we thereby incapacitated for duty? Yes. *How to perform that which is good I find not,* Romans 7:18. And estranged from it? Yes. *They are all estranged from me,* Ezekiel 14:5.

Is the nature of man defiled by the fall? Yes. *We are all as an unclean thing,* Isaiah 64:6. Doth this defilement extend to both the inward and outward man? Yes. *It is a filthiness both of flesh and spirit,* 2 Corinthians 7:1. Doth it extend to all the faculties of the inward man? Yes. *Their mind and conscience is defiled,* Titus 1:15. And to all the members of the outward man? Yes. *For we yield our members as servants to uncleanness and to iniquity,* Romans 6:19. Do we now commit sin naturally? Yes. *We drink iniquity like water,* Job 15:16. And delight in it? Yes. *It is sweet in the mouth,* Job 20:12. Is this the case of little children? Yes. *For foolishness is bound up in the heart of a child,* Proverbs 22:15. And of all mankind? Yes. *For the whole world lieth in wickedness,* 1 John 5:19.

Is corrupt nature contrary to the being and perfections of God? Yes. *The carnal mind is enmity against God,* Romans 8:7. And to the law of God? Yes. *It is not subject to the law of God, neither indeed can be,* Romans 8:7. And to the grace of God? Yes. *For the flesh lusteth against the spirit, and the spirit against the flesh, and these are contrary the one to the other*, Galatians 5:17. And are the worst men's actions a copy of the best men's hearts? Yes. *For as in water face answereth to face, so the heart of man to man*, Proverbs 27:19.

Q 22. What is the misery of that estate whereinto man fell?
A. All mankind by their fall lost communion with God, are under his wrath and curse, and so made liable to all miseries in this life, to death itself, and to the pains of hell for ever.

Is fallen man rendered unworthy of communion with God? Yes. *For what communion hath light with darkness*, 2 Corinthians 6:14. And unfit for it? Yes. *For can two walk together unless they are agreed*, Amos 3:3. And is he excluded from it? Yes. *Your iniquities have separated between you and your God*, Isaiah 59:2. But may not this breach be repaired? Yes. *Ye who sometimes were far off are made nigh by the blood of Christ*, Ephesians 2:13.

Is fallen man under God's wrath? Yes. *And were by nature the children of wrath even as others*, Ephesians 2:3. Will this wrath certainly find out those who are the subjects of it? Yes. *There is no escaping*, Ezra 9:14. Is it therefore a dreadful thing to be exposed to it? Yes. *Who can stand before his indignation*, Nahum 1:6. And are the saints sensible that it is so? Yes. *Rebuke me not in thy wrath*, Psalm 38:1.

Is fallen man under God's curse? Yes. *As many as are of the works of the law, are under the curse*, Ephesians 3:11. Is there a curse upon the bodies of the wicked? Yes. *It shall come into their bowels like water, and like oil into their bones*, Psalm 109:18.

And upon their labors? Yes. *Ye looked for much, and lo it came to little,* Haggai 1:9. And upon their families? Yes. *The curse of the Lord is in the house of the wicked,* Proverbs 3:33. And upon their enjoyments? Yes. *I will curse your blessings, yea I have cursed them already,* Malachi 2:2. Does this curse extend to sinners of every degree? Yes. *It goeth forth over the face of the whole earth, and cutteth off on every side,* Zechariah 5:3.

Are fallen men subject to many internal and spiritual evils? Yes. *This is thy wickedness, because it is bitter, because it reacheth unto thine heart,* Jeremiah 4:18. Are they subject to the tyranny of Satan? Yes. *He worketh in the children of disobedience,* Ephesians 2:2. And to judicial blindness? Yes. *God hath given them the spirit of slumber, eyes that they should not see,* Romans 11:8. And to hardness of heart? Yes. *Having their conscience seared,* 1 Timothy 4:2. And to vile affections? Yes. *For this cause God gave them up to vile affections,* Romans 1:26. And to strong delusions? Yes. *God shall send them strong delusion to believe a lie,* 2 Thessalonians 2:11. And to great distress and perplexity of mind? Yes. *Terrors take hold of him as waters, a tempest stealeth him away in the night,* Job 27:20.

Is fallen man subject to many external evils? Yes. *Many sorrows shall be to the wicked,* Psalm 32:10. Is he exposed to bodily diseases? Yes. *The Lord shall smite thee with a consumption, and with a fever,* Deuteronomy 28:22. And to toil and labor? Yes. *In the sweat of thy face shalt thou eat bread,* Genesis 3:19. And to crosses and disappointments? Yes. *Thou shalt build, but I will throw down,* Malachi 1:4. And to contempt and reproach? Yes.

Thou shalt become a proverb and a byword, Deuteronomy 28:37. Is all this a sad inheritance from our first parents? Yes. *For man is born to trouble as the sparks fly upwards,* Job 5:7.

Are all mankind by the fall become liable to death? Yes. *The wages of sin is death,* Romans 6:23. Doth sin make death terrible? Yes. *The sting of death is sin,* 1 Corinthians 15:56. And that even to the saints? Yes. There are some of them, *who through fear of death are all their life-time subject to bondage,* Hebrews 2:15.

Have we by sin forfeited the happiness of heaven? Yes. *The foolish shall not stand in thy sight,* Psalm 5:5. And incurred the pains of hell? Yes. *Let them go down quick into hell,* Psalm 55:15. And are those pains everlasting? Yes. *Who shall be punished with everlasting destruction,* 2 Thessalonians 1:9. And is this the due desert of sin? Yes. *For it is a righteous thing with God to recompense tribulation,* 2 Thessalonians 1:6.

Q 23. Did God leave all mankind to perish in the estate of sin and misery?
A. God having out of his mere good pleasure, from all eternity, elected some to everlasting life, did enter into a covenant of grace, to deliver them out of the estate of sin and misery, and to bring them into an estate of salvation by a Redeemer.

Shall any of the human race be recovered from the ruins of the fall? Yes. *A remnant shall be saved,* Romans 9:27. Is the salvation of this remnant certain? Yes. *The purpose of God according to election shall stand,* Romans 9:11. Are all others left to perish in their sins? Yes. *The rest were blinded,* Romans 11:7. But is God's decree the impulsive cause of their ruin? No. *For when lust hath conceived, it bringeth forth sin, and sin when it is finished bringeth forth death,* James 1:15.

Are all the saints the objects of God's eternal choice? Yes. *God hath from the beginning chosen you,* 2 Thessalonians 2:13. And are they chosen to happiness as the end? Yes. *For God hath not appointed us to wrath, but to obtain salvation,* 1 Thessalonians 5:9. And to sanctification as the means? Yes. *Ye are chosen to salvation through sanctification,* 2 Thessalonians 2:13. Are they chosen in Christ? Yes. *According as he hath chosen us in him,* Ephesians 1:4. And is it a certain number that is thus chosen? Yes. *The Lord knoweth them that are his,* 2 Timothy 2:19.

Doth the decree of election extend but to a few comparatively? Yes. *Few are chosen,* Matthew 20:16. But does it extend to some of all nations? Yes. *Thou hast redeemed us to God out of every kindred and tongue, and people, and nation,* Revelation 5:9. And to some of the chief of sinners? Yes. Paul *was a chosen vessel, yet the chief of sinners,* Acts 9:15, and 1 Timothy 1:15. And to all that are willing to come to Christ? Yes. *Him that cometh to me, I will in no wise cast out,* John 6:37. Is this then an encouragement to use the means? Yes. *Strive to enter in at the strait gate,* Luke 13:24.

Is the decree of election founded upon God's sovereign pleasure? Yes. *I will have mercy upon whom I will have mercy,* Romans 9:15. And upon nothing in the creature? No. *Ye have not chosen me, but I have chosen you,* John 15:16. Is it secret? Yes. It is called *the mystery of his will,* Ephesians 1:9. And firm and irrevocable? Yes. *The foundation of God standeth sure,* 2 Timothy 2:19.

Doth God execute all special grace through Christ? Yes. *We are blessed with all spiritual blessings in Christ*, Ephesians 1:3. Were there mutual engagements for this purpose between the Father and Son? Yes. *The counsel of peace shall be between them both*, Zechariah 6:13. Were all the promises of the covenant primarily made to Christ? Yes. Hence they are called *the sure mercies of David*, Isaiah 55:3. Were all the conditions of it exacted from him? Yes. *The Lord that laid on him the iniquity of us all*, Isaiah 53:6. Did Christ freely undertake the work of our redemption? Yes. *Lo I come to do thy will, O God*, Hebrews 10:7. And did the Father engage for the success of his undertaking? Yes. *He shall see the travail of his soul and be satisfied*, Isaiah 53:11.

Are the saints in covenant given to Christ? Yes. *Thine they were, and thou gavest them me*, John 17:6. Are they given to him to be redeemed? Yes. *To redeem them that were under the law*, Galatians 4:5. And to be called? Yes. *Them I must bring*, John 10:16. And to be preserved? Yes. *Those that thou gavest me I have kept*, John 17:12. And to be finally glorified? Yes. *Thou hast given him power over all flesh, that he should give eternal life to as many as thou hast given him*, John 17:2. And shall all this be certainly accomplished? Yes. *The pleasure of the Lord shall prosper in his hand*, Isaiah 53:10.

Could we be saved by the first covenant? No. *For if there had been a law which could have given life, verily righteousness should have been by the law*, Galatians 5:21. Is the new covenant then a great privilege? Yes. *It is good tidings of great joy*, Luke 2:10. And should we embrace it as such? Yes. *It should be all our salvation, and all our desire*, 2 Samuel 23:5.

Q 24. Who is the Redeemer of God's elect?

A. The only Redeemer of God's elect is the Lord Jesus Christ; who, being the eternal Son of God, became man, and so was and continueth to be God and man in two distinct natures, and one person for ever.

Is Christ a Redeemer? Yes. *I know that my Redeemer liveth,* Job 19:25. Doth he redeem from sin? Yes. *He gave himself for us, that he might redeem us from all iniquity,* Titus 2:14. And from the curse? Yes. *He hath redeemed us from the curse of the law,* Galatians 3:13. And from everlasting misery? Yes. *We shall be saved from wrath through him,* Romans 5:9. Doth he redeem by price? Yes. *Who gave himself a ransom,* I Timothy 2:6. And by power? Yes. *He led captivity captive,* Ephesians 4:8.

Is Christ in a special manner the Redeemer of God's elect? Yes. *He gathereth together in one the children of God that are scattered abroad,* John 11:52. Did the elect then need a Redeemer? Yes, *for we ourselves were sometimes foolish and disobedient,* Titus 3:3. Is he the only Redeemer of God's Elect? Yes. *Neither is there salvation in any other,* Acts 4:12. Is he the only one that could be their Redeemer? Yes. *None can by any means redeem his brother, nor give to God a ransom for him,* Psalm 49:7. And need they no other? No. *For he is mighty to save,* Isaiah 63:1.

Is Christ the Son of God? Yes. *Thou art Christ the Son of the living God,* Matthew 16:16. Is he the only begotten Son? Yes. *He was the only begotten of the Father,* John 1:14. And his beloved Son? Yes. *I will send my beloved Son, it may be they will reverence him,* Luke 20:13. Is the Son of the same nature with the Father? Yes. *He is the express image of his Person,* Hebrews 1:3. And equal to him? Yes. *He is the man his fellow,* Zechariah 13:7. Is this a mystery which we cannot comprehend? Yes. *What is his name, and what is his Son's name, if though canst tell,* Proverbs 30:3.

Did Christ the Son of God assume our nature? Yes. *The word was made flesh,* John 1:14. Are the Deity and humanity united in the person of Christ? Yes. *He is Emmanuel, God with us,* Matthew 1:23. Are the two natures distinct, though united? Yes. *Of whom as concerning the flesh, Christ came, who is God,* Romans 9:5. Is not the human nature then absorbed by the divine? No. *He is the man Christ Jesus,* 1 Timothy 2:5. And will this union between the two natures still continue? Yes. *Because he continueth for ever, he hath an unchangeable priesthood,* Hebrews 7:24.

Do the two natures in Christ form any more than one person? No. *For the saints shall reign in life by one Jesus Christ,* Romans 5:17. And is the person of Christ a glorious person? Yes. *We beheld his glory,* John 1:14. Is the doctrine of Christ's incarnation an important article of the Christian religion? Yes. *Great is the mystery of godliness, God manifest in the flesh,* 1 Timothy 3:16. Should we therefore receive it? Yes. *For he that confesseth not that Jesus Christ is come in the flesh, is not of God,* 1 John 4:3. And rejoice in it? Yes. *Our souls should magnify the Lord, and our spirits rejoice in God our Saviour,* Luke 1:46.

Q 25. How did Christ, being the Son of God become man?
A. Christ the Son of God became man by taking to himself a true body, and a reasonable soul; being conceived by the power of the Holy Spirit in the womb of the Virgin Mary, and born of her, yet without sin.

Did Christ assume a body? Yes. *A body hath thou prepared me*, Hebrews 10:5. Was this a true human body? Yes. *For he was made in the likeness of men*, Philippians 2:7. Had it all the properties of a body like ours? Yes. *Handle me and see, for spirit hath not flesh and bones as ye see me have*, Luke 24:39. Was it liable to sinless infirmities? Yes. *He was hungry and weary*, Matthew 4:2, John 4:6. Was it capable of suffering? Yes. *He hath reconciled us in the body of his flesh through death*, Colossians 1:21. And was it requisite that he should assume such a body? Yes. *For in all things it behooved him to be made like unto his brethren*, Hebrews 2:17.

Had Christ a real human soul? Yes. *Thou shalt make his soul an offering for sin*, Isaiah 53:10. Was it a rational soul? Yes. *For he increased in wisdom*, Luke 2:52. And endowed with natural passions? Yes. *My soul is exceeding sorrowful*, Matthew 26:28. And capable of separation from the body? Yes. *He poured out his soul unto death*, Isaiah 53:12. Was Christ's human nature greatly abased? Yes. *I am a worm, and no man*, Psalm 22:6. And greatly exalted? Yes, *For in him dwelleth all the fullness of the Godhead, bodily*, Colossians 2:9.

Did Christ come unto the world in an ordinary way? No. *For the Lord hath created a new thing in the earth*, Jeremiah 31:22. Was he conceived by the power of the Holy Ghost? Yes. *The Holy Ghost shall come upon thee, and the power of the Highest shall overshadow thee*, Luke 1:35. And born of a virgin? Yes. *Behold a Virgin shall conceive and bear a Son*, Isaiah 7:14. Had Christ a reputed father? Yes. *Is not this Joseph's Son*, Luke 4:22. But was he no more than a reputed father? No. *For as his mother Mary was espoused to Joseph (before they came together)* *she* *was* *found* *with* *child* *by* *the* *Holy Ghost*, Matthew 1:18.

Was Christ born at the appointed time? Yes. *When the fullness of time was come, God sent forth his Son*, Galatians 4:4. And at the appointed place? Yes. *To you is born this day in the city of David a Saviour*, Luke 2:11. And of the appointed stock? Yes. *For he took upon him the seed of Abraham*, Hebrews 2:16. Did the prophets foretell his birth? Yes. *As God spake by the mouth of his holy prophets*, Luke 1:70. And did the angels celebrate it? Yes. *There was a multitude of the heavenly host praising God*, Luke 2:13.

Was Christ perfectly holy? Yes. *He was holy, harmless and undefiled*, Hebrews 7:26. Was he free from the original corruption? Yes. *The prince of this world cometh, and hath nothing in me*, John 14:30. And from an act of sin? Yes. *He did no sin*, 1 Peter 2:22. Was it necessary that he should be so? Yes. *Such a High Priest became us*, Hebrews 7:26. Would his sufferings otherwise have been ineffectual? Yes. *For he must through the eternal Spirit offer himself without spot*, Hebrews 9:14.

Q 26. What offices doth Christ execute as our Redeemer?
A. Christ as our Redeemer executeth the offices of a prophet, of a priest, and of king, both in his estate of humiliation and exaltation.

Is the Saviour of the elect the anointed of God? Yes. *God thy God hath anointed thee with the oil of gladness above thy fellows*, Psalm 45:7. Is he therefore called Christ? Yes. *We have found the Messiah (that is being interpreted the Christ)*, John 1:41. Was Christ appointed to his work? Yes. *He was fore-ordained before the foundation of the world*,

1 Peter 1:20.   Was he furnished with sufficient authority to enter upon it? Yes. *Him hath God the Father sealed,* John 6:27. Was he suitably qualified for the discharge of it? Yes. *God gave not the spirit by measure to him,* John 3:34. Was he owned and approved in it? Yes. *This is my beloved Son in whom I am well pleased.* Matthew 3:17. And did he put the finishing hand to it? Yes. *I have finished the work that thou gavest me to do,* John 17:4.

Was our salvation the great end of what Christ did and suffered? Yes. *He suffered the just for the unjust, that he might bring us to God,* 1 Peter 3:18.   Is he therefore to his people all they need? Yes. *Christ is all,* Colossians 3:11. Is he a prophet? Yes. *He shall be called the Prophet of the Highest.* Luke 1:76.[3] Is he a priest? Yes. *He is the High-Priest of our profession,* Hebrews 3:1. Is he a king? Yes. *I have set my King upon my holy hill of Zion,* Psalm 2:6.

Doth Christ execute these offices wisely? Yes. *My Servant shall deal prudently,* Isaiah 52:13.   And faithfully?   Yes.   *He was faithful to him that appointed him,* Hebrews 3:2. And diligently? Yes. *Wot ye not that I must be about my Father's business?* Luke 2:49. And successfully? Yes. *He shall not fail nor be discouraged,* Isaiah 42:4.

Did Christ execute these offices in his state of humiliation? Yes. *I have glorified thee on the earth,* John 17:4. And doth he execute them in his state of exaltation? Yes. *He now appears in the presence of God for us,* Hebrews 9:24.   Where Christ effectually executes one office, doth he execute all? Yes. *For he is both a Prince and a Saviour,* Acts

---

[3] This reference speaks of John the Baptist, not Jesus Christ. The following are more to the point: *Deuteronomy 18:15; Matthew 17:5; Acts 3:22-26; Hebrews 1:1,2.*

5:31. And is he to be received in all? Yes. *Is Christ divided?* I Corinthians 1:13.

Q 27. How doth Christ execute the office of a prophet?
A. Christ executeth the office of prophet in revealing to us, by his word and Spirit, the will of God for our salvation.

Was Christ's prophetical office foretold under the Old Testament? Yes. *The Lord thy God will raise up unto thee, from the midst of thee, a prophet like unto me,* Deuteronomy 18:15. Was Moses then a great prophet? Yes. *There arose not a prophet since in Israel like unto Moses,* Deuteronomy 34:10. Was Christ like unto Moses raised up from amongst his brethren? Yes. *For he was taken from among men,* Hebrews 5:1. Was he like Moses in meekness? Yes. *Learn of me for I am meek,* Matthew 11:29. And in faithfulness? Yes. *All things that I have heard of the Father, I have made known unto you,* John 15:15. Did he like Moses confirm his doctrine by miracles? Yes. *The works that I do, bear witness of me,* John 5:36. But was he greater than Moses? Yes. *For Moses was faithful as a servant, but Christ as a Son,* Hebrews 3:5.

Did Christ as a prophet foretell future events? Yes. *The testimony of Jesus is the spirit of prophecy,* Revelation 19:10. Did he open the way of salvation by himself? Yes. *Grace and truth came by Jesus Christ,* John 1:17. Did he make a fuller discovery of a future state than had been made before? Yes. *Life and immortality are brought to light by the gospel,* 2 Timothy 1:10. Did he reveal the whole will of God? Yes. *I have given them the words which though gavest unto me,* John 17:8.

Was Christ a divine teacher? Yes. *We know that thou art a teacher come from God,* John 3:2. Was he a plain teacher? Yes. *Now speakest though plainly,* John 16:29. Was he a prudent teacher? Yes. *He taught them as they were able to bear,* Mark 4:33. Was he an affectionate teacher? Yes. *They wondered at the gracious words that proceeded out of his mouth,* Luke 4:22. Was he a powerful teacher? Yes. *He taught them as one having authority,* Matthew 7:29. Was he an eloquent teacher? Yes. *He had the tongue of the learned,* Isaiah 50:4. But was his success in teaching equal to his qualifications for it? No. *All day long I have stretched forth my hands to a disobedient and gainsaying people,* Romans 10:21.

Did Christ execute the office of a prophet before his incarnation? Yes. *For he went and preached to the sprits in prison,* 1 Peter 3:19. Did he execute this office whilst upon earth? Yes. *Jesus went about teaching in their synagogues,* Matthew 4:23. And doth he execute it in heaven? Yes. *He speaketh from heaven,* Hebrews 12:25. Doth Christ reveal the will of God objectively by his word? Yes. *These things are written that ye might believe,* John 20:31. And subjectively by his Spirit? Yes. *When the spirit of truth is come, he will guide you unto all truth,* John 16:13. And is the latter as well as the former necessary to our salvation? Yes. *For if any man have not the Spirit of Christ he is none of his,* Romans 8:9.

Should we learn of this teacher? Yes. *Hear ye him,* Matthew 17:5. And is it at our peril if we do not? Yes. *Every soul that will not hear that Prophet shall be destroyed from among the people,* Acts 3:23.

Q 28. How doth Christ execute the office of a priest?
A. Christ executeth the office of priest in his once offering up himself a sacrifice to satisfy divine justice

and reconcile us to God, and in making continual intercession for us.

Is Christ a priest? Yes. *After the similitude of Melchisedec there ariseth another priest,* Hebrews 7:15. Is he an high-priest? Yes, *Having an High Priest over the house of God,* Hebrews 10:21. Is he a great high-priest? Yes. *We have a great High-Priest,* Hebrews 4:14. Is he so in his person? Yes. *For he is made higher than the heavens,* Hebrews 7:26. Is he so on account of the great trust reposed in him? Yes. *For he is an High-Priest of good things to come by a greater and more perfect tabernacle,* Hebrews 9:11. And on account of the great solemnity of his installment? Yes. *It was by an oath,* Hebrews 7:20. And in respect to the continuance of his office? Yes. *The Lord sware and will not repent, 'thou art a Priest for ever after the order of Melchisedec,'* Hebrews 7:21.

Doth the priesthood of Christ suppose man's guilt? Yes. *For if one died for all, then were all dead,* 2 Corinthians 5:14. And man's impotency? Yes. *There were none to make up the hedge or stand in the gap,* Ezekiel 22:30. Doth it imply Christ's deity? Yes. *We have a great High Priest, Jesus the Son of God,* Hebrews 4:14. And his humanity? Yes. *For he that sanctifieth and they that are sanctified are both of one,* Hebrews 2:11. Doth it also imply the Father's designation? Yes. *No man taketh this honour to himself, but he who is called of God as was Aaron,* Hebrews 5:4.

Did Christ as a priest make satisfaction for the sins of his people? Yes. *He made reconciliation for iniquity,* Daniel 9:24. Did he do this by sacrifice? Yes. *For without shedding of blood there is no remission,* Hebrews 9:22. And by the sacrifice of himself? Yes. *He hath put away sin by the sacrifice of himself,* Hebrews 9:26. Was it necessary that this sacrifice should be offered? Yes. *For it was necessary that the patterns of things in the heavens should be purified by these, but the heavenly things themselves, with better sacrifices than these,* Hebrews 9:23. But is it necessary that it should be repeated? No. *For this man after he had offered one sacrifice for sins for ever, sat down on the right hand of God,* Hebrews 10:12.

Was the oblation of Christ a voluntary one? Yes. *No man taketh my life from me, but I lay it down of myself,* John 10:18. And was it a precious one? Yes. *For the redemption of the soul is precious,* Psalm 49:8. And was it complete and satisfactory? Yes. *He gave himself for us an offering and a sacrifice to God for a sweet-smelling savour,* Ephesians 5:2.

Doth Christ as a priest make intercession? Yes. *If any man sin, we have an Advocate with the Father,* 1 John 2:1. Is he an able Advocate? Yes. *The Lord hath laid help upon One that is mighty,* Psalm 89:19. Is he a wise and skillful advocate? Yes. *He is of a quick understanding in the fear of the Lord,* Isaiah 11:3. Is he a righteous Advocate? Yes. *He is Jesus Christ the righteous,* 1 John 2:1. Is he a kind and affectionate Advocate? Yes. *He is a merciful and faithful High Priest,* Hebrews 2:17. Is he a constant Advocate? Yes. *He ever liveth to make intercession for us,* Hebrews 7:25. Is he a successful Advocate? Yes. *I know that thou heareth me always,* John 11:42. And is he the only Advocate? Yes. *There is but one Mediator between God and man,* 1 Timothy 2:5.

Is the advocateship of Christ confined to those for whom he died? Yes. *I pray not for the world,* John 17:9. And doth it extend to every individual of those?

Yes. *I have prayed for thee that thy faith fail not,* Luke 22:32. Should this encourage prayer? Yes. *Let us come boldly to the throne of grace,* Hebrews 4:16. And does it afford matter of joy in every condition of life? Yes. *These things I speak that they might have my joy fulfilled in themselves,* John 17:13.

Q 29. How doth Christ execute the office of king?
A. Christ executeth the office of a king, in subduing us to himself, in ruling, and defending us, and in restraining and conquering all his and our enemies.

Is Christ a King? Yes. *There is another King, one Jesus,* Acts 17:7. Doth Christ execute the kingly office? Yes. *The government shall be upon his shoulder,* Isaiah 9:6. And is he duly qualified so to do? Yes. *He is the Lamb with seven horns and seven eyes,* Revelation 5:6. Is he King as Mediator? Yes. *He hath authority to execute judgment, because he is the Son of Man,* John 5:27. And is his Mediatorial government founded upon the performance of his Mediatorial engagements? Yes. *Because he humbled himself and became obedient unto death, even the death of the cross, therefore God hath highly exalted him,* Philippians 2:8,9.

Is Christ a powerful King? Yes. *All power is given to him both in heaven and earth,* Matthew 28:18. Is he a merciful King? Yes. *He is meek and having salvation,* Zechariah 9:9, Matthew 21:5. Is he a universal King? Yes. *He is Governor among the nations,* Psalm 22:28. Is he a righteous King? Yes. *A king shall reign in righteousness,* Isaiah 32:1. And is he a rightful one? Yes. *Unto him was given dominion and glory and a kingdom,* Daniel 7:14. Should we then submit to his authority? Yes. *Take my yoke upon you,* Matthew 11:29.

Is Christ in an especial manner the King of saints? Yes. *Just and true are thy ways, thou King of Saints,* Revelation 15:3. Are such naturally the subjects of another kingdom? Yes. *Other lords besides thee have had the dominion over us,* Isaiah 26:13. But are they in due time rescued and delivered? Yes. *Even the captives of the mighty shall be taken away, and the prey of the terrible shall be delivered,* Isaiah 49:25. And doth Christ govern those whom he hath thus subdued? Yes. *For out of thee shall come a Governor that shall rule my people Israel,* Matthew 2:6.

Is Christ King over the church? Yes. *Is not the Lord in Zion, is not he King in her,* Jeremiah 8:19. Doth he enact laws there? Yes. *Teaching them to observe all things whatsoever I have commanded you,* Matthew 28:20. Doth he commission officers? Yes. *He gave some apostles and some prophets,* Ephesians 4:11. And does he resent the introduction of any thing without his authority? Yes. *In their setting their threshold by my threshold, and their post by my post, they have defiled my holy name,* Ezekiel 43:8.

Doth Christ as a King preserve his subjects? Yes. *We are preserved in Christ Jesus,* Jude ver. 1. And protect them? Yes. *As birds flying so he defends Jerusalem,* Isaiah 31:5. And punish their faults? Yes. *Whom he loveth he chasteneth,* Hebrews 12:6. And reward their faithful services? Yes. *His reward is with him,* Revelation 22:12.

Doth Christ exercise his Kingly power in restraining his enemies? Yes. *I will put my hook in thy nose, and my bridle in thy lips,* Isaiah 37:29. And in subduing them? Yes. *He hath spoiled principalities and powers,* Colossians 2:15. And in destroying them? Yes. *He will break them with a rod of iron, and dash them in pieces like a potter's vessel,* Psalm 2:9. Will the conquest of the saints' enemies be gradual? Yes. *I will drive them out by little and little,* Exodus 23:30. But will it be total? Yes. *For he must reign till he hath put all enemies under his feet,* 1 Corinthians 15:25.

Q 30. Wherein did Christ's humiliation consist?

A. Christ's humiliation consisted in his being born, and that in a low condition, made under the law, undergoing the miseries of this life, the wrath of God, and the cursed death of the cross; in being buried, and continuing under the power of death for a time.

Did Christ humble himself? Yes. *He made himself of no reputation,* Philippians 2:7. And was it requisite that he should do so? Yes. *For thus it was written and thus it behoved Christ to suffer,* Luke 24:46. Did he humble himself in his birth? Yes. *He took upon him the form of a servant,* Philippians 2:7. Was he born of a poor stock? Yes. *He was a root out of a dry ground,* Isaiah 53:2. And in a poor place? Yes. *Bethlehem was little among the thousands of Judah,* Micah 5:2. Was he poorly provided for? Yes. *She brought forth her first born, and wrapped him in swaddling clothes and laid him in a manger,* Luke 2:7. Was this widely different from his former estate? Yes. *For he was rich, though for our sakes he became poor,* 2 Corinthians 8:9.

Was Christ made under the law? Yes. *He was made of a woman, made under the law,* Galatians 4:4. Was he circumcised? Yes. *He was circumcised the eighth day,* Luke 2:21. Was he thereby obligated to keep the whole law? Yes. *For I testify again to every man that is circumcised, that he is a debtor to do the whole law,* Galatians 5:3. And did he actually keep it? Yes. *Which of you convinceth me of sin,* John 8:46.   Did he observe the ceremonial as well as the moral law? Yes. *Then went he up also unto the feast,* John 7:10. And did he not only obey the precepts of the law, but bear the penalties of it? Yes. *He was made a curse for us,* Galatians 3:13.

Did Christ undergo the miseries of this life? Yes. *He was a man of sorrows,* Isaiah 53:3. Were his temptations a trouble to him? Yes. *He suffered, being tempted,* Hebrews 2:18.   And his little success? Yes. *He was grieved for the hardness of their hearts,* Mark 3:5.   And the sorrows of his friends? Yes. *For when he saw Mary weeping, he groaned in his Spirit and was troubled.* John 11:33. And the contradictions of his enemies? Yes. *They said, 'he deceiveth the people,'* John 7:12. Were his miracles slandered? Yes. *He casteth out devils by Beelzebub the prince of devils,* Matthew 12:24. And were his best actions misrepresented? Yes. *Behold a gluttonous man and a wine-bibber, a friend of publicans and sinners,* Luke 7:34.

Was Christ unknown to the world? Yes. *Whom none of the princes of this world knew,* 1 Corinthians 2:8. Was he despised? Yes. *He was despised and rejected of men,* Isaiah 53:3. Was he reproached? Yes. *He was a reproach of men,* Psalm 22:6. Was he persecuted? Yes. *The Jews took up stones to stone him,* John 10:31. Had he any fixed abode? No. *The Son of man hath not where to lay his head,* Luke 9:58. Had he any certain maintenance? No. *For he was hungry and had nothing to eat,* Mark 11:12. Were his countrymen unkind? Yes. *He came to his own and his own received him not,* John 1:11. Did many of his friends prove false? Yes. *Many of his disciples went back and walked no more with him,* John 6:66. And were those on whom he bestowed favours unthankful? Yes. *Were there not ten cleansed, but where are the nine,* Luke 17:17.

Was Christ's death another instance of his humiliation? Yes. *He humbled himself and became obedient unto death,* Philippians 2:8. Was his death a painful one? Yes. *It was the death of the cross,* ibid. Was it a shameful one? Yes. *For he endured the cross, despising the shame,* Hebrews 12:2. Was it a cursed one? Yes. *For cursed is every one that hangeth on a tree,* Galatians 3:13. Did he suffer in his body? Yes. *For we are sanctified thro' the offering of the body of Jesus Christ once for all,* Hebrews 10:10. Did he suffer in his feeling? Yes. *They pierced his hands and his feet,* Psalm 22:16. And in his taste? Yes. *They gave him vinegar mingled with gall,* Matthew 27:34. And in his sight? Yes. *They wagged their heads at him,* Matthew 27:39. And in his hearing? Yes. *They that passed by reviled him,* ibid. And in his smelling? Yes. *They brought him to Golgotha, that is to say, the place of a skull,* Matthew 27:33. Did he also suffer in his soul? Yes. *Now is my soul troubled,* John 12:27. And was this the sorest of all his suffering? Yes. *He was in an agony,* Luke 22:44.

Did Christ suffer from the Father? Yes. *He was smitten of God,* Isaiah 53:4. And from Satan? Yes. *Thou shalt bruise his heel,* Genesis 3:15. And from men? Yes. *This is your hour and the power of darkness,* Luke 22:53. Was he betrayed by one disciple? Yes. *The devil put it into the heart of Judas Iscariot to betray him,* John 13:2. And forsaken by the rest? Yes. *All his disciples forsook him and fled,* Matthew 26:56. Was he falsely accused? Yes. *They sought false witness against him,* Matthew 26:59. And unjustly condemned? Yes. *For Pilate said, 'I find no fault in him,'* Luke 23:4. And inhumanly executed? Yes. *For he was scourged, crowned with thorns, and made to bear his own cross,* Matthew 27:26, 29, John 19:17.

Did Christ die to display the justice and holiness of God? Yes. *To declare his righteousness that he might be just,* Romans 3:26. And to represent the great evil and malignity of sin? Yes. *And for sin, he condemned sin in the flesh,* Romans 8:3. And to set us an example of patience and resignation to the divine will? Yes. *For as much as Christ hath suffered for us in the flesh, arm yourselves likewise with the same mind,* 1 Peter 4:1. And to glorify that law which man hath broken? Yes. *He hath magnified the law and made it honourable,* Isaiah 42:21. And to destroy Satan? Yes. *That through death he might destroy him that had the power of death, even the devil,* Hebrews 2:14. And to break the power of sin? Yes. *Our old man is crucified with Christ, that the body of sin might be destroyed,* Romans 6:6. And to bring in a justifying righteousness? Yes. *By his knowledge shall my righteous servant justify many, for he shall bear their iniquities,* Isaiah 53:11. And to procure us a title to heaven? Yes. *For the saints shall reign in life by one Christ Jesus,* Romans 5:17. Was it for the elect that Christ suffered and died? Yes. *For he loved the church and gave himself for it,* Ephesians 5:25.

Was Christ buried? Yes. *And that he was buried,* 1 Corinthians 15:4. Was he buried at another's expense? Yes. *And when Joseph had taken the body he wrapped it in a clean linen cloth, and laid it in his own tomb*, Matthew 27:59,60. Did he continue under the power of death for a time? Yes. *So shall the Son of Man be three days and three nights in the heart of the earth*, Matthew 12:40. And was this a part of Christ's humiliation? Yes. *Thou hast bought me into the dust of death*, Psalm 22:15.

Should the sufferings of Christ make sinners tremble? Yes. *If they do these things in a green tree, what shall be done in the dry*, Luke 23:31. And the saints rejoice? Yes. *God forbid that I should glory, save in the cross of our Lord Jesus Christ*, Galatians 6:14.

Q 31. Wherein consisteth Christ's exaltation?
A. Christ's exaltation consisteth in his rising again from the dead on the third day, in ascending up into heaven, in sitting at the right hand of God the Father, and in coming to judge the world at the last day.

Was Christ's resurrection the first step to his exaltation? Yes. *He was buried and rose again*, 1 Corinthians 15:4. Was it foretold that Christ would rise? Yes. *Thou wilt not suffer thy Holy One to see corruption*, Psalm 16:10. Was it necessary that he should rise? Yes. *He loosed the pains of death, because it was not possible that he should be holden by it*, Acts 2:24. Is it certain that he did rise? Yes. *He shewed himself alive by many infallible proofs*, Acts 1:3. Have we the testimony of Christ's apostles for this? Yes. *Whereof we are witnesses*, Acts 3:15. And of his enemies? Yes. *Some of the watch shewed unto the chief priests all things that were done*, Matthew 28:11. And of the angels? Yes. *He is not here, he is risen*, Matthew 28:6. And of himself? Yes. *I am he that liveth and was dead, and behold I am alive for evermore*, Revelation 1:18. Was he seen after his resurrection? Yes. *He was seen of Cephas, then of the twelve, after that he was seen of above five hundred brethren at once*, 1 Corinthians 15:5. May it then be depended upon as matter of fact? Yes. *For in the mouth of two or three witnesses every word shall be established*, Matthew 18:16.

Did Christ rise by his own power? Yes. *Destroy this temple, and in three days I will raise it up again*, John 2:19. And at the precise time? Yes. *God raised him up on the third day*, Acts 10:40. And with great majesty? Yes. *Behold the angel of the Lord descended from heaven and came and rolled back the stone from the door*, Matthew 28:2,3. Did he rise with the same body in which he was crucified? Yes. *Behold my hands and my feet*, Luke 24:39. Did he rise as a public person? Yes. *As the first fruits of them that slept*, 1 Corinthians 15:20. And did he rise to die no more? Yes. *Death hath no more dominion over him*, Romans 6:9.

Did Christ stay some time upon earth after his resurrection? Yes. *He was seen of them forty days*, Acts 1:3. Did he improve this time for the instruction of his disciples? Yes. *He gave commandments unto the apostles whom he had chosen*, Acts 1:2. And after that was he received up into heaven? Yes. *He ascended far up above all heavens*, Ephesians 4:10. Did he ascend for the good of the church? Yes. *That he might fill all things*, ibid. And for his own glory? Yes. *Ought not Christ to have suffered these things, and to enter into his glory*, Luke 24:26.

Did Christ ascend in public view? Yes. *Whilst they beheld he was taken up*, Acts 1:9. And in a cloud? Yes. *A cloud received him out of their sight*, Acts 1:9.

Did he ascend with great pomp? Yes. *He was attended with the chariots of God, even thousands of angels,* Psalm 68:17. Did he depart with a blessing in his mouth? Yes. *It came to pass while he blessed them he was parted from them,* Luke 24:51. And did he meet with a welcome whither he went? Yes. *He came to the Ancient of Days, and they brought him before him,* Daniel 7:13.

Doth Christ sit at the right hand of God? Yes. *He is set on the right hand of the throne of the Majesty in the heavens,* Hebrews 8:1. And hath he a right to sit there? Yes. *For the Lord said unto him, 'Sit thou at my right hand,'* Psalm 110:1. Doth Christ's sitting at God's right hand denote the completion of his work? Yes. *When he had once offered one sacrifice for sins, he sat down on the right hand of God,* Hebrews 10:12. Does it imply dignity and honour? Yes. *To which of the angels said he at any time, 'Sit thou on my right hand,'* Hebrews 1:13. And authority and power? Yes. *He sits at the right hand of power,* Matthew 26:64. And safety and security? Yes. *Thy right hand shall save me,* Psalm 138:7. And joy and satisfaction? Yes. *For at God's right hand are pleasures for evermore,* Psalm 16:11. Doth it also imply the continuance of this his state? Yes. *For he shall reign over the house of Jacob for ever,* Luke 1:33. Should this be a motive to us to have our hearts in heaven? Yes. *Seek those things which are above, where Christ sitteth at the right hand of God,* Colossians 3:1.

Will Christ come again? Yes. *This same Jesus, who is now taken up from you into heaven, shall so come,* Acts 1:11. Will he come quickly? Yes. *Yet a little while and he who shall come will come and will not tarry,* Hebrews 10:37. Will he come suddenly? Yes.

For the day of the Lord cometh as a thief in the night, 1 Thessalonians 5:2. Will he come publicly? Yes. *Every eye shall see him,* Revelation 1:7. Will his coming be glorious and magnificent? Yes. *'Tis the glorious appearance of the great God and our Saviour Jesus Christ,* Titus 2:13. Should the saints then long for and desire his coming? Yes. *Looking for and hasting unto the day of the Lord,* 2 Peter 3:12.

Will Christ come as a judge? Yes. *He shall judge the quick and dead at his appearing,* 2 Timothy 4:1. Is he an able and understanding judge? Yes. *He shall not judge after the sight of the eyes,* Isaiah 11:3. Is he a righteous and impartial judge? Yes. *He loveth righteousness and hateth wickedness,* Psalm 45:7. Will he be to the wicked a terrible judge? Yes. *He will come in flaming fire taking vengeance on them that know not God,* 2 Thessalonians 1:8. Will he be a peremptory and inflexible judge? Yes. *He will not alter the thing that is gone out of his lips,* Psalm 89:34. Is the time of judgment known? No. *Of that day and hour knoweth no man,* Mark 13:32. But is it fixed and determined? Yes. *For God hath appointed a day in which he will judge the world in righteousness by the man whom he hath ordained,* Acts 17:31. Will that be a joyous day to the saints? Yes. *For he will then be glorified in his saints, and admired in all them that believe,* 2 Thessalonians 1:10.

Q 32. How are we made partakers of the redemption purchased by Christ?

A. We are made partakers of the redemption purchased by Christ, by the effectual application of it to us by his Holy Spirit.

Is there a redemption wrought out for the people of God? Yes. *He sent redemption unto his people,* Psalm 111:9. Is Christ the author of this redemption? Yes. *He obtained eternal redemption for us*, Hebrews 9:12. Is his blood the price of it? Yes. *We are redeemed with the precious blood of Christ*, 1 Peter 1:18,19. Do many expect redemption in another way? Yes. *Because I am innocent, surely his anger shall turn from me*, Jeremiah 2:35. But is this the only way? Yes. *For other foundations can no man lay than that which is laid, which is Jesus Christ*, 1 Corinthians 3:11.

Do all partake of the redemption purchased by Christ? No. *Some have neither part nor lot in this matter*, Acts 8:21. Do all partake of it who pretend to it? No. *Thou hast a name that thou livest and art dead*, Revelation 3:1. Do all believers partake of it? Yes. *We are made partakers of Christ*, Hebrews 3:14. Do such receive the Redeemer? Yes. *To as many as received him gave he power to become the sons of God*, John 1:12. Do they receive him in all his offices? Yes. *Ye have received Christ Jesus the Lord*, Colossians 2:6. And do any receive this of themselves? No. *For a man can receive nothing, except it be given him from above*, John 3:27.

Is it necessary that redemption be applied to us? Yes. *Who of God is made unto us redemption*, 1 Corinthians 1:30. Is this a great and effectual work? Yes. *For there is an exceeding greatness of power manifested to us-ward who believe*, Ephesians 1:19. Is it a work within us? Yes. *'Tis Christ in us, the hope of glory*, Colossians 1:27. Is it the work of the Spirit? Yes. *'Tis the Spirit that quickens*, John 6:63. Is it wrought only upon the elect? Yes. *The election hath obtained it*, Romans 11:7. And shall all those be partakers of this redemption to whom it is effectually applied? Yes. *He that believeth on the Son hath everlasting life*, John 3:36.

Q 33. How doth the Spirit apply to us the redemption purchased by Christ?

A. The Spirit applieth to us the redemption purchased by Christ, by working faith in us, and thereby uniting us to Christ, in our effectual calling.

Is the application of redemption limited by the purpose of God? Yes. *It shall be given to them for whom it is prepared of my Father,* Matthew 20:23. And by the purchase of Christ? Yes. *Ye believe not because ye are not of my sheep,* John 10:26. And by the operations of the Spirit? Yes. *For we are saved by the washing of regeneration, and by the renewing of the Holy Ghost,* Titus 3:5.

Is faith necessary in order to our participation of the blessings of redemption? Yes. *He that believeth not is condemned already,* John 3:18. Is it the great thing necessary? Yes. *Only believe, all things are possible to him that believeth,* Mark 5:36 and 9:23. Is it therefore bestowed upon all God's redeemed ones? Yes. *They have all obtained the like precious faith,* 2 Peter 1:1. Is the same measure of faith bestowed upon every one? No. *For unto every one of us is given grace according to the measure of the gift of Christ,* Ephesians 4:7. But does weak faith have interest in gospel privileges as well as strong? Yes. *For the righteousness of God is unto all, and upon all them that believe, and there is no difference,* Romans 3:22.

Are all true believers united to Christ? Yes. *I in them and thou in me that they may be made perfect in one,* John 17:23. Are the souls of believers united to Christ? Yes. *He that is joined to the Lord is one spirit,* 1 Corinthians 6:17. And their bodies? Yes. *Know ye not that your bodies are the members of Christ,* 1 Corinthians 6:15. Is this a vital union?

Yes. *Because I live, ye shall live also,* John 14:19. Is it a lasting and indissolvable union? Yes. *I will betroth thee to me for ever,* Hosea 2:19. But is it an inexplicable and mysterious one? Yes. *This is a great mystery,* Ephesians 5:32.

Are we vitally united to Christ by the Spirit? Yes. *We are an habitation of God through the Spirit,* Ephesians 2:23. And that in our effectual calling? Yes. *We are called into the fellowship of his Son Jesus Christ,* 1 Corinthians 1:9. But is there a union prior to our effectual calling? Yes. For we read of the *grace given us in Christ before the world began,* 2 Timothy 1:9.

Are all the saints effectually called? Yes. *They are preserved and called,* Jude ver. 1. Is God the author of this call? Yes. *He hath called us out of darkness into his marvelous light,* 1 Peter 2:9. Is grace the motive of it? Yes. *It pleased God who called me by his grace,* Galatians 1:15. Is the gospel the means of it? Yes. *Whereunto he called you by our gospel,* 2 Thessalonians 2:14. Is glory the end of it? Yes. *Who hath called you to his kingdom and glory,* 1 Thessalonians 2:12. Should we then examine our title to this privilege? Yes. *Make your calling and election sure,* 2 Peter 1:10. And endeavor to improve it? Yes. *Walk worthy of the vocation wherewith ye are called,* Ephesians 4:1.

Q 34. What is effectual calling?

A. Effectual calling is the work of God's Spirit, whereby convincing us of our sin and misery, enlightening our minds in the knowledge of Christ, and renewing our wills, he doth persuade and enable us to embrace Jesus Christ freely offered to us in the gospel.

Is there an outward call given to all men? Yes. *Unto you, O men, I call,* Proverbs 8:4. Does God call by his words of creation? Yes. *For there is no speech nor language where their voice is not heard,* Psalm 19:3. And by his words of providence? Yes. *The Lord's voice crieth unto the city,* Micah 6:9. And by his word? Yes. *He sent forth his servants to call them that were bidden,* Matthew 22:3. And by the common motions of his Spirit? Yes. *My Spirit shall not always strive with man,* Genesis 6:3. But is this call always effectual? No. *They would not come,* Matthew 22:3.

Are the special calls of the Spirit the fruits of electing love? Yes. *Whom he predestinated, them he also called,* Romans 8:30. Are they attended with the mighty power of God? Yes. *Our gospel came not unto you in word only, but also in power,* 1 Thessalonians 1:5. And yet suitable to the nature of man? Yes. *I drew them with the cords of a man,* Hosea 11:4. And are they always effectual? Yes. *They shall come,* John 6:37.

Are all that are effectually called convinced of sin? Yes. *When the commandment came, sin revived,* Romans 7:9. Are they convinced of sin in the heart? Yes. *They shall know every man the plague of his own heart,* 1 Kings 8:38. And of sin in the life? Yes. *Thou makest me to possess the iniquities of my youth,* Job 13:26. Are they especially convinced of gross and leading sins? Yes. *Who was before a persecutor,* 1 Timothy 1:13. Do they see sin in the glass of the law? Yes. *For by the law is the knowledge of sin,* Romans 3:20. And in the glass of the divine perfections? Yes. *Now mine eye seeth thee, I abhor myself,* Job 42:5, 6. And in the glass of Christ's sufferings? Yes. *They shall look upon me whom they have pierced, and mourn,* Zechariah 12:10. Do they see sin to be exceeding sinful? Yes. *Know therefore and see that it is an evil thing,* Jeremiah 2:19. And exceeding hateful? Yes. *I hate every false way,* Psalm 119:104. And exceeding hurtful? Yes. *I find more bitter than death the woman whose heart is snares and nets,* Ecclesiastes 7:26. And is such a conviction the fruit of the Spirit? Yes. *For when he is come he will reprove the world of sin,* John 16:8.

Are all such convinced of their misery? Yes. *Woe is me, for I am undone,* Isaiah 6:5. And of the equity of God's judgments? Yes. *O Lord, righteousness belongeth to thee,* Daniel 9:7. And of their helplessness in themselves? Yes. *We cannot stand before thee because of this,* Ezra 9:15. Will such a conviction produce horror? Yes. *The jailor came trembling,* Acts 16:29. And shame? Yes. *We lie down in our shame,* Jeremiah 3:25. And humble silence? Yes. *He putteth his mouth in the dust,* Lamentations 3:29. And earnest enquiry? Yes. *Lord, what wilt thou have me to do,* Acts 9:6.

Is such a conviction necessary? Yes. *For the whole need not a physician,* Matthew 9:12. But is it all that is necessary? No. *For he has torn and he will heal us,* Hosea 6:1. Does the same spirit then that has begun the work carry it on? Yes. *For he will perfect that which concerneth us,* Psalm 138:8. Doth he enlighten our minds? Yes. *He shines into our hearts,* 2 Corinthians 4:6. Doth he particularly enlighten them into the knowledge of Christ? Yes. *He giveth light of the knowledge of the glory of God in the face of Jesus Christ,* ibid. And of the things of Christ? Yes. *He shall take of mine and shew it unto you,* John 16:14,15.

Is that knowledge which the Spirit affords inward and experimental? Yes. *Wisdom entereth into the heart,* Proverbs 2:10.   Is it attended with the greatest certainty? Yes. *We believe and are sure that thou art Christ, the Son of the living God.* John 6:69. Is it an operative and effectual knowledge? Yes. *It bringeth forth fruit,* Colossians 1:6. Is it an abiding knowledge? Yes. *The anointing which you have received of him abideth in you,* 1 John 2:7.   Should it therefore be earnestly coveted and sought after? Yes. *I count all things but loss for the excellency of the knowledge of Christ Jesus our Lord,* Philippians 3:8.

Is this illumination of the understanding attended with a determination of the will? Yes. *He shall make ready a people prepared for the Lord,* Luke 1:17.   Is the perverse will rendered pliable? Yes. *I will take the stony heart out of their flesh, and will give them an heart of flesh,* Ezekiel 11:19.   And the rebellious will obedient? Yes. *Every thought is brought into captivity to the obedience of Christ,* 2 Corinthians 10:5.   And is this also the work of God? Yes. *It is he that worketh in us to will,* Philippians 2:13.

Doth the soul thus awakened and enlightened venture itself upon Christ? Yes. *Every man that hath heard and learned of the Father, cometh unto me,* John 6:45.   And that immediately? Yes. *Christ said, 'follow me,' and he arose and followed him,* Matthew 9:9.   And resolutely? Yes. *Tho he slay me, yet will I trust him,* Job 13:15.   Is Christ proposed in the word as an able Saviour? Yes. *He is able to save to the uttermost, all that come unto God thro' him,* Hebrews 7:25.   And as a willing Saviour? Yes. *This man receiveth sinners,* Luke 15:2.   And do the actions of faith in the soul answer to the discoveries made of Christ in the word? Yes. *So we preached and so ye believed,* 1 Corinthians 15:1.

Is the whole work of grace in conversion represented by a call? Yes. *Called to be saints,* 1 Corinthians 1:2. Is this a secret call? Yes. *The kingdom of God cometh not with observation,* Luke 17:20. And a mysterious one? Yes. *For we know not what is the way of the spirit,* Ecclesiastes 11:5. And a personal one? Yes. *I have called thee by thy name,* Isaiah 43:1. And a free and gracious one? Yes. *Of his own will begat he us,* James 1:18. Should God therefore have the glory of it? Yes. *Not unto us, not unto us, but unto thy name give glory, for thy mercy, and for thy truth's sake,* Psalm 115:1.

Q 35. What benefits do they that are effectually called partake of in this life?
A. They that are effectually called do in this life partake of justification, adoption, sanctification, and the several benefits which in this life do either accompany or flow from them.

Is effectual calling of great advantage? Yes. *Godliness is profitable unto all things,* 1 Timothy 4:8. Is it of immediate advantage? Yes. *If ye be willing and obedient ye shall eat the good of the land,* Isaiah 1:19. And of eternal advantage? Yes. *For it hath the promise not only of the life that now is, but of that which is to come,* 1 Timothy 4:8. Doth it bring one into a state of grace? Yes. *Such are not under the law, but under grace.* Romans 6:15. And into a state of comfort? Yes. *We who have believed do enter into rest,* Hebrews 4:3. And into a state of holiness? Yes. *God hath not called us to uncleanness, but to holiness,* 1 Thessalonians 4:7. And is it an earnest of everlasting glory? Yes. *For God will give grace and glory, and no good thing will he withhold from those who walk uprightly,* Psalm 84:11.

Are those who are effectually called justified? Yes. *Whom he called them he also justified*, Romans 8:30. Is this a great privilege? Yes. *Blessed is the man to whom the Lord imputeth not iniquity*, Psalm 32:2. Is it the certain and enduring privilege of all the saints? Yes. *There is no condemnation to them that are in Christ Jesus*, Romans 8:1. And are all others excluded? Yes. *They are in the gall of bitterness and in the bond of iniquity*, Acts 8:23.

Are all those that are effectually called adopted? Yes. *Ye are all the children of God by faith in Jesus Christ*, Galatians 3:26. Is this a great instance of love in God? Yes. *Behold what manner of love the Father hath bestowed upon us, that we should be called the sons of God*, 1 John 3:1. And a great blessing to men? Yes. *For if children, then heirs*, Romans 8:17. Are such also sanctified? Yes. *They are sanctified in Christ Jesus*, 1 Corinthians 1:2. And without this would their happiness be incomplete? Yes. *For without holiness none shall see the Lord*, Hebrews 12:14.

Have those who are effectually called a title to all other covenant blessings? Yes. *All things are yours*, 1 Corinthians 3:22. And may they take the comfort of them? Yes. *As having nothing and yet possessing all things*, 2 Corinthians 6:10. And is this their case without exception? Yes. *For the same Lord over all is rich unto all that call upon him*, Romans 10:12.

Q 36. What is justification?
A. Justification is an act of God's free grace, wherein he pardoneth all our sins, and accepteth us as righteous in his sight, only for the righteousness of Christ imputed to us, and received by faith alone.

Is justification an act of God? Yes. *It is God that justifieth,* Romans 8:33. And of his free grace? Yes. *Being justified by his grace, we are made heirs,* Titus 3:7. Doth this grace set aside all merit in the creature? Yes. *For if by grace, then it is no more of works,* Romans 11:6. But does it set aside all merit in Christ? No. *For we are justified freely by his grace, through the redemption that is in Jesus Christ,* Romans 3:24.

Does justification include in it the forgiveness of sins? Yes. *We have redemption through his blood, the forgiveness of sins,* Ephesians 1:7. Is remission of sins an act of power? Yes. *The Son of Man hath power on earth to forgive sin,* Matthew 9:6. And of grace? Yes. *I will be merciful to their unrighteousness,* Hebrews 8:12. And of justice? Yes. *If we confess our sins, he is faithful and just to forgive us our sins,* 1 John 1:9. Does God forgive sin as a Father? Yes. *I will spare them as a man spareth his son that serveth him,* Malachi 3:17. And as a Sovereign? Yes. *Who is a God like unto thee, that pardoneth iniquity,* Micah 7:18. Doth he pardon many sins? Yes. *Her sins which are many are all forgiven,* Luke 7:47. And great sins? Yes. *Though your sins have been as scarlet they shall be as white as snow,* Isaiah 1:18. But doth every sin need a pardon? Yes. *For if he will contend with us, we cannot answer him one of a thousand,* Job 9:3.

Doth justification include in it the acceptance of our persons? Yes. *He hath made us accepted in the Beloved,* Ephesians 1:6. And of our services? Yes. *God had respect to Abel and to his offering,* Genesis 4:4. Doth God look upon justified ones with complacency? Yes. *His countenance doth behold the upright,* Psalm 11:7. And speak of them with approbation? Yes. *Thou art all fair my love, there is no spot in thee,* Song of Solomon 4:7. And treat them with intimacy and endearment? Yes. *The secret of the Lord is with them that fear him, and he will shew them his covenant,* Psalm 25:14.

Were the ceremonial sacrifices insufficient for man's justification? Yes. *For they could not take away sin,* Hebrews 10:14. And are moral duties as insufficient now? Yes. *For by the works of the law shall no flesh be justified,* Galatians 2:16. Are duties after faith as insufficient as those before? Yes. *For all our righteousnesses are as filthy rags,* Isaiah 64:6. Is therefore an attempt to be justified in this way a glaring instance of folly and ignorance? Yes. *For they being ignorant of God's righteousness go about to establish a righteousness of their own,* Romans 10:3. And will it issue in utter ruin and destruction? Yes. *This shall ye have of mine hand; ye shall lie down in sorrow,* Isaiah 50:11.

Are we justified only for the righteousness of Christ? Yes. *Not having my own righteousness, which is of the law, but that which is through the faith of Christ,* Philippians 3:9. Did Christ perform what the law required? Yes. *There was no guile found in his mouth,* 1 Peter 2:22. And is this a part of our justifying righteousness? Yes. *By the obedience of one many are made righteous,* Romans 5:19. Did he suffer what the law threatened? Yes. *For he was bruised for our iniquities,* Isaiah 53:5. And is this the other part of it? Yes. *Thou wast slain and hast redeemed us to God by thy blood,* Revelation 5:9. Is this righteousness satisfactory to God? Yes. *The Lord is well pleased for his righteousness sake,* Isaiah 42:21. And sufficient for man? Yes. *For grace reigns through righteousness unto eternal life by Jesus Christ our Lord,* Romans 5:21. And shall it never be abrogated? No. *My righteousness shall not be abolished,* Isaiah 51:6.

Doth this righteousness become ours by imputation? Yes. *David describeth the blessedness of the man to whom God imputeth righteousness without works,* Romans 4:6. And does this imputation depend on any act in the creature? No. *For it is the gift of righteousness,* Romans 5:17. Must the righteousness of Christ be received as well as imputed? Yes. *We have received the atonement,* Romans 5:11. And is faith the instrument of receiving it? Yes. *God hath set forth Christ to be a propitiation through faith in his blood,* Romans 3:25. Is justification the less of grace because it is through faith? No. *Therefore it is of faith, that it might be by grace,* Romans 4:16.

Doth this doctrine glorify the divine wisdom? Yes. *Herein God hath abounded towards us in all wisdom and prudence,* Ephesians 1:8. And magnify the divine goodness? Yes. *Herein is love, not that we loved God, but that he loved us, and sent his Son to be a propitiation for our sins,* 1 John 4:10. Doth it contribute to the comfort of afflicted consciences? Yes. *For being justified by faith, we have peace with God.* Romans 5:1. And to destroy pride and vain glory? Yes. *Where is boasting then? It is excluded, by what law? Of works, nay but by the law of faith,* Romans 3:27. Is it a powerful motive to holiness and practical religion? Yes. *It is a doctrine according to godliness,* 1 Timothy 6:3. And an everlasting foundation for thankfulness and praise? Yes. *I will greatly rejoice in the Lord, for he hath clothed me with the robe of righteousness,* Isaiah 61:10.

Q 37. What is adoption?

A. Adoption is an act of God's free grace, whereby we are received into the number and have a right to all the privileges of the sons of God.

Are some the sons of God by creation? Yes. *All the sons of God shouted for joy.* Job 38:7. And others by an external profession? Yes. *Let my Son go that he may serve me,* Exodus 4:23. But are the saints so by adoption? Yes. *We receive the adoption of Sons,* Galatians 4:5. Is Christ the medium of our adoption? Yes. *We are predestinated to the adoption of children by Jesus Christ,* Ephesians 1:5. And the exemplar of it? Yes. *God hath predestinated us to be conformed to the image of his Son,* Romans 8:29. And the end of it? Yes. *That he might be the first born among many brethren,* Romans 8:29. And is grace the motive of it? Yes. *It is according to the good pleasure of his will, to the praise of the glory of his grace,* Ephesians 1:5, 6.

Do the saints receive the nature of Sons? Yes. *They are made partakers of a divine nature,* 2 Peter 1:4. And the Spirit of Sons? Yes. *Because ye are sons God hath sent forth the Spirit of his Son into your hearts,* Galatians 4:6. And the provision of sons? Yes. *They shall want no good thing,* Psalm 34:10. And the inheritance of sons? Yes. *Wherefore thou art no more a servant, but a son, and if a son then an heir of God, through Christ,* Galatians 4:7.

Are God's children the objects of his pity? Yes. *As a father pitieth his children, so the Lord pitieth them that fear him,* Psalm 103:13. And of his care? Yes. *I have nourished and brought up children,* Isaiah 1:2. Are they strongly defended? Yes. *His children shall have a place of refuge,* Proverbs 14:26. And honourably attended? Yes. *He shall give his angels charge over thee, to keep thee in all thy ways,* Psalm 91:11. And if chastened, is it in love? Yes. *Whom the Lord loveth he chasteneth, and scourgeth every son whom he receiveth,* Hebrews 12:6.

Should God's children then go to him as a Father? Yes. *I will arise and go to my Father,* Luke 15:18. And reverence him as a Father? Yes. *If I be a Father, where is mine honour,* Malachi 1:6. And imitate him? Yes. *Be ye perfect, as your heavenly Father is perfect,* Matthew 5:48. And obey him? Yes. *As obedient children,* 1 Peter 1:14. And submit to his chastisement? Yes. *My son, despise not the chastening of the Lord,* Hebrews 12:5.

Have all the saints one Father? Yes. *Have we not all one Father?* Malachi 2:10. Should they therefore love as brethren? Yes. *Add to godliness brotherly kindness,* 2 Peter 1:7. And is the neglect hereof a great sin? Yes. *Why do we deal treacherously every man against his brother,* Malachi 2:10.

Q 38. What is sanctification?

A. Sanctification is the work of God's free grace, whereby we are renewed in the whole man after the image of God, and are enabled more and more to die unto sin, and live unto righteousness.

Are all that are justified sanctified? Yes. *For Christ is made both righteousness and sanctification,* 1 Corinthians 1:30. Is it necessary that they should be so? Yes. *For nothing that defileth shall enter into the kingdom of heaven,* Revelation 21:27. And is it the will of God that they shall be so? Yes. *This is the will of God, even your sanctification,* 1 Thessalonians 4:3. Is Christ's death the meritorious cause of their sanctification? Yes. *He gave himself for us, that he might purify us a peculiar people to himself,* Titus 2:14. And is the Spirit the efficient cause of it? Yes. *'Tis called sanctification of the Spirit,* 2 Thessalonians 2:13. And is the word the instrumental cause of it? Yes. *Sanctify them through thy truth, thy word is truth,* John 17:17. But is the grace of God the original source from which this blessing flows? Yes. *Thy time was the time of love, then washed I thee with water, yea and I thoroughly washed away thy blood,* Ezekiel 16:8, 9.

Is sanctification more than an external reformation? Yes. *Ye make clean the outside of the cup and of the platter, but within are full of extortion and excess,* Matthew 23:25. Is it more than civility and good nature? Yes. *For he who had this yet lacked one thing,* Mark 10:21. Is it more than conviction? Yes. *For Ahab humbled himself,* 1 Kings 21:29. Is it more than an outward profession? Yes. *For some have the form of godliness who deny the power,* 2 Timothy 3:5.

Does sanctification imply an universal change? Yes. *Old things are past away, and all things are become new,* 2 Corinthians 5:17. Doth it extend to the inward man? Yes. *We are renewed in the spirit of our mind,* Ephesians 4:23. Is the understanding enlightened? Yes. *Ye were darkness, but now are ye light,* Ephesians 5:8. And the will subdued? Yes. *Thy people shall be willing in the day of thy power,* Psalm 60:3. And the affections spiritualized? Yes. *They are set on things above,* Colossians 3:2. Doth it also extend to the outward man? Yes. *Having our bodies washed with pure water,* Hebrews 10:22.

Is the saint renewed after the image of God? Yes. *Put on the new man, which is renewed after the image of him that created him,* Colossians 3:10. And after the pattern of Christ? Yes. *My little children of whom I travail in birth till Christ be formed in you,* Galatians 4:19. Doth he live in the exercise of every grace? Yes. *The life that I live in the flesh I live by the faith of the Son of God,* Galatians 2:20. And would he be found in the practice of every duty? Yes. *Fervent in spirit, serving the Lord,* Romans 12:11.

Is sin mortified in those that are sanctified? Yes. *They that are Christ's have crucified the flesh,* Galatians 5:24. Is this a difficult work? Yes. We read of *resisting unto blood striving against sin,* Hebrews 12:4. But is it a needful work? Yes. *If thy hand or thy foot offend thee, cut it off, for it is better for thee to enter into life halt or maimed than to be cast into everlasting fire,* Matthew 18:8. And can it only be performed under a divine influence? Yes. *If ye through the Spirit do mortify the deeds of the body, ye shall live,* Romans 8:13.

Do those that are dead unto sin live unto righteousness? Yes. *Being dead to sin we live unto righteousness,* 1 Peter 2:24. Is the work of sanctification imperfect in the present life? Yes. *Not as though I had already attained,* Philippians 3:12. But is it progressive? Yes. *The path of the just is like a shining light, shining more and more,* Proverbs 4:18. And will it be complete above? Yes. *When that which is perfect is come, then that which is in part shall be done away.* 1 Corinthians 13:10.

Q 39. What are the benefits which in this life do accompany or flow from justification, adoption, and sanctification?
A. The benefits which in this life do accompany or flow from justification, adoption, and sanctification, are assurance of God's love, peace of conscience, joy in the Holy Spirit, increase of grace, and perseverance therein to the end.

Hath a full assurance of God's love been attained by Christians in the present life? Yes. *We have known and believed the love which God hath to us,* 1 John 4:16. Is this assurance built upon the testimony of the Spirit? Yes. *The Spirit itself beareth witness with our sprits that we are the children of God,* Romans 8:16. And upon the testimony of conscience? Yes. *Our rejoicing is this, the testimony of our conscience,* 2 Corinthians 1:12. And upon the concurrent testimony of the word? Yes. *That we through patience and comfort of the Scripture might have hope,* Romans 15:4. Do all the saints attain to this assurance? No. *There are some who walk trembling after the Lord,* Hosea 11:10. And may those that have attained to it, lose it? Yes. *By thy favour thou hast made my mountain to stand strong, thou hideth thy face, and I was troubled,* Psalm 30:7. Should those that want assurance wait for it? Yes. *I will wait upon the Lord that hideth his face,* Isaiah 8:17. And hope for it? Yes. *Hope thou in God, for I shall yet praise him.* Psalm 42:11. And labour for it? Yes. *Shew the same diligence unto the full assurance of hope unto the end,* Hebrews 6:11. And should those who have it be thankful for it? Yes. *I will joy in the God of my salvation,* Habakkuk 3:18. And improve it? Yes. *Thy loving kindness is before mine eyes, and I have walked in thy truth,* Psalm 26:3.

Is peace of conscience the privilege of the saints? Yes. *My peace I give unto you,* John 14:27. And of none but the saints? No. *For there is no peace saith my God to the wicked,* Isaiah 57:21. Doth this peace follow upon our justification? Yes. *Son, be of good cheer, thy sins be forgiven thee,* Matthew 9:2. Is it the fruit of our sanctification? Yes. *'Tis peace in believing,* Romans 15:13. And is it the usual concomitant of a regular course of obedience? Yes. *Great peace have they that love thy law, and nothing shall offend them*, Psalm 119:165.   Is this a great privilege to those who possess it? Yes. *For if our hearts condemn us not, then have we confidence towards God*, 1 John 3:21. Doth it preserve them in life? Yes. *The peace of God shall keep your hearts and minds*, Philippians 4:7. And support them in death? Yes. *The end of that man is peace*, Psalm 37:37. And follow them into the other world? Yes. *They shall enter into peace*, Isaiah 57:2.

Have the saints joy in the Holy Ghost? Yes. *For believing we rejoice with joy unspeakable and full of glory*, 1 Peter 1:8. Are precious promises given that they might rejoice? Yes. *These things I speak that they might have my joy fulfilled in themselves*, John 17:13. And a gospel ministry settled? Yes. *Not that we have dominion over your faith, but are helpers of your joy*, 2 Corinthians 1:24. And comfortable prospects afforded? Yes. *We rejoice in hope of the glory of God*, Romans 5:2. Is it therefore the duty of such to rejoice? Yes. *Rejoice evermore*, 1 Thessalonians 5:16. And of none but such? No. *Rejoice not, O Israel, for joy, as other people, for thou hast gone a whoring from thy God*, Hosea 9:1.

Is it the saints' duty to grow in grace? Yes. *Grow in grace*, 2 Peter 3:18. Is it their desire thus to grow? Yes. *Lord, increase our faith*, Luke 17:5. And is it certain that they shall grow? Yes. *They shall grow as the vine*, Hosea 14:7. Do the saints grow in all grace? Yes. *For they grow up unto him in all things, which is the head, even Christ*, Ephesians 4:15. But does this growth more visibly appear in some graces than in others? Yes. Thus the apostle tells the Thessalonians, that *their faith grew exceedingly, and their charity towards each other abounded*, 2 Thessalonians 1:3.

Shall true believers persevere unto the end? Yes. *They shall be holden up, for God is able to make them to stand,* Romans 14:4.   Shall they be kept from fundamental errors?   Yes.   *For they are established in the truth,* 2 Peter 1:12.   And retain the vital principle of grace implanted in their souls? Yes.   *For it is that good part that shall not be taken away,* Luke 10:42.   And never relapse into a settled course of wickedness?   No.   *For we are not of them that draw back unto perdition,* Hebrews 10:39.

May a profession of religion be renounced?   Yes.   *Demas hath forsaken me,* 2 Timothy 4:10.   May great gifts be lost? Yes.   *His arm shall be clean dried up, and his right eye be utterly darkened,* Zechariah 11:17.   May appearances of grace vanish?   Yes.   *From him that hath not shall be taken away, even that which he seemeth to have,* Luke 8:18.   And may real grace decline? Yes. *Thou hast left thy first love,* Revelation 2:4.   But may it be totally lost?   No.   *His seed remaineth in him,* 1 John 3:9.

Q 40. What benefits do believers receive from Christ at their death?
A. The souls of believers are at their death made perfect in holiness, and do immediately pass into glory; and their bodies being still united to Christ, do rest in their grave till the resurrection.

Do believers die as well as others?   Yes.   *Your fathers where are they, and the prophets do they live for ever?*   Zechariah 1:5.   Must they die as well as others?   Yes.   *Knowing that shortly I must put off this tabernacle,* 2 Peter 1:14.   Would they not live if they could?   No.   *I would not live always,* Job. 7:16.   But is there a manifest difference between their death and that of others?   Yes.   *For precious in the sight of the Lord is the death of his saints,* Psalm 116:15.

Is death an advantage to the saints?   Yes.   *To die is gain,* Philippians 1:21.   Doth the soul die with the body? No. *For men may kill the body, but they are not able to kill the soul,* Matthew 10:28. Doth it sleep with the body? No. *For it returns to God who gave it,* Ecclesiastes 12:7. Does it immediately enter upon a separate state? Yes. *For when we are absent from the body, we are present with the Lord,* 2 Corinthians 5:8.

Doth death release the saints from all their sorrows? Yes. *They shall no more say, I am sick,* Isaiah 33:24. And free them from all their remaining corruptions? Yes. *For they are without fault before the throne of God,* Revelation 14:5. And set them at an eternal distance from all their spiritual enemies? Yes. *For the accuser of the brethren is cast down,* Revelation 12:10. And put an end to all their trials and labours? Yes. *They rest from their labours,* Revelation 14:13. And introduce them into a state of absolute perfection? Yes. *For the spirits of just men are made perfect,* Hebrews 12:23.

Do believers at death enter upon a state of perfect knowledge? Yes. *For here we see thru a glass darkly, but then face to face,* 1 Corinthians 13:12. And of perfect holiness? Yes. *For they have washed their robes, and made them white in the blood of the Lamb,* Revelation 7:14. And of complete glory? Yes. *Thou shalt guide me by thy counsel and afterward receive me to glory,* Psalm 73:24. Are they received into a glorious place? Yes. *For it is enlightened with the glory of God, and the Lamb is the Light thereof,* Revelation 21:23. Are they joined with glorious company? Yes. *They are come to an innumerable company of angels, to God the judge of all, and to Jesus the Mediator of the new covenant,* Hebrews 12:22, 23. Do they wear a glorious image? Yes. *I shall be satisfied when I awake in thy likeness,* Psalm 17:15. Are they employed in glorious work? Yes. *They serve God day and night, in his temple*, Revelation 7:15. And do they receive a glorious reward? Yes. *Ye shall receive a crown of glory, that fadeth not away*, 1 Peter 5:4.

Are the bodies of believers committed to the grave? Yes. *Then shall the dust return to the earth as it was*, Ecclesiastes 12:7. Is the grave the common receptacle of mankind? Yes. *Then shall dust return to the earth as it was*, Ecclesiastes 12:7. Hath a decent interment been sometimes denied to wicked men? Yes. *He shall be buried with the burial of an ass*, Jeremiah 22:19. But is it promised to the saints? Yes. *Thou shalt go to thy fathers in peace, thou shalt be buried in a good old age*, Genesis 15:15. Is the grave a resting place to such? Yes. *They shall rest in their beds*, Isaiah 57:2. And do they sometimes long for that resting place? Yes. *O that thou wouldst hide me in the grave*, Job 14:13. And provide for it? Yes. *Give me a possession of a burying place*, Genesis 23:4.

Doth death separate the saints from the love of God? No. *Neither death nor life can separate us from the love of God*, Romans 8:38. Or dissolve their union with Christ? No. *For they sleep in Jesus*, 1 Thessalonians 4:14. May they therefore meet it without fear? Yes. *O death, where is thy sting, O grave where is thy victory?*, 1 Corinthians 15:55.

Q 41. What benefits do believers receive from Christ at the resurrection?

A. At the resurrection believers, being raised up in glory, shall be openly acknowledged, and acquitted in the Day of Judgment, and made perfectly blessed, both in soul and body, in the full enjoyment of God to all eternity.

Is it possible that there should be a resurrection? Yes. *Why should it be thought a thing incredible to you, that God should raise the dead?*, Acts 26:8. Is it certain that there shall be a resurrection? Yes. *For many of them* (i.e. the multitude of them) *that sleep in the dust shall awake*, Daniel 12:2. Has there already been a resurrection? Yes. *For the graves were opened and many bodies of the saints which slept arose*, Matthew 27:52. Is this work ascribed to the Father? Yes. *For he which raised up the Lord Jesus shall raise up us also*, 2 Corinthians 4:14. And to the Son? Yes. *As the Father raiseth up the dead and quickeneth them, so the Son quickeneth whom he will*, John 5:22. And to the Spirit? Yes. *He will quicken your mortal bodies by his Spirit*, Romans 8:11. And shall the saints rise first? Yes. *The dead in Christ shall rise first*, 1 Thessalonians 4:16.

Will the same bodies be raised again? Yes. *In my flesh I shall see God*, Job 19:26. But will they be very different from what they are now? Yes. *That which thou sowest is not that body which shall be, so also is the resurrection of the dead*, 1 Corinthians 15:37,38,42. Will they be free from all natural weaknesses? Yes. *For they are sown in weakness but they are raised in power*, 1 Corinthians 15:43. Will they be free from all moral defilements? Yes. *For blessed and holy is he, that hath part in the first resurrection*, Revelation 20:6. Will they be endowed with activity and vigour? Yes. *It is sown a natural body, it is raised a spiritual body.* 1 Corinthians 15:44. Will they be rendered incorruptible and immortal? Yes. *For this corruptible shall put on incorruption, and this mortal put on immortality*, 1 Corinthians 15:53. Will they in all these respects resemble the glorious body of Christ? Yes. *He will change our vile body, and fashion it like unto his glorious body*, Philippians 3:21.

And will those who are found alive at Christ's second coming undergo a change equivalent to the resurrection? Yes. *We shall not all sleep, but we shall all be changed*, 1 Corinthians 15:51.

Will the saints be gathered together at the day of judgment? Yes. *Gather together my saints to me*, Psalm 50:5. And will this be the work of angels? Yes. *He shall send his angels and they shall gather together his elect from the four winds*, Matthew 24:31. Will they be separated from the wicked? Yes. *As the shepherd divideth the sheep from the goats*, Matthew 25:32. And will this be a final separation? Yes. *Between us and you there is a great gulf fixed*, Luke 16:26. Will they accompany Christ to judgment? Yes. *Behold he cometh with ten thousand of his saints*, Jude ver. 14. And be assessors with him in it? Yes. *Ye shall sit upon twelve thrones, judging the twelve tribes of Israel*, Matthew 19:28. And testify their approbation of all his proceedings? Yes. *They will say, 'hallelujah, Salvation and glory unto the Lord our God, for true and righteous are his judgments,'* Revelation 19:1,2. Will the saints be openly acknowledged in the day of judgment? Yes. *Him will I confess before my Father which is in heaven*, Matthew 10:32. And openly acquitted? Yes. *Well done good and faithful servant*, Matthew 25:23. And openly rewarded? Yes. *Enter thou into the joy of thy Lord*, ibid. Will their good works be then remembered? Yes. *I was an hungred and ye gave me meat*, Matthew 25:35. And their evil ones forgotten? Yes. *The iniquity of Israel shall then be sought for, and there shall be none*, Jeremiah 50:20.

Will heaven be the place of the saints residence? Yes. *Elijah went up by a whirlwind into heaven*, 2 Kings 2:11. Is it prepared for them? Yes. *I go to prepare a place for you,* John 14:2. And promised to them? Yes. *It is eternal life which God that cannot lie hath promised,* Titus 1:2. Will they in heaven see God? Yes. *Blessed are the pure in heart, for they shall see God,* Matthew 5:8. Will this be a transforming vision? Yes. *They shall be like him, for they shall see him as he is,* 1 John 3:2. And an abiding one? Yes. *So shall we be for ever with the Lord,* 1 Thessalonians 4:17. Is this enough to comfort them under all the sorrows and afflictions of life? Yes. *Wherefore comfort one another with these words,* 1 Thessalonians 4:18.

Q 42. But what shall be done to the wicked at their death?
A. The souls of the wicked shall, at their death, be cast into the torments of hell, and their bodies lie in their graves, till the resurrection and judgment of the great day.

Must the wicked die as well as the righteous? Yes. *For it is appointed unto all men once to die,* Hebrews 9:27. Must they die though they would not? Yes. *For the wicked is driven away in his wickedness,* Proverbs 14:32. Doth death often come upon them unexpected? Yes. *When they cry peace and safety, then sudden destruction cometh upon them,* 1 Thessalonians 5:3. And does it find them unprepared? Yes. *While they went to buy, the bridegroom came,* Matthew 25:10.

Do the souls of the wicked at death go into a place of torments? Yes. *In hell he lifted up his eyes being in torment,* Luke 16:23. And lie under the wrath of God? Yes. *For the Lord shall swallow them up in his wrath,* Psalm 21:9. And under the agonies of an accusing conscience? Yes. *There the worm dieth not,* Mark 9:46. Have they some presages of this before hand? Yes. *They have a fearful looking for of judgment and fiery indignation*, Hebrews 10:27. And will their misery be equal to their fears? Yes. *For according to thy fear, so is thy wrath*, Psalm 90:11.

Will all things round about them conspire to make them miserable? Yes. *For terrors shall make them afraid on every side*, Job 18:11. Will the saints pity them? No. *For the righteous shall see, and fear, and laugh at them*, Psalm 52:6. Will partnership in misery alleviate their pains? No. *For they shall be amazed one at another, their faces shall be as flames*, Isaiah 13:8. Shall they have a sad remembrance of their former abundance? Yes. *Son remember that thou in thy life-time received thy good things*, Luke 16:25. And a distant prospect of the heavenly happiness? Yes. *They shall see Abraham, Isaac and Jacob in the kingdom of heaven and themselves thrust out*, Luke 13:28. And will all this tend to fill them with inexpressible anguish, and horror, fury, and despair? Yes. *There shall be weeping, and gnashing of teeth*, Matthew 13:42.

Is there any possibility for the wicked to escape? No. *How can ye escape the damnation of hell?*, Matthew 23:33. Cannot they escape by cunning? No. *God taketh the wise in their own craftiness*, Job 5:13. Nor by power? No. *For by strength shall no man prevail*, 1 Samuel 2:9. Nor by flight? No. *Can any hide himself in secret places, that I shall not see him?* Jeremiah 23:24. Nor by numbers? No. *For though hand join in hand, yet the wicked shall not be unpunished*, Proverbs 11:21. Will hell then be large enough to hold the whole number of the ungodly? Yes. *For God hath made it deep and large*, Isaiah 30:33.

Are the bodies of the wicked lodged in the grave? Yes. *Like sheep they are laid in the grave*, Psalm

49:14. Doth the grave consume them? Yes. *So shall the grave consume those that have sinned*, Job 24:19. Does it mar their beauty? Yes. *Death shall feed on them*, Psalm 49:14. And rob them of their glory? Yes. *His glory shall not descend after him*, Psalm 49:17. And blot out their memory? Yes. *He shall be no more remembered*, Job 24:20. Are they reserved there to the Day of Judgment? Yes. *God reserveth the unjust unto the Day of Judgment to be punished*, 2 Peter 2:9. And shall they then be brought forth? Yes. *They shall be brought forth to the day of wrath*, Job 21:30.

Q 43. What shall be done to the wicked, at the Day of Judgment?
A. At the Day of Judgment the bodies of the wicked, being raised out of their graves, shall be sentenced, together with their souls, to unspeakable torments with the devil and his angels for ever.

Will the wicked rise again? Yes. *There shall be a resurrection both of the just and of the unjust*, Acts 24:15. Will they rise at Christ's call? Yes. *They shall hear his voice and come forth*, John 5:28. Will it be a shameful resurrection to such? Yes. *They shall awake to everlasting shame and contempt*, Daniel 12:2. And a dreadful one? Yes. *They shall come forth to the resurrection of damnation*, John 5:29. And will the judgment follow? Yes. *The Lord cometh to execute judgment*, Jude ver. 15.

Is the Day of Judgment called a great day? Yes. *It is that great day of God Almighty*, Revelation 16:14. Will it be a day of discover? Yes. *The Lord will bring to light the hidden things of darkness*, 1 Corinthians 4;5. And of conviction? Yes. *To convince all that are ungodly*, Jude ver. 15. And of recompense? Yes. *He shall recompense tribulation to them that trouble you,* 2 Thessalonians 1:6. And of wrath? Yes. *The great day of his wrath is come,* Revelation 6:17. Would sinners be glad not to appear on that day? Yes. *They will say to the mountains and rocks fall on us, and hide us from the face of him that sitteth upon the throne,* Revelation 6:16. But must they appear? Yes. *I saw the dead both small and great stand before God,* Revelation 20:12.

Will the judgment be public? Yes. *He shall call to the heavens from above, and to the earth,* Psalm 50:4. And impartial? Yes. *For there is no respect of persons with God,* Romans 2:11. And very strict? Yes. *For God will bring every work into judgment,* Ecclesiastes 12:14. Will it extend to the thoughts? Yes? *For God will judge the secrets of men by Jesus Christ,* Romans 2:16. And to the words? Yes. *By thy words thou shalt be justified, and by thy words, condemned,* Matthew 12:37. And to sins of omission? Yes? *I was hungry and you gave me no meat,* Matthew 25:42. And to sins of commission? Yes. *For he that doth wrong shall receive for the wrong that he hath done,* Colossians 3:25. Will sentence be immediately passed? Yes. *Then shall he say to those on his left hand, 'Depart from me ye cursed,'* Matthew 25:41. And as speedily executed? Yes. *These shall go away into everlasting punishment,* Matthew 25:46.

Will hell be the place of the sinner's torment? Yes. *The wicked shall be turned into hell,* Psalm 9:17. And God the inflictor of it? Yes. *Upon the wicked he will rain snares, fire and brimstone, a horrible tempest,* Psalm 11:6. And devils their companions in it? Yes. *Depart into everlasting fire, prepared for the devil and his angels,* Matthew 25:41. And will the body as well as the soul be the subject of it? Yes. *The whole body shall be cast into hell,* Matthew 5:29.

Will the misery of the damned be unmixed? Yes. *The wrath of God is poured out without mixture,* Revelation 14:10. And extreme? Yes. *It is wrath to the uttermost,* 1 Thessalonians 2:16. And intolerable? Yes. *Can thine heart endure?,* Ezekiel 22:14. And without inter-mission? Yes. *They have no rest, day nor night,* Revelation 14:11. And without end? Yes. *The smoke of their torment ascendeth up for ever and ever,* ibid. Will this be the portion of all the wicked? Yes. *For indignation, and wrath, tribulation, and anguish shall be upon every soul that doth evil,* Romans 2:9.

Q 44. What is the duty which God requireth of man?
A. The duty which God requireth of man is, obedience to his revealed will.

Hath God revealed his will? Yes. *He hath shewed his word unto Jacob, his statutes and his judgments unto Israel,* Psalm 147:19. Hath he revealed it plainly? Yes. *So that he may run which readeth it,* Habakkuk 2:2. And fully? Yes. *I have not shunned to declare to you the whole counsel of God,* Acts 20:27. Should we therefore seek to be acquainted with it? Yes. *Lead me in thy truth and teach me,* Psalm 25:5.

Is obedience to God's revealed will a duty? Yes. *And now, O Israel, what doth the Lord thy God require of thee, but to walk in his ways,* Deuteronomy 10:12. Is it the duty of all? Yes. *Give ear all ye inhabitants of the world, both low and high, rich and poor,* Psalm 49:1,2. But especially of the redeemed? Yes. *Ye are bought with a price, therefore glorify God in your body, and in your spirit, which are God's,* 1 Corinthians 6:20. And is it their whole duty? Yes. *Let us hear the conclusion of the* matter, fear God and keep his commandments, for this is the whole duty of man, Ecclesiastes 12:13.

Is it reasonable that God should be obeyed? Yes. *It is our reasonable service*, Romans 12:1. Is obedience due to him as our Creator? Yes. *Thou art my servant; I have formed thee*, Isaiah 44:21. And as our preserver? Yes. *Is he not thy Father that hath bought thee, hath he not made and established thee?*, Deuteronomy 32:6. And as our Master? Yes. *If I be a Master, where is my fear?* Malachi 1:6. And as our Sovereign? Yes. *All the ends of the earth shall remember and turn unto the Lord, for the kingdom is the Lord's*, Psalm 22:27,28. Should God's commands therefore take place of men's? Yes. *Whether it be right in the sight of God to hearken unto you, more than unto God, judge ye*, Acts 4:19.

Q 45. What did God at first reveal to man for the rule of his obedience?
A. The rule which God at first revealed to man for his obedience, was the moral law.

Were there positive institutions under the Old Testament? Yes. *There were meats, and drinks, and diverse washings and carnal ordinances*, Hebrews 9:10. Were these suited to the infant state of the church? Yes. *Even so we when we were children, were in bondage under the elements of the world*, Galatians 4:3. But are they now abolished? Yes. *For they were only imposed till the time of reformation*, Hebrews 9:10. Is it our great mercy to be free from them? Yes. *For they were a yoke which neither our fathers nor we were able to bear*, Acts 15:10. Do we owe this liberty to Christ? Yes. *For the priesthood being changed, there is made of necessity a change also of the law*, Hebrews 7:12.

And should we stand fast in it? Yes. *Be not entangled again with the yoke of bondage,* Galatians 5:1.

Are there positive institutions under the gospel? Yes. *For I have received of the Lord, which I also delivered unto you,* 1 Corinthians 11:23. And should these be observed? Yes. *And keep the ordinances as I delivered them unto you,* 1 Corinthians 11:2. But is the moral law the principal rule of obedience? Yes. *The Lord our God made a covenant with us in Horeb,* Deuteronomy 5:2.

Was this law originally written upon the heart of man? Yes. *They shew the work of the law, written in their hearts,* Romans 2:15. Doth natural conscience influence this law? Yes. *For the Gentiles, which have not the law, do by nature the things contained in the law,* Romans 2:14. Did the Gentiles then sin by breaking this law? Yes. *What they know naturally in these things, they corrupt themselves,* Jude ver. 10. And will they be punished for the breach of it? Yes. *They that have sinned without law shall perish without the law,* Romans 2:12. But is this law more fully revealed in the word? Yes. *The Lord made not this covenant with our fathers, but with us, even us, who are all of us here alive this day,* Deuteronomy 5:3.

Should we subscribe to the excellency of the law? Yes. *The law is holy, just, and good,* Romans 7:12. And enquire into its uses? Yes. *Wherefore then serveth the law,* Galatians 3:19. Are the saints under the law as a covenant of works? No. *We are not under the law, but under grace,* Romans 6:15. But are they under it as a rule of life? Yes. *Being not without law to God,* 1 Corinthians 9:21. Is it universally binding? Yes. *I esteem all thy precepts concerning all things to be right,* Psalm 119:128.

And perpetually so? Yes. *Do we then make void the law through faith, God forbid,* Romans 3:31.

Doth the law curb sin? Yes. *It was made not for the righteous man but for the lawless and disobedient,* 1 Timothy 1:9. And instruct in duty? Yes. *For the end of the commandment is charity,* 1 Timothy 1:5. Doth it convince of sin? Yes. *I had not known sin but by the law,* Romans 7:7. And aggravate sin? Yes. *The law entered that the offence might abound,* Romans 5:20. And beget fear? Yes. *It gendereth unto bondage,* Galatians 4:24. And silence carnal objections? Yes. *I through the law am dead to the law,* Galatians 2:19. And lead the sinner to Christ? Yes. *The law is our school-master, to bring us to Christ,* Galatians 3:24. Is the law then of great advantage if rightly used? Yes. *For we know that the law is good if a man use it lawfully,* 1 Timothy 1:8.

Q 46. Where is the moral law summarily comprehended?
A. The moral law is summarily comprehended in the Ten Commandments.

Was the moral law in force before the Ten Commandments were given? Yes. *For Abraham commanded his children to keep the way of the Lord,* Genesis 18:19. Were any parts of it published before? Yes. *Whoso sheddeth man's blood, by man shall his blood be shed,* Genesis 9:6. But was it at last summed up in the Ten Commandments? Yes. *He declared unto you his covenant, even Ten Commandments,* Deuteronomy 4:13. Were these commandments spoken? Yes. *Ye heard a voice,* Deuteronomy 4:12. And did God speak them? Yes. *God spake all these words, saying,* Exodus 20:1. Were they written? Yes. *What is written in the law?* Luke 10:25. And did God write them? Yes. *The writing was the writing of God,* Exodus 32:16.

Was Christ concerned in giving the law? Yes. *He spake to our fathers in Mount Sinai,* Acts 7:38. Was it given by the hands of Moses? Yes. *For the law was given by Moses,* John 1:17. And by the ministration of angels? Yes. *They received the law by the disposition of angels,* Acts 7:53.

Was the law given with much pomp? Yes. *The Lord came from Sinai and rose up from Seir, and came with ten thousands of his saints,* Deuteronomy 33:2. And with great terror? Yes. *There were lightnings and thunderings, and the noise of the trumpet and the mountain smoking,* Exodus 20:18. Was the sight hereof terrible to Moses himself? Yes. *He said, 'I exceedingly fear and quake,'* Hebrews 12:21. And did it strike an awe upon the people? Yes. *When the people saw it they removed and stood afar off,* Exodus 20:18. Is it necessary then that what was delivered with so much terror should be obeyed with fear? Yes. *We must serve God, acceptably with reverence and godly fear,* Hebrews 12:28.[4]

Q 47. What is the sum of the Ten Commandments?
A. The sum of the Ten Commandments is, to *love the Lord our God, with all our heart, with all our soul, with all our strength, and with all our mind; and our neighbour as ourselves.*

Were the Ten Commandments written originally in two tables? Yes. *The Lord said, 'hew thee out two tables of stone, and I will write upon the tables',* Deuteronomy 10:1. Is love to God inclusive of all the duties of the first table? Yes. *It is the first and great commandment,* Matthew 22:38. And is love to

---

[4] The moral law is so called, because it is a rule founded upon the perfections of God, having its general principles in the light of nature, and given to mankind as intelligent and social creatures, for the direction of their manners and behaviour.

our neighbour inclusive of all the duties of the second? Yes. *The second is like unto it, thou shalt love thy neighbour as thyself,* Matthew 22:39. Is the whole law then fulfilled in love? Yes. *For love is the fulfilling of the law,* Romans 13:10.

Is it our duty to love God? Yes. *Take good heed to yourselves that ye love the Lord your God,* Joshua 23:11. Is there in him every thing that is lovely? Yes. *How great is his beauty,* Zechariah 9:17. And will he return our love? Yes. *I love them that love me,* Proverbs 8:17. And reward it? Yes. *For eye hath not seen what God hath prepared for them that love him,* 1 Corinthians 2:9.

Should we discover our love to God in frequent thoughts of him? Yes. *My meditation of him shall be sweet,* Psalm 104:34. And in earnest desires after him? Yes. *My soul thirsteth for thee, my flesh longeth for thee,* Psalm 63:2. And in sorrow for his absence? Yes. *Why hidest thou thyself,* Psalm 10:1. And in an unfeigned submission to his providential will? Yes. *I was dumb, I opened not my mouth,* Psalm 39:9. And in a conscientious obedience to all his commands? Yes. *This is the love of God that we keep his commandments,* 1 John 5:3. And in a due resentment against whatsoever offends him? Yes. *Do not I hate them that hate thee, and am I not grieved with those that rise up against thee,* Psalm 139:21.

Should our love to God be rational and judicious? Yes. *That your love might abound yet more and more, in knowledge and in all judgment,* Philippians 1:9. And upright and sincere? Yes. *Grace be with them that love the Lord Jesus Christ in sincerity,* Ephesians 6:24. And strong and vehement? *Yes I am sick of love,* Song of Solomon 2:5. And supreme and superlative? Yes. *He that loveth father and mother more than me, is not worthy of me,* Matthew 10:37. And constant and abiding? Yes. *Keep yourselves in the love of God,* Jude ver. 21.

Must our love be confined to God? No. *He that loveth God must love his brother also,* 1 John 4:21. Should we seek the good of others? Yes. *Charity seeketh not her own,* 1 Corinthians 13:5. And lend a compassionate ear to their complaints? Yes. *To the afflicted pity should be shewn,* Job 6:14. And supply their necessities? Yes. *We should not withhold the poor from his desire, nor cause the eye of the widow to fail,* Job 31:16. And reprove their sins? Yes. *Thou shalt in any wise rebuke thy neighbour,* Leviticus 19:17. And pray for them? Yes. *Pray one for another,* James 5:16. And even venture our lives for them if it be necessary? Yes. *We ought to lay down our lives for the brethren,* 1 John 3:16.

Should we love others as Christ hath loved us? Yes. *And walk in love as Christ also loved us,* Ephesians 5:2. And as we love ourselves? Yes. *Thou shalt love thy neighbour as thyself,* Matthew 19:19. Should we love them as sincerely? Yes. *Let us not love in word, but in deed and in truth,* 1 John 3:18. And as fervently? Yes. *Above all things have fervent charity among yourselves,* 1 Peter 4:8. And as constantly? Yes. *Let brotherly love continue,* Hebrews 13:1. Doth it hence follow that we should do to others as we would be done by? Yes. *Whatsoever ye would that men should do to you, do ye even unto them,* Matthew 7:12.

Is love, Christ's new commandment? Yes. *A new commandment I give unto you, that ye love one another,* John 13:34. Is it a test of our discipleship? Yes. *By this shall all men know that ye are my* disciples, *if ye love one another,* John 13:35.   Is it placed at the top of the Christian graces? Yes. *The greatest of these is charity,* 1 Corinthians 13:13. And is it a grace that will continue and accompany us to heaven? Yes. *Now abideth charity,* ibid.

Q 48. What is the preface to the Ten Commandments? A. The preface to the Ten Commandments is in these words; *I am the Lord thy God which have brought thee out of the land of Egypt, out of the house of bondage.*

Were the children of Israel under peculiar obligations to God? Yes. *He brought them out of the land of Egypt, and out of the house of bondage,* Exodus 20:2.   Were the children of Israel then in Egypt? Yes. *These are the names of the children of Israel which came into Egypt,* Exodus 1:1.   Were they there as strangers? Yes. *Ye were strangers in the land of Egypt,* Exodus 22:21.   Were they there as bond slaves? Yes. *Thou wast a bondman in the land of Egypt,* Deuteronomy 15:15.   And were they long there? Yes. *We have dwelt in Egypt a long time,* Numbers 20:15.

Did God bring them out of Egypt? Yes. *I made you to go out of Egypt,* Judges 2:1.   And that miraculously? Yes. *Ye have seen all that the Lord did before your eyes in the land of Egypt, the signs and those great miracles,* Deuteronomy 29:2,3.   And in haste? Yes. *Thou camest out of Egypt in haste,* Deuteronomy 16:3.   And at the appointed time? Yes. *In the self same day all the hosts of the Lord went out from the land of Egypt,* Exodus 12:41.   Did this oblige them to thankfulness? Yes. *It was a night to be much observed to the Lord,* Exodus12:42.   And to obedience? Yes. *When I brought thee out of the land of Egypt, I said, 'obey my voice,'* Jeremiah 7: 22-23.

Q 49. What doth the preface to the Ten Commandments teach us?

A. The preface to the Ten Commandments teacheth us that because God is the Lord, and our God and redeemer, therefore we are bound to keep all his commandments.

Is God the Lord? Yes. *I am the Lord, that is my name,* Isaiah 42:8. Is this a name betokening authority? Yes. *The Lord Most High is terrible, he is a great King,* Psalm 47:2. Is it therefore an obligation upon us to keep his commands? Yes. *Ye shall therefore keep my statutes and my judgments, I am the Lord,* Leviticus 18:5. Is he our God? Yes. *O Lord thou art our God,* 2 Chronicles 14:11. Is he so by covenant? Yes. *I entered into covenant with thee, and thou becamest mine,* Ezekiel 16:8. And by our choice? Yes. *Ye have chosen you the Lord,* Joshua 24:22. Is this a reason why we should keep his commandments? Yes. *Thou shalt love the Lord thy God and keep his charge,* Deuteronomy 11:1. And is it a reason obligatory to Gentiles as well as Jews? Yes. *For is he the God of the Jews only? Is he not also of the Gentiles? Yea of the Gentiles also,* Romans 3:29.

Is God our Redeemer? Yes. *All flesh shall know that I the Lord am thy Saviour and thy Redeemer,* Isaiah 49:26. Hath he redeemed us from outward troubles? Yes. *The angel that redeemed me from all evil, bless the lads,* Genesis 48:16. And from our spiritual enemies? Yes. *We are delivered out of the hands of our enemies,* Luke 1:74. And from the bondage of sin? Yes. *He shall redeem Israel from all their iniquities,* Psalm 130:8. And from eternal wrath? Yes. *Who hath delivered us from the wrath to come,* 1 Thessalonians 1:10.

Are we then in gratitude bound to obey God? Yes. *Truly I am thy servant, I am thy servant, thou hast*

loosed my bonds, Psalm 116:16.   And in justice?
Yes. *For ye are not your own,* 1 Corinthians 6:19.
And are we guilty not only of horrid ingratitude, but
of great impiety if we do not?   Yes. *For will a man
rob God?,* Malachi 3:8.[5]

Q 50. Which is the first commandment?
A. The first commandment is, *Thou shalt have no other
gods before me.*

Is the belief and worship of a Deity one of the
principles of natural religion?   Yes. *For all people
will walk every one in the name of their god,* Micah
4:5.   But is it more strongly inculcated in the divine
word?   Yes. *Worship the Lord,* Psalm 29:2.

Did the sin of having many gods prevail in the early
ages of the world?   Yes. *Wherefore hast thou stolen
my gods,* Genesis 31:30.   And were God's own
people soon infected with it?   Yes. *Up make us
gods,* Exodus 32:1.   Is this too absolutely forbidden
in the first commandment?   Yes. *For the first of all
the commandments is this, hear O Israel the Lord our
God is one Lord,* Mark 12:29.   And was it severely
punished in those that were guilty of it?   Yes. *For
the Lord plagued the people because they made the
calf,* Exodus 32 & ult.

Q 51. What is required in the first commandment?
A. The first commandment requireth us to know and
acknowledge God to be the only true God and our
God, and to worship and glorify him accordingly.

Is it our duty to know God? Yes. *Know thou the God
of thy fathers,* 1 Chronicles 28:9.   And   to

---

[5] A national covenant being a thing peculiar to the Jewish
economy: what is said under the foregoing answer can only with
propriety be applied to real saints, under the gospel dispensation.

acknowledge him? Yes. *In all thy ways acknowledge him,* Proverbs 3:6. Should we do this by a humble fear of him? Yes. *I fear God,* Genesis 42:18. And by a hearty confidence in him? Yes. *I trust in thee,* Psalm 25:2. And by an entire submission to him? Yes. *Submit yourselves unto God,* James 4:7.

Should we acknowledge God as our God? Yes. *One shall say, 'I am the Lord's',* Isaiah 44:5. And as the only true God? Yes. *Ye turned from idols to serve the living and true God,* 1 Thessalonians 1:9. Should we do this publicly and in the face of the world? Yes. *And hast professed a good profession before many witnesses,* 1 Timothy 6:12. Should we do it with judgment and understanding? Yes. *Choose ye this day whom ye will serve,* Joshua 24:15. Should we do it joyfully and without regret? Yes. *The jailor rejoiced believing in God with all his house,* Acts 16:34. Should we do it sincerely and without deceit? Yes. *Son give me thine heart,* Proverbs 23:26. Should we do it entirely and without reserve? Yes. *Caleb hath wholly followed the Lord,* Deuteronomy 1:36. Should we do it resolutely and without hesitation? Yes. *Nay but we will serve the Lord,* Joshua 24:21. And should we do it fixedly and without revolt? Yes. *So will we not go back from thee,* Psalm 80:18.

Should we give up ourselves to the will of God? *Yes. Here am I, let him do to me as seemeth him good,* 2 Samuel 15:26. And surrender ourselves to his government? Yes. *By thee only will we make mention of thy name,* Isaiah 26:13. And devote ourselves to his service? Yes. *Yield yourselves unto the Lord, and serve the Lord your God,* 2 Chronicles 30:8. And has God a just right to all this? Yes. *Of thine own have we given unto thee,* 1 Chronicles 29:14.

Is it enough that we verbally devote ourselves to the Lord? No. *For we must vow and pay unto the Lord our God*, Psalm 76:11. Must we therefore worship him? Yes. *We are a holy priesthood to offer up spiritual sacrifices unto God*, 1 Peter 2:5. Must we do this with the inward man? Yes. *Bless the Lord, O my soul*, Psalm 103:1. And with the whole man? Yes. *All that is within me bless his holy name*, ibid. And with a view to Christ? Yes. *Their sacrifices shall be accepted upon mine altar*, Isaiah 56:7. And by the assistance of the Spirit? Yes. *Strengthened with might by his Spirit in the inward man*, Ephesians 3:16. And in the way of his own appointments? Yes. *For in vain do they worship me teaching for doctrines the commandments of men*, Matthew 15:9.

Should we also glorify God? Yes. *Glorify God in your body, and in your spirit*, 1 Corinthians 6:20. Should we do this by a constant attendance on his ordinances? Yes. *All nations shall come and worship before thee, and shall glorify thy name*, Psalm 86:9. And by a humble confession of our sins? Yes. *My son, give glory to God, and make confession to him*, Joshua 7:19. And by a regular course of obedience? Yes. *Herein is my Father glorified, if ye bring forth much fruit*, John 15:8. And if called thereto by suffering for his sake? Yes. *This spake he signifying by what death he should glorify God*, John 21:19. And will this in the end redound to our own advantage? Yes. *For them that honor me, I will honor*, 1 Samuel 2:30.

Q 52. What is forbidden in the first commandment?
A. The first commandment forbiddeth the denying, or not worshipping and glorifying the true God, as God and our God, and the giving of that worship and glory to any other, which is due unto him alone.

Is it a sin to deny God? Yes. *They deny the only Lord God,* Jude ver. 4. May God be denied in his attributes? Yes. *They say, 'How doth God know, and is there knowledge in the Most High?'* Psalm 73:11. And in his authority? Yes. *Who is Lord over me?,* Psalm 12:4. And in his providence? Yes. *They say the Lord will not do good, neither will he do evil,* Zephaniah 1:12. And in his truths? Yes. *They bring in damnable heresies, denying the Lord that bought them,* 2 Peter 2:1. And may God be practically denied even where he is doctrinally owned? Yes. *They profess that they know God, but in works they deny him,* Titus 1:16.

Is ignorance of God a great sin? Yes. *They know not the way of the Lord,* Jeremiah 5:4. And forgetfulness of God? Yes. *Thou hast forgotten God that formed thee,* Deuteronomy 32:18. And distrust of God? Yes. *Is the Lord among us, or is he not?* Exodus 17:7. And contempt of God? Yes. *Wherefore do the wicked contemn God?* Psalm 10:13. And any abatement of affection toward him? Yes. *I have somewhat against thee because thou hast left thy first love,* Revelation 2:4.

Is it a sin to neglect the worship of God? Yes. *Thou hast not called upon me, O Jacob,* Isaiah 43:22. Or to divide it? Yes. *They swear by the Lord, and swear by Malcham,* Zephaniah 1:5. Or to be remiss in it? Yes. *Their heart was not right with him,* Psalm 78:37. Or to perform it for selfish ends? Yes. *Did ye at all fast unto me, even to me,* Zechariah 7:5.

Is idolatry a very heinous sin? Yes. *Neither be ye idolaters, as were some of them,* 1 Corinthians 10:7. Were the Gentiles idolaters? Yes. *Ye have seen their idols, wood and stone,* Deuteronomy 29:17. Were they guilty of the grossest idolatry? Yes. *They sacrificed to devils, and not to God,* 1 Corinthians 10:20.   Are the Papists idolaters?   Yes.   For they do honor to one *who sitteth in the temple of God, shewing himself that he is God,* 2 Thessalonians 2:4.   But is there such a thing as heart idolatry?   Yes.   *These men have set up their idols in their hearts,* Ezekiel 14:3.   Are proud men idolaters?   Yes.   *Thine heart is lifted up, and thou hast said, 'I am a god,'* Ezekiel 28:2.   And covetous men? Yes.   *Mortify covetousness which is idolatry,* Colossians 3:5.   And sensualists?   Yes.   *Whose god is their belly,* Philippians 3:19.   Is undue flattery also a kind of idolatry?   Yes.   *The people said, 'it is the voice of God, and not of man,'* Acts 12:22.   Is this a sin that God will correct in this world?   Yes.   *Ye shall bear the sins of your idols,* Ezekiel 23:49.   And will he severely punish it in the world to come?   Yes.   *For idolaters shall not inherit the kingdom of God,* 1 Corinthians 6:9.

Q 53. What are we especially taught by these words before me, in the first commandment?

A. These words *before me,* in the first commandment teach us, that God, who seeth all things, taketh notice of and is much displeased with the sin of having any other god.

Doth God see all our actions?   Yes.   *If we should say the darkness shall cover us, even the night shall be light about us,* Psalm 139:11.   Doth he see our most secret duties?   Yes.   *Your Father which seeth in secret will reward you openly,* Matthew 6:4.   Doth he see our most secret sins?   Yes.   *He hath set our secret sins in the light of his countenance,* Psalm 90:8.   And should this dissuade from sin?   Yes. *How can I do this great wickedness, and sin against God?* Genesis 39:9.

Do idolaters often flatter themselves that God doth not see them? Yes. *They do it in the dark, and say the Lord seeth us not,* Ezekiel 8:12. But doth God see them? Yes. *If we have stretched out our hands to a strange god, shall not God search this out?,* Psalm 44:20,21. Is this an aggravation of their sin? Yes. *They provoke me to anger continually to my face,* Isaiah 65:3. And should it be a preservative against it? Yes. *We must serve God with a perfect heart, for the Lord searcheth all hearts,* 1 Chronicles 28:9.

Is idolatry spiritual robbery? Yes. *I am the Lord, and my glory I will not give to another,* Isaiah 42:8 And spiritual adultery? Yes. *Thou hast gone a whoring from thy God,* Hosea 9:1. Is God therefore greatly displeased with it? Yes. *They provoked him in jealously with strange gods,* Deuteronomy 32:16. And is this a reason why we should be aware of it? Yes. *For who knoweth the power of his anger,* Psalm 90:11.

Q 54. Which is the second commandment?
A. The second commandment is, *Thou shalt not make unto thee any graven image, or any likeness of anything that is in heaven above, or that is in the earth beneath, or that is in the water under the earth; thou shalt not bow down thyself to them, nor serve them: for I the Lord thy God am a jealous God, visiting the iniquity of the fathers upon the children unto the third and fourth generation of them that hate me; and shewing mercy unto thousands of them that love me, and keep my commandments.*

Should we be careful to avoid idolatry? Yes. *Take heed, lest ye corrupt yourselves, and make you a graven image,* Deuteronomy 4:15,16. And that in all the instances of it? Yes. *The similitude of any figure, the likeness of male or female, the likeness of a beast or winged fowl,* Deuteronomy 4:16,17. And in all the approaches to it? Yes. *Make no mention of the names of other gods, neither let it be heard out of thy mouth,* Exodus 23:13.

Is idolatry an infatuating sin? Yes. *They are mad upon their idols,* Jeremiah 50:38. And a spreading sin? Yes. *For Asia and the whole world worshipped the goddess Diana,* Acts 19:27. Was it therefore necessary, that the prohibition of it should be enforced and repeated? Yes. *For precept must be upon precept, and line upon line,* Isaiah 28:10. And is it forbidden in the New Testament as well as the old? Yes. *That they should not worship idols of gold, and silver, and stone, and wood,* Revelation 9:20.

Q 55. What is required in the second commandment?
A. The second commandment requireth the receiving, observing, and keeping pure and entire all such religious worship and ordinances, as God hath appointed in his word.

May civil honor be given to creatures? Yes. *Thy Father's children shall bow down before thee,* Genesis 49:8. But is divine worship due only to God? Yes. *Him only shalt thou serve,* Matthew 4:10. Is the light of nature sufficient to direct us in the worship of God? No. *Whom ye ignorantly worship,* Acts 17:23. Should we therefore have recourse to the written word? Yes. *And Joshua built an altar to the Lord, as it is written in the book of the law of Moses,* Joshua 8:31.

Should all God's ordinances be received? Yes. *Receive, I pray thee, the law from his mouth,* Job 22:22. And observed? Yes. *Ye shall observe my statutes,* Leviticus 19:37. And kept pure without adulteration? Yes. *Add thou not unto his words,* Proverbs 30:6. And entire without diminution?

Yes. *Ye have not kept my ways, but have been partial in my law,* Malachi 2:9. Is this especially the duty of ministers? Yes. *The good thing which was committed to thee keep,* 2 Timothy 1:14.

May not our own fancies be the rule of our worship? No. *Remember the commandments of the Lord, and seek not after your own heart, and your own eyes,* Numbers 15:39. Nor the customs of men? No. *After the doings of the land of Egypt, and after the doings of the land of Canaan, ye shall not do,* Leviticus 18:3. Nor the prescriptions of superiors? No. *Be it known unto thee, O King, that we will not serve thy gods,* Daniel 3:18. Should we therefore keep close to God's Word as our rule? Yes. *And look that thou make them after the pattern,* Exodus 25:40. Nor be affrighted therefrom by the greatest reproaches or sufferings? No. *None of these things move me,* Acts 20:24.

Q 56. What is forbidden in the second commandment?
A. The second commandment forbiddeth the worshipping of God by images, or any other way not appointed in his word.

Is it a sin to worship any creature? Yes. *They served the creature more than the Creator,* Romans 1:25. Or the image of any Creature? Yes. *Cursed be the man that maketh any graven or molten image, an abomination unto the Lord,* Deuteronomy 27:15. May we not worship the host of heaven? No. *Lest when thou seest the sun and the moon and the stars, thou shouldst be driven to worship them,* Deuteronomy 4:19. Nor great and good men? No. *Why do ye these things, we are also men of like passions with you,* Acts 14:15. Nor good angels? No. *Let no man beguile you of your reward, by a voluntary humility and worshipping of angels,* Colossians 2:18.

Is it a sin to plead for idols? Yes. *Will ye plead for Baal?* Judges 6:31. Or pray to them? Yes. *One shall cry to him yet he cannot answer,* Isaiah 46:7. Or trust in them? Yes. *They shall be greatly ashamed that trust in graven images,* Isaiah 42:17. Or attribute any thing to them? Yes. *Lest thou shouldst say, 'My idol hath done them,'* Isaiah 48:5. Or give them any part of religious worship? Yes. *If my heart hath been secretly enticed, or my mouth has kissed my hand, this were an iniquity, to be punished by the Judge,* Job 31:27,28.

Is it a sin to worship the true God by images? Yes. *Take ye therefore good heed unto yourselves, for ye saw no manner of similitude,* Deuteronomy 4:15,16. Can we form any image of God in our minds? No. *To whom will ye liken God,* Isaiah 40:18. Is it impossible then to form it with our hands? Yes. *For we must not think that the Godhead is like unto gold or silver, or stone graven by art or man's device,* Acts 17:29. Do those therefore that attempt it put a great affront upon him? Yes. *They change the glory of the incorruptible God into an image, made like unto corruptible man,* Romans 1:23.

Doth this commandment forbid all superstitious practices in worship? Yes. *In all things ye are too superstitious,* Acts 17:22. And all sinful compliances with the invention of men? Yes. *Touch not, take not, handle not after the commandments and doctrines of men,* Colossians 2:21,22. Does it particularly condemn the idolatry of the papists in worshipping a consecrated host? Yes. *For it is bread that we break,* 1 Corinthians 10:16. Is it enough that these things are not expressly forbidden? No. *They offered strange fire, which the Lord commandeth them not,* Leviticus 10:1.

Q 57. What are the reasons annexed to the second commandment?

A. The reasons annexed to the second commandment are, God's sovereignty over us, his propriety in us, and the zeal he hath to his own worship.

Is God the Lord? Yes. *I am the Lord,* Leviticus 19:4. Is that a reason why we should worship him? Yes. *Let us kneel before the Lord our Maker,* Psalm 95:6. And is idolatry therefore an act of rebellion against him? Yes. *We have rebelled by departing from thee,* Daniel 9:5. Is he our God? Yes. *I am the Lord your God,* Leviticus 24:22. Is that also a reason why we should worship him? Yes. *We will serve the Lord for he is our God,* Joshua 24:18. And cleave unto him? Yes. *For hath a nation changed their gods,* Jeremiah 2:11. And is it a breach of covenant if we do not? Yes. *They will turn unto other gods, and serve them, and break my covenant,* Deuteronomy 31:20.

Is God a jealous God? Yes. *The Lord thy God is a jealous God amongst you,* Deuteronomy 6:15. Doth jealously imply the height of anger and indignation? Yes. *God is jealous, the Lord revengeth, and is furious,* Nahum 1:2. And doth nothing stir up the jealousy of God more than idolatry? No. *They have moved me to jealousy with that which is not god, they have provoked me to anger with their vanities,* Deuteronomy 32:21.

Will God visit the iniquity of such? Yes. *Shall I not visit them for these things,* Jeremiah 5:9. And that upon their children? Yes. *Thou recompensest the iniquity of the fathers, into the bosom of their children,* Jeremiah 32:18. And their children's children? Yes. *To the third and fourth generation,*

Exodus 34:7.   But will his judgments fall most heavily on those who make their fathers sins their own? Yes. *Behold ye are risen up in your fathers stead, an increase of sinful men to augment yet the fierce anger of the Lord,* Numbers 32:14.

Amidst the most general apostasy are there some that love God and keep his commandments? Yes. *I have left me seven thousand in Israel, that have not bowed to Baal,* 1 Kings 19:18. And may such expect to be exempted from desolating judgments when they come? Yes. *Go set a mark on the forehead of them that sigh and cry,* Ezekiel 9:4. And to meet with peculiar tokens of the divine regard? Yes. *For the mercy of the Lord is from everlasting to everlasting, upon all them that fear him,* Psalm 103:17.

Q 58. Which is the third commandment?
A. The third commandment is, *Thou shalt not take the name of the Lord thy God in vain; for the Lord will not hold him guiltless that taketh his name in vain* .

By God's name are we to understand his nature? Yes. *My name is in him;* (speaking of Christ) Exodus 23:21.   And his essential properties? Yes. *I will make all my goodness to pass before thee, and I will proclaim the name of the Lord,* Exodus 33:19.   And his titles? Yes. *If they shall say, 'what is his name?' What shall I answer? And God said, 'I am that I am,'* Exodus 3:13,14. And any thing whereby he maketh himself known? Yes. *I have manifested thy name, unto the men thou gavest me,* John 17:6.

Should we reverence the name of God? Yes. *That thou mayest fear this glorious and fearful name, the Lord thy God,* Deuteronomy 28:58. And trust in it? Yes. *The name of the Lord is a strong tower, the righteous runneth into it and is safe*, Proverbs 18:10. And walk in it? Yes. *We will walk in the name of the Lord our God, for ever and ever*, Micah 4:5. And should we do this by no other name? No. *I will take away the names of Baalim out of her mouth*, Hosea 2:17.

Hath God a great regard for his own name? Yes. *For how should my name be polluted*, Isaiah 48:11. Is it therefore a great sin for us to be careless of it? Yes. *Neither shalt thou profane the name of thy God: I am the Lord*, Leviticus 18:21.

Q 59. What is required in the third commandment?
A. The third commandment requireth the holy and reverent use of God's names, titles, attributes, ordinances, word and works.

Should we make profession of God's name? Yes. *O Lord, we are called by thy name*, Jeremiah 14:9. And be sincere in our profession? Yes. *They shall ask the way to Zion with their faces thitherward*, Jeremiah 50:5. And be careful to credit and maintain it? Yes. *Thou hast kept my word and hast not denied my name*, Revelation 3:8.

Should we use the name of God in prayer? Yes. *I will call on the name of the Lord*, Psalm 116:17. And in praise? Yes. *Let them praise thy great name*, Psalm 99:3. And in Christian conversation? Yes. *I will declare thy name unto my brethren*, Psalm 22:22. But should we do it with the profoundest humility? Yes. *Behold I have taken upon me to speak unto God, who am but dust and ashes*, Genesis 18:27. And with great seriousness and deliberation? Yes. *Be not rash with thy mouth*, Ecclesiastes 5:2.

Should we give glory to God in his word? Yes. *For he hath magnified his word above all his name*, Psalm 138:2.

And in his works? Yes. *Let them declare his works with rejoicing*, Psalm 107:22. And in his worship? Yes. *For God is greatly to be feared in the assemblies of his saints, and to be held in reverence by all them that are about him*, Psalm 89:7.

Is it lawful to swear? Yes. *An oath for confirmation is the end of all strife*, Hebrews 6:16. But should we be cautious in swearing? Yes. *We should fear an oath*, Ecclesiastes 9:2. And conscientious? Yes. *Thou shalt swear in truth, in judgment, and in righteousness*, Jeremiah 4:2. Doth an oath bind the soul? Yes. *If a man swear an oath to bind his soul with a bond*, Numbers 30:2. Should we therefore look upon ourselves as bound by it? Yes. *David spared Mephibosheth, Jonathan's son, because of the oath of the Lord*, 2 Samuel 21:7. And that though it is to our detriment? Yes. *The good man sweareth to his own hurt, and changeth not*, Psalm 15:4.

Q 60. What is forbidden in the third commandment?
A. The third commandment forbiddeth all profaning and abusing of any thing whereby God makes himself known.

Is it a great sin to profane God's name? Yes. *They profaned my holy name*, Ezekiel 36:20. Is it a profanation of God's name to use it as an expletive in discourse? Yes. *Let your communication be yea, yea, and nay, nay, for whatsoever is more than these cometh of evil*, Matthew 5:37. Or as a charm? Yes. *As those exorcists who said, 'we adjure you by Jesus,'* Acts 19:13. Or as a sanction for cruelty? Yes. *Your brethren that hated you and cast you out, said, 'Let the Lord be glorified'*, Isaiah 66:5. Is God's name also profaned by putting a slight upon sacred things? Yes. *'Cursed be he that voweth and sacrificeth to the*

Lord, a corrupt thing, for I am a great King,' saith the Lord, 'and my name is dreadful,' Malachi 1:14.

Is blasphemy a breach of this commandment? Yes. *Foolish people have blasphemed thy name,* Psalm 74:18. And hypocrisy? Yes. *For unto the wicked God saith, 'what hast thou to do to declare my statutes,'* Psalm 50:16. Is this a great sin? Yes. *Their heart is divided; now shall they be found faulty,* Hosea 10:2. And a destructive sin? Yes. *The hypocrites in heart heap up wrath,* Job 36:13. Should we therefore be careful to avoid it? Yes. *Beware of the leaven of the Pharisees, which is hypocrisy,* Luke 12:1.

Is this commandment broken by sinful and unnecessary lots? Yes. *They cast pur, that is the lot, before Haman from day to day,* Esther 3:7. And by profane cursing? Yes. *Out of the same mouth proceedeth blessing and cursing, my brethren these things ought not to be,* James 3:10. And by rash swearing? Yes. *Above all things my brethren, swear not,* James 5:12. And by false swearing? Yes. *Ye shall not swear by my name falsely,* Leviticus 19:12.

Is it a great sin to swear falsely? Yes. *For it blasphemeth that worthy name, by which we are called,* James 2:7. Is it a sin that brings a curse upon the persons who are guilty of it? Yes. *Will ye steal, murder, and swear falsely, therefore I will cast you out of my sight,* Jeremiah 7:9,15. And upon their families? Yes. *It shall enter into the house of him that sweareth falsely by my name,* Zechariah 5:4. And upon the land? Yes. *Because of swearing the land mourns,* Jeremiah 23:10.

Q 61. What is the reason annexed to the third commandment?

A. The reason annexed to the third commandment is, that however the breakers of this commandment may escape punishment from men, yet the Lord our God will not suffer them to escape his righteous judgment.

Do the breakers of this commandment often escape punishment from men? Yes. *Men hear cursing, and bewrayeth it not,* Proverbs 29:24.   And are they therefore secure?   Yes.   *Because sentence is not speedily executed, therefore their heart is fully set in them to do evil,* Ecclesiastes 8:11.   But do those who connive at this sin thereby become partners in it? Yes. *If a soul hear the voice of swearing and do not utter it, he shall bear his iniquity,* Leviticus 5:1.

Do such hope to escape the judgments of God? Yes. *They belch out with their mouths, and say, 'who doth hear?'* Psalm 59:7.   But shall they escape them? No. *Surely mine oath which he hath despised, I will recompense upon his own head,* Ezekiel 17:19.

Shall hypocrites be punished? Yes. *Woe unto you hypocrites,* Matthew 23:13.   And mockers?   Yes. *Behold ye despisers, wonder and perish,* Acts 13:41. And covenant breakers?   Yes.   *Surely in the place where the King dwelleth, who made him King, and whose covenant he brake, he shall die,* Ezekiel 17:16.   And those who use God's name in a vain manner? Yes. *For every idle word that men speak they must give an account,* Matthew 12:36.   Shall such be punished in this world? Yes. *The Lord will make their plagues wonderful,* Deuteronomy 28:59. And in the world to come? Yes. *They treasure up wrath against the day of wrath,* Romans 2:5.

Q 62. What is the fourth commandment?

A. The fourth commandment is, *Remember the Sabbath day to keep it holy: six days shalt thou labour and do all thy work; but the seventh day is the Sabbath of the Lord thy God, in it thou shalt not do any work, thou, nor thy son, nor thy daughter, nor thy man-servant, nor thy maid-servant, nor thy cattle, nor the stranger that is within thy gates: for in six days the Lord made heaven and earth, the sea, and all that in them is, and rested the seventh day; wherefore the Lord blessed the Sabbath day and hallowed it.*

Is labour necessary as well as rest? Yes. *Six days shalt thou labor,* Deuteronomy 5:13. Doth labor tend to plenty? Yes. *The soul of the diligent shall be made fat,* Proverbs 13:4. And does it add sweetness to our gettings? Yes. *The sleep of the laboring man is sweet,* Ecclesiastes 5:12. Doth idleness tend to poverty? Yes. *It shall clothe a man with rags,* Proverbs 23:21. And expose to many temptations? Yes. *They learn to be idle, and not only idle but tattlers also, and busy bodies, speaking things which they ought not,* 1 Timothy 5:13. Is it therefore forbidden under the severest penalties? Yes. *This is commanded you, that if any would not work, neither should he eat,* 2 Thessalonians 3:10. And doth it hence appear that a multiplicity of unnecessary holy days, is both a nuisance and a sin? Yes. *Ye observe days and months, and times, and years, I am afraid of you,* Galatians 4:10,11.

Should every returning seventh day be set apart to the services of religion? Yes. *'From one Sabbath to another shall all flesh come and worship before me,' saith the Lord,* Isaiah 66:23. But should our religion be confined to that day? No. *For every day will I bless thee,* Psalm 145:2. Must children keep the

Sabbath? Yes. *Thou and thy son, and thy daughter,* Exodus 20:10. And servants? Yes. *That thy man servant and thy maid servant may rest as well as thou,* Deuteronomy 5:14. And our cattle? Yes. *I saw some lading asses on the Sabbath-day and I testified against them,* Nehemiah 13:15. Hath the Sabbath a reference to God's resting from the works of creation? Yes. *On the seventh day God ended his works,* Genesis 2:2. Should we therefore on this day remember him in his works? Yes. *Worship him that made heaven, and earth, and the sea, and the fountains of water,* Revelation 14:7. Doth it point out an eternal rest? Yes. *There remaineth a rest,* (or the keeping of a Sabbath[6]) *for the people of God,* Hebrews 4:9. Should we therefore keep that rest in view, and labor to attain it? Yes. *Let us labor therefore to enter into that rest,* Hebrews 4:11.

Q 63. What is required in the fourth commandment?
A. The fourth commandment requireth the keeping holy to God one whole day in seven to be a Sabbath to himself.

Is it the will of God that we should take special notice of the Sabbath? Yes. *Remember the Sabbath-day,* Exodus 20:8. Should we remember it before it comes? Yes. *For we read of the preparation of the Sabbath,* Mark 15:42. And when it comes? Yes. *Eat that to-day for to-day is a Sabbath unto the Lord,* Exodus 16:25. And after it is over? Yes. *I had gone with the multitude that kept holy day,* Psalm 42:4.

Must we keep holy the Sabbath-day? Yes. *Hallow my Sabbaths,* Ezekiel 20:20. Must we keep it by holy rest? Yes. *Six days may work be done, but in*

---

[6] Σαββατισμὸς

the seventh is the Sabbath of rest, Exodus 31:13. And by holy services? Yes. *The people of the land shall worship at the door of his gate in the Sabbath,* Ezekiel 46:3. And with holy affections? Yes. *This is the day which the Lord hath made, we will rejoice and be glad in it,* Psalm 118:24.

Must the Sabbath that we keep be a common day, consisting of twenty-four hours? Yes. *For the evening and the morning were the first day,* Genesis 1:5. Should not the Sabbath then be begun and ended in the evening? No. *For we read that the Sabbath ended when it began to dawn towards the first day of the week,* Matthew 28:1.

Q 64. Which day of the seven hath God appointed to be the weekly Sabbath?
A. Before the resurrection of Christ, God appointed the seventh day of the week to be the weekly Sabbath; and the first day of the week ever since, to continue to the end of the world, which is the Christian Sabbath.

Was the Sabbath appointed from the beginning of the world? Yes. *God blessed the seventh day and sanctified it,* Genesis 2:2. And was it observed before the giving of the law? Yes. *Tomorrow is the rest of the holy Sabbath,* Exodus 16:23. Was it particularly enforced upon the Israelites? Yes. *I gave them my Sabbaths,* Ezekiel 20:12. And that in commemoration of their delivery out of Egypt? Yes. *Remember that thou wast a servant in Egypt, and that the Lord thy God brought thee out from thence, therefore he commanded thee to keep the Sabbath-day,* Deuteronomy 5:15. But is it obligatory on Christians? Yes. *Pray that your flight be not on the Sabbath-day,* Matthew 24:20.

Was the Jewish Sabbath kept on the seventh day of the week? Yes. *For he spake on the seventh day this wise,* Hebrews 4:4. But had Christ a power to alter it? Yes. *For the Son of Man is Lord even of the Sabbath-day,* Matthew 12:8. Is such an alteration hinted at in the Old Testament? Yes. *It shall be that upon the eighth day and so forward the priests shall make your burnt offerings,* etc. *and I will accept you, saith the Lord God,* Ezekiel 43:27.[7] And did it actually take place after Christ's resurrection? Yes. *For on the first day of the week, the disciples came together to break bread,* Acts 20:7. And does their example carry in it, the force of a command? Yes. *Wherefore I beseech you be ye followers of me,* 1 Corinthians 4:16.

Did Christ rise upon the first day? Yes. *He rose early on the first day of the week,* Mark 16:9. And did he then rest from his labors? Yes. *He ceased from his own works, as God did from his,* Hebrews 4: 10. Did he honor this day with his presence? Yes. *The same day at evening, being the first day of the week, came Jesus, and stood in the midst,* John 20:19. And did he renew his visit the next first day? Yes. *After eight days, when the disciples were within and Thomas with them, came Jesus,*[8] John 20:26. And was this a mark

---

[7] Most, if not all expositors agree, that these chapters at the end of Ezekiel refer to the form, order and worship of the gospel church, (though there may be some difficulty in making the application) and then by the eighth day here spoken of, it seems most natural to understand the first day of the week, or Christian Sabbath, in the stated returns of it. See Dr. Gill, upon the place.

[8] Almost all the nations of the world, except the English, reckon their days inclusively, and so did the ancient Hebrews. 'Tis observable, that we read of no other assembling of the disciples between the days spoken of John 20:19 and 26, which is somewhat surprising, if we suppose the seventh day to have been kept by them as the Sabbath. Surely they would have then met on that day, and Christ would have dignified it by his presence.

of his approbation? Yes. *For he meeteth them that remember him in his ways,* Isaiah 64:5.

Was this day dignified by a new title? Yes. *It was called the Lord's Day,* Revelation 1:10. Did the Spirit bestow his extraordinary gifts on this day? Yes. *For it was on the day of Pentecost, which was the morrow after the seventh day,* Acts 2:1; cf. Leviticus 23:6. Does he on it confer his special grace? Yes. *I was in the Spirit on the Lord's Day,* Revelation 1:10.

Did the primitive Christians assemble on this day? Yes. *Upon the first day of the week let every one lay by him in store,* 1 Corinthians 16:1,2. And was this a public and not a private collection? Yes. *That there be no gatherings when I come,*[9] ibid. Is their practice then a rule? Yes. *Ye became followers of the churches of Christ,* 1 Thessalonians 2:14.

Do we upon this day commemorate a more glorious creation than the first? Yes. *Behold I create new heavens and a new earth, and the former shall not be remembered, nor come into mind,* Isaiah 65:17. And celebrate a more eminent deliverance than that of the children of Israel out of Egypt? Yes. *The days came that they shall no more say, 'the Lord liveth which brought up the children of Israel out of the land of Egypt',* Jeremiah 23:7. Should we therefore join with our fellow Christians in keeping this day? Yes. *For if any man will be contentious we have no such custom, neither the churches of Christ,* 1 Corinthians 11:16. But is not this a direct breach of the fourth commandment? No. For that only says, *Six days shalt thou labor, but the seventh* (i.e., the day following the six) *is the Sabbath,* Exodus 20:10. If the

---

[9] Such charitable contributions were well adapted to times of public worship, see Dr. Gill on the Place, as also Isa 58:7, 8.

matter was more disputable than it is, should not the superior advantage of keeping the first day in the present circumstances of things have some weight? Yes. *For the Sabbath was made for man, and not man for the Sabbath,* Mark 2:27.

Q 65. How is the Sabbath to be sanctified?

A. The Sabbath is to be sanctified by a holy resting all that day, even from such worldly employments and recreations as are lawful on other days; and spending the whole time in the public and private exercises of God's worship, except so much as is to be taken up in the works of necessity and mercy.

Must we sanctify the Sabbath? Yes. *Keep the Sabbath to sanctify it,* Deuteronomy 5:12. Must the whole Sabbath be sanctified? Yes. *When the gates of Jerusalem began to be dark, before the Sabbath I commanded that they should be shut, and that they should not be opened till after the Sabbath,* Nehemiah 13:19.

Must we keep the Sabbath as a day of rest? Yes. *It is a Sabbath of rest,* Leviticus 23:3. And do no work thereon? No. *Ye shall do no work therein,* ibid. Must we avoid those labors which are permitted on other days? Yes. *Take heed to yourselves and bear no burden on the Sabbath-day,* Jeremiah 17:21. And which are required on other days? Yes. *Six days shall ye gather manna, but on the seventh which is the Sabbath, there shall be none,* Exodus 16:26. And does this extend to the most busy seasons of the year? Yes. *For in earing time, and in harvest thou shalt rest,* Exodus 34:21. Is buying and selling therefore unlawful on the Sabbath-day? Yes. *I testified against them in the day that they sold victuals,* Nehemiah 13:15.

Should public worship be maintained on the Sabbath-day? Yes. *It is an holy convocation,* Leviticus 23:3. And should we make conscience of attending upon it? Yes. *Not forsaking the assembling of yourselves together,* Hebrews 10:25. And that early? Yes. *Early will I seek thee,* Psalm 63:1. And late? Yes. *Bless the Lord, all ye servants of the Lord, which by night stand in the house of the Lord,* Psalm 134:1. But should we confine our religious services to the house of God? No. *It is the Sabbath of the Lord in all our dwellings,* Leviticus 23:3.

Is prayer a part of Sabbath service? Yes. *On the Sabbath-day we went to the river's side, where prayer was wont to be made,* Acts 16:13. And singing of psalms? Yes. We have *a psalm or song for the Sabbath day,* Psalm 92. And reading the word? Yes. *The prophets are read every Sabbath day,* Acts 13:27. And hearing? Yes. *The next Sabbath day came almost the whole city together to hear the word,* Acts 13:44. And Christian conversation? Yes. *They talked together of all those things that had happened,* Luke 24:14.

Should we keep the Sabbath with reverence? Yes. *Keep thy foot when thou goest into the house of God,* Ecclesiastes 5:1. And with diligence? Yes. *We must lay hold on the Sabbath to keep from polluting it,* Isaiah 56:2. And must we honor God in all the duties of it? Yes. *We must call the Sabbath honorable and honor him,* Isaiah 58:13. Are men apt to watch how we keep the Sabbath? Yes. *As he went into the house of one of the chief Pharisees on the Sabbath day they watched him,* Luke 14:1. And should this make us circumspect? Yes. *Lead me in a plain path because of mine enemies* (margin reads, *observers,*) Psalm 27:11.

Are works of charity and mercy to be done on the Sabbath day? Yes. *Ought not this woman to be loosed from this bond on the Sabbath day*, Luke 13:16. And works of necessity? Yes. *Jesus went on the Sabbath through the corn and his disciples were an hungred and began to pluck the ears of corn to eat*, Matthew 12:1. Are Christians obliged to the same strictness in keeping the Sabbath as the Jews? Yes. *Ye have been called unto liberty*, Galatians 5:13. But should they be careful not to abuse their liberty? Yes. *Use not your liberty for an occasion to the flesh*, ibid. And is conscience as directed by the word the only judge in this case? Yes. *Happy is he that condemneth not himself in that which he alloweth*, Romans 14:22.

Q 66. What is forbidden in the fourth commandment?
A. The fourth commandment forbiddeth the omission or careless performance of the duties required, and the profaning the day by idleness, or doing that which is in itself sinful, or by unnecessary thoughts, words, or works, about worldly employments or recreations.

Is the Sabbath profaned by the neglect of it? Yes. *They hid their eyes from my Sabbaths, and I am profaned amongst them*, Ezekiel 22:26. And by unnecessary journeys, visits, and the like? Yes. *Abide ye every man in his place, let no man go out of his place on the seventh day*, Exodus 16:29. And by pastimes and diversions? Yes. *Not finding thine own pleasure*, Isaiah 58:13. And by idle and unprofitable discourse? Yes. *Not speaking thine own words*, Isaiah 58:13. And especially by those actions which are at all times unlawful? Yes. *Thy have committed adultery in the same day, and have profaned my Sabbaths*, Ezekiel 23:37,38.

Do those profane the Sabbath who perform duties of it carelessly? Yes. *Ye brought that which was torn, and lame, and sick,* Malachi 1:13. Or hypocritically? Yes. *Their heart is far from me,* Matthew 15:8. Or reluctantly? Yes. *As Doeg who was detained before the Lord,* 1 Samuel 21:7. Or who are weary of it? Yes. *They say, 'when will the new moon be gone, that we may fell corn, and the Sabbath that we may set forth wheat,'* Amos 8:5.

Q 67. What are the reasons annexed to the fourth commandment?
A. The reasons annexed to the fourth commandment, are God's allowing us six days of the week for our own lawful employments, his challenging a special propriety in the seventh, his own example, and his blessing the Sabbath day.

Hath God allowed us six days to work in? Yes. *Six days may work be done,* Exodus 31:15. And ought we to work on those six days? Yes. *There are six days on which men ought to work,* Luke 13:14. Is it highly reasonable then that we should devote a seventh to God? Yes. *For his commandments are not grievous,* 1 John 5:3.

Doth God challenge a special propriety in the Sabbath-day? Yes. *It is the Sabbath of the Lord thy God,* Deuteronomy 5:14. And is that a reason why we should devote it to him? Yes. *Render unto God the things that are God's,* Matthew 22:21. Did God himself observe the Sabbath? Yes. *For the seventh day he rested and was refreshed,* Exodus 31:17. And ought we to imitate him? Yes. *Be ye followers of God as dear children,* Ephesians 5:1. Did Christ observe the Sabbath? Yes. *He was teaching in one of the synagogues on the Sabbath,* Luke 13:10. And should we follow his example? Yes. *Let this mind be in you, which was also in Christ Jesus,* Philippians 2:5.

Is the due observation of the Sabbath attended with many blessing? Yes. *Then shalt thou delight thyself in the Lord, and I will cause thee to ride upon the high places of the earth,* Isaiah 58:14. Doth it bring blessings upon particular persons and families? Yes. *To the eunuchs that keep my Sabbaths, I will give a place in my house, and a name better than of sons and daughters,* Isaiah 56:4,5. And upon the state? Yes. *If you hallow the Sabbath day, and do no work thereon, then shall this city remain for ever,* Jeremiah 17:24,25. And upon the church? Yes. *Then they shall come from the cities of Judah, and from the plain, bringing burnt offerings and meat-offerings and sacrifices of praise unto the house of the Lord,* Jeremiah 17:26. Will a profanation of the Sabbath expose to God's severest wrath? Yes. *They greatly polluted my Sabbaths, then I said I would pour out my fury on them,* Ezekiel 20:13. Is it in effect a violation of the whole law? Yes. *They rebelled against me, and walked not in my statutes, they polluted my Sabbaths,* Ezekiel 20:21. And may those that break Sabbaths expect to lose them? Yes. *I will cause her Sabbaths to cease,* Hosea 2:11.

Q 68. Which is the fifth commandment?
A. The fifth commandment is, *Honor thy father and thy mother; that thy days may be long in the land which the Lord thy God giveth thee.*

Is piety towards God a necessary branch of true religion? Yes. *Add to patience, godliness,* 2 Peter 1:6. And is righteousness towards men a branch of the same? Yes. *Follow that which is good to all men,* 1 Thessalonians 5:15. Does the law of God require both? Yes. *To do justly, to love mercy, and to walk humbly with God,* Micah 6:8. Doth the grace of the gospel teach both? Yes. *To live soberly, righteously and godly*, Titus 2:12. Have good men practiced both? Yes. *Herein do I exercise myself to have always a conscience void of offence toward God and toward men*, Acts 24:16. Ought these two therefore never to be separated? No. *For what God hath joined together, let no man put asunder*, Matthew 19:6.

Are kings and supreme governors included under the general title of fathers? Yes. *Blessed be the kingdom of our father David*, Mark 11:10. And pastors of churches? Yes. *Ye have not many fathers, for in Christ Jesus I have begotten you thru the gospel*, 1 Corinthians 4:15. And masters of families? Yes. *Naaman's servants said unto him, 'my Father,'* 2 Kings 5:13. And all superiors either in age and office, or in gifts and endowments? Yes. *Hear ye children the instruction of a father*, Proverbs 4:1. And is proper respect due to all these according to their different characters and stations? Yes. *Render therefore honor to whom honor is due*, Romans 13:7.

Q 69. What is required in the fifth commandment?
A. The fifth commandment requireth the preserving the honour and performing the duties belonging to every one in their several places and relations, as superiors, inferiors, or equals.

Should children reverence their parents? Yes. *Ye shall fear every man his father and his mother*, Leviticus 19:3. And obey their instructions? Yes. *Children obey your parents in the Lord*, Ephesians 6:1. And submit to their corrections? Yes. *The fathers of our flesh corrected us, and we gave them reverence*, Hebrews 12:9. And seek their consent in disposing of themselves? Yes. *Jacob obeyed his father and mother, and went to Padan-Aram for a wife*, Genesis 28:7. Is it their duty thankfully to acknowledge the favors they have received from them? Yes. *I was my father's son, tender and only beloved in the sight of my mother*, Proverbs 4:3. And if possible to requite them? Yes. *Let them shew piety at home, and requite their parents*, 1 Timothy 5:4. And do these duties extend to those that are only our parents in law? Yes. *So Moses hearkened to the voice of his father-in-law, and did all that he had said*, Exodus 18:24.

Should parents provide for their children? Yes. *What man is there among you, who if his son ask bread, will give him a stone*, Matthew 7:9. And instruct them? Yes. *Train up a child in the way he should go*, Proverbs 22:6. And correct them when needful? Yes. *The rod and reproof give wisdom*, Proverbs 29:15. But should they abstain from severity and passion? Yes. *Parents, provoke not your children to anger*, Colossians 3:21. Is it the duty of parents to pray for their children? Yes. *Give unto Solomon, my son, a perfect heart*, 1 Chronicles 29:19. And to pray with them? Yes. *Thus David returned to bless his household*, 2 Samuel 6:20. And to set them a good example? Yes. *I will walk within my house with a perfect heart*, Psalm 101:2. And to keep a watchful eye over them? Yes. *It may be my sons have sinned and cursed God in their hearts*, Job 1:5. And will this in the end turn to their own advantage? Yes. *For he that begetteth a wise child shall have joy of him*, Proverbs 23:24.

Should servants honor their masters? Yes. *They must count them worthy of all honor*, 1 Timothy 6:1. And obey them? Yes. *Ye servants obey in all things your masters*, Colossians 3:22. And be just and faithful to them? Yes. *Shewing all good fidelity*, Titus 2:10. And patiently bear their reproofs and corrections? Yes. *Not answering again*, Titus 2:9. Is this subjection due even to froward masters? Yes. *To the froward also*, 1 Peter 2:18. And is it equally so to believing ones? Yes. *They that have believing masters let them not despise them, but rather do them service*, 1 Timothy 6:2.

Should masters be just to their servants? Yes. *Masters give to your servants that which is just and good*, Colossians 4:1. And gentle? Yes. *Forbearing threatening*, Ephesians 6:9. But should they be careful to maintain their authority? Yes. *For the earth is disquieted for a servant when he reigneth*, Proverbs 30:22.

Is it the duty of husbands to love their wives? Yes. *Husbands love your wives*, Ephesians 5:25. And of wives to submit to their husbands? Yes. *Wives submit yourselves unto your own husbands*, Ephesians 5:22. Is it the duty of husbands and wives to be pleasing to one another? Yes. *He that is married careth how to please his wife, and she that is married how to please her husband*, 1 Corinthians 7:33,34. And to be mutually helpful to one another in their religious concerns? Yes. *How knowest thou, O wife, whether thou shalt save thy husband, or how knowest thou, O man, whether thou shalt save thy wife*, 1 Corinthians 7:16.

Is there a duty due from subjects to their magistrates? Yes. *Honor the King*, 1 Peter 2:17. And from magistrates to their subjects? Yes. *He that ruleth over men must be just*, 2 Samuel 23:3. Is there a duty due from people to their ministers? Yes. *Obey them that have the rule over you, and submit yourselves*, Hebrews 13:17. And from ministers to their people? Yes. *Feed the flock of God, which is among you*, 1 Peter 5:2.

Is it the duty of inferiors to honor their superiors? Yes. *Thou shalt rise up before the hoary head, and honor the face of the old man,* Leviticus 19:32. And to endeavor to improve by them? Yes. *They waited for me as for the rain,* Job 29:23. Is it the duty of superiors to carry it respectfully towards their inferiors? Yes. *Condescend to men of low estate,* Romans 12:16. And to seek their edification? Yes. *The fruit of the righteous is a tree of life,* Proverbs 11:30.

Should neighbors shew themselves neighborly? Yes. *Let every one please his neighbor for his good,* Romans 15:2. And friends behave themselves friendly? Yes. *A man that hath friends must shew himself friendly,* Proverbs 18:24. And brethren carry themselves in a brotherly manner? Yes. *Behold, how good and pleasant a thing it is for brethren to dwell together in unity,* Psalm 133:1. And does a failure on one side justify a failure on the other? No. *See that none render evil for evil unto any man,* 1 Thessalonians 5:15.

Q 70. What is forbidden in the fifth commandment?
A. The fifth commandment forbiddeth the neglecting of, or doing any thing against the honour and duty which belongeth to every one in their several places and relations.

Is it a sin for children to be irreverent to their parents? Yes. *Cursed be he that setteth light by father or mother,* Deuteronomy 27:16. Or disobedient? Yes. *The eye that mocketh at his father, and despiseth to obey his mother, the ravens of the valley shall pick it out, and the young eagles shall eat it,* Proverbs 30:17. Or wasteful? Yes. *He that wasteth his father, or chaseth away his mother causeth shame*, Proverbs 19:26. Or incorrigible? Yes. *'Why do ye such things?'*, *notwithstanding they hearkened not to the voice of their Father*, 1 Samuel 2:25. Is it a sin for parents not to love their children? Yes. *Such are without natural affection*, Romans 1:31. Or to be remiss in their education? Yes. *His sons make themselves vile, and he restraineth them not*, 1 Samuel 3:13.

Is it a sin for inferiors to be rude and undutiful to their superiors? Yes. *For the child to behave himself proudly against the ancient, and the base against the honorable*, Isaiah 3:5. And for superiors to be harsh and uncivil to inferiors? Yes. *Who say to the poor, stand thou there, or sit thou under my footstool*, James 2:3. Is it a sin for equals to affect the pre-eminency? Yes. *There was a strife among the disciples which of them should be accounted the greatest*, Luke 22:24. Or to be vexatious and quarrelsome? Yes. *Lest there be debates, wraths, and envyings*, 2 Corinthians 12:20.

Q 71. What is the reason annexed to the fifth commandment?
A. The reason annexed to the fifth commandment is a promise of long life and prosperity (as far as it shall serve for God's glory, and their own good) to all such as keep this commandment.

Have some good men been cut off in the midst of their days? Yes. *He weakened my strength in the way; he shortened my days*, Psalm 102:23. But is this always in mercy? Yes. *They are taken away from the evil to come*, Isaiah 57:1. Have some wicked men lived to a great age? Yes. *The wicked live and become old*, Job 21:7. And is this always in judgment? Yes. *For the sinner being a hundred years old shall be accursed,* Isaiah 65:20.   But are good people of all others most likely to enjoy the comforts of this world?   Yes.   *There is no want to them that fear him,* Psalm 34:9.   And to live long in it?   Yes.   *What man is he that desireth life, and loveth many days, let him depart from evil and do good,* Psalm 34:12,14.   And shall this blessing be granted as far as it is for God's glory and their own good? Yes.   *They have failed not aught of any good thing the Lord had spoken, all came to pass.*   Joshua 21:45. And if denied in this world shall it be bestowed in the next?   Yes.   *For this is the promise, which he hath promised us, even eternal life,* 1 John 2:25.

Is long life and happiness a blessing peculiarly vouchsafed to dutiful and obedient children?   Yes. *My son keep my commandment, for length of days and long life, and peace, shall they add unto thee,* Proverbs 3:1,2.   And denied to the unruly and disobedient?   Yes.   *There shall not be an old man in thy house,* 1 Samuel 2:31.

Q 72. What is the sixth commandment?
A. The sixth commandment is, *Thou shalt not kill.*

Are the lives of men in their own nature precious? Yes.   *The life is more than meat,* Matthew 6:25.   Hath God therefore set a hedge round about them?   Yes.   *Of every man will I require the life of man,* Genesis 9:5. And was it needful that he should do so?   Yes.   *For out of the heart proceed murders,* Matthew 15:19.

Q 73. What is required in the sixth commandment?
A. The sixth commandment requireth all lawful endeavours to preserve our own life and the life of others.

Is self-preservation a part of the law of nature? Yes. *Skin for skin, all that a man hath will he give for his life,* Job 2:4. But has this law been broken? Yes. For some *choose strangling and death rather than life,* Job 7:15. Was it therefore necessary that it should be enforced by an express command? Yes. *Do thyself no harm,* Acts 16:28.

Should we use all lawful methods for the preservation of our health? Yes. *Use a little wine for thy stomach's sake,* 1 Timothy 5:23. Should we for this purpose be moderate in the use of meats and drinks? Yes. *When thou sittest to eat with a ruler, put a knife to thy throat,* Proverbs 23:1,2. And avoid all unnecessary acts of mortification? Yes. *Be not righteous overmuch, for why shouldest thou destroy thyself?* Ecclesiastes 7:16. And defend ourselves against violence? Yes. *He that hath no sword, let him sell his garments, and buy one,* Luke 22:36. And from persecution? Yes. *When they persecute you in one city fly to another,* Matthew 10:23. And not causelessly run into danger? No. *Let not thy voice be heard amongst us, lest angry fellows run upon thee, and thou lose thy life,* Judges 18:25.

Should whatsoever we do for the preservation of our own lives be with an eye to God's glory? Yes. *That whether we live, we might live unto the Lord,* Romans 14:8. Is it therefore unlawful to commit sin even to save life? Yes. *For he that so saveth his life, shall lose it,* Matthew 16:25.

Should we be careful of the lives of others? Yes. *Judah said, 'what profit is it if we slay our brother?',* Genesis 37:26. Should we pray for their health? Yes. *I wish above all things that thou mayest prosper and be in health,* 3 John, ver. 2. And discover designs to their prejudice? Yes. *When Paul's sister's son heard of their lying in wait, he went and told Paul,* Acts 23:16. And hide them from the unjust fury of their enemies? Yes. *As Obadiah hid the prophets of the Lord by fifties in a cave,* 1 Kings 18:4. And avoid every thing whereby their lives might be endangered? Yes. *Thou shalt make a battlement for thy roof that thou bring not blood upon thine house, if any man fall from thence,* Deuteronomy 22:8.

Should magistrates defend the innocent? Yes. *They must deliver them that are drawn out to death,* Proverbs 24:11. And rich men succor the poor? Yes. *The blessing of him that was ready to perish came upon me,* Job 29:13. Should we be careful of giving offence? Yes. *If it be possible live peaceably with all men,* Romans 12:18. And equally so of taking it? Yes. *Dearly beloved avenge not yourselves,* Romans 12:19.

Q 74. What is forbidden in the sixth commandment?
A. The sixth commandment absolutely forbiddeth the taking away of our own life, or the life of our neighbour unjustly, or whatsoever tendeth thereunto.

Is it a sin to destroy ourselves? Yes. *Why shouldst thou die before thy time,* Ecclesiastes 7:17. Is this often the fruit of pride? Yes. *When Ahitophel saw that his counsel was not followed,* he went *and hanged himself,* 2 Samuel 17:23. And of envy? Yes. *Envy is the rottenness of the bones,* Proverbs 14:30. And of passion? Yes. *I do well to be angry, even unto death,* Jonah 4:9. And of uncleanness? Yes. *He that committeth fornication sinneth against his own body,* 1 Corinthians 6:18. And of intemperance? Yes. *At last it biteth like a serpent, and stingeth like an adder,* Proverbs 23:32. And of immoderate care and sorrow? Yes. *For the sorrow of the world worketh death*, 2 Corinthians 7:10.

Is this an encroachment upon God's prerogative? Yes. For it is *he that that killeth and maketh alive*, Deuteronomy 32:39.   And a compliance with Satan's temptations? Yes. *For he was a murderer from the beginning*, John 8:44.   But may we not expose our lives for the sake of a good conscience? Yes. *They loved not their lives unto death*, Revelation 12:11.   And hazard them in a good cause? Yes. *Zebulon and Naphtali jeoparded their lives in the high places of the field*, Judges 5:18.

Is it a breach of this command for magistrates to take away the lives of capital offenders? No. *Thou shalt do according to the sentence, and the man that will do presumptuously, even that man shall die*, Deuteronomy 17:10,12.   Or for one man to kill another in lawful war? No. *Smite Amalek, and slay both man and woman, infant and suckling*, 1 Samuel 15:3.   Or by accident? No. *Whoso killeth his neighbor ignorantly, whom he hated not in time past, shall flee to the city of refuge*, Deuteronomy 14:4,5.   Or in his own defense? No. *For if a thief be found breaking up and be smitten that he die, then shall no blood be shed for him*, Exodus 22:2.

But is willful murder a great sin? Yes. *It was said by them of old time thou shalt not kill*, Matthew 5:21.   Is it a crying sin? Yes. *The voice of thy brother's blood crieth to me from the ground*, Genesis 4:10.   Is it a sin that calls for present punishment? Yes. *Thou shalt take him from mine altar that he may die*, Exodus 21:14.   And exposes to future damnation? Yes. *For no murderer hath eternal life*, 1 John 3:15.   Ought we therefore to pray that God would keep us from it? Yes. *Deliver me from blood guiltiness, O God,* Psalm 51:14.

Is it a breach of this commandment to counsel the death of others? Yes. *Thou hast slain him with the sword of the children of Ammon,* 2 Samuel 12:9. Or to consent to it? Yes. *Ye by wicked hands have crucified and slain,* Acts 2:23. Or to be any ways accessory to it? Yes. *I have sinned, in that I have betrayed innocent blood,* Matthew 27:4. Or to rejoice at it? Yes. *If I have rejoiced at the destruction of him that hated me,* Job 31:29. Or being in power to neglect to punish it? Yes. *Ye shall take no satisfaction for the life of a murderer, but he shall surely be put to death, so shall ye not pollute the land,* Numbers 35:31,32.

Is unjust and immoderate anger a breach of this commandment? Yes. *Whoso is angry with his brother without a cause, is in danger of the judgment,* Matthew 5:22. And foul and provoking language? Yes. *Whosoever shall say unto his brother 'Racha,' or thou fool, shall be in danger of hell fire,* ibid. And malice and hatred? Yes. *He that hateth his brother is a murderer,* 1 John 3:15. And is there such a thing as soul-murder? Yes. *If thou givest him not a warning his blood will I require at thine hand,* Ezekiel 3:18.

Q 75. Which is the seventh commandment?
A. The seventh commandment is, *Thou shalt not commit adultery.*

Is adultery a sin which some are much inclined to? Yes. *They were as fed horses, every one neighing after his neighbor's wife,* Jeremiah 5:8. Is it necessary therefore that it should be forbidden? Yes. *The law was made for whoremongers,* 1 Timothy 1:10. Was it forbidden under the Old Testament? Yes. *Thou shalt not be with thy neighbor's wife to defile thyself with her*, Leviticus 18:20. And is it forbidden under the New? Yes. *For this is the will of God, that you should abstain from fornication*, 1 Thessalonians 4:3. And is it contrary to the law of nature? Yes. For Abimelech calls adultery *a great sin*, Genesis 20:9.

Q 76. What is required in the seventh commandment?
A. The seventh commandment requireth the preservation of our own and our neighbors chastity, in heart, speech, and behavior.

Is it our duty to keep our bodies pure? Yes. We must *possess our vessels in sanctification and honor, and not in the lust of concupiscence*, 1 Thessalonians 4:4. Should our thoughts be chaste? Yes. *Lust not after her beauty in thine heart*, Proverbs 6:25. And in words? Yes. *Let no corrupt communication proceed out of your mouth*, Ephesians 4:29. And our behaviour? Yes. *Having a chaste conversation coupled with fear*, 1 Peter 3:2. Should we be careful of our own chastity? Yes. We must *cleanse ourselves from all filthiness both of flesh and spirit*, 2 Corinthians 7:1. And of that of others? Yes. *And it came to pass as she spake to Joseph day by day, that he hearkened not unto her to lie by her*, Genesis 39:10.

Should we for this purpose keep a strict watch over our senses? Yes. *I made a covenant with mine eyes*, Job 31:1. And study the rules of sobriety and temperance? Yes. *I keep under my body and bring it into subjection*, 1 Corinthians 9:27. And addict ourselves to some lawful calling? Yes. *Thus Joseph went into the house to do his business*, Genesis 39:11. And avoid loose and wanton company? Yes. *Come not nigh the door of her house*, Proverbs 5:8.

And if other means prove ineffectual should we marry? Yes. *If they cannot contain let them marry,* 1 Corinthians 7:9.   Is it therefore a sin in the papists to forbid marriage to the clergy?   Yes. *Forbidding to marry,* 1 Timothy 4:3.

Q 77. What is forbidden in the seventh commandment?
A. The seventh commandment forbiddeth all unchaste thoughts, words, and actions.

Is adultery a very great sin?   Yes.   It is called an *abomination,* Ezekiel 22:11.   Doth it waste the body? Yes.   *And thou mourn at last when thy flesh and thy body are consumed,* Proverbs 5:11.   And wrong the soul?   Yes.   *Abstain from fleshly lusts, that war against the soul,* 1 Peter 2:11.   And bring a blot upon the character?   Yes.   *A wound and dishonor shall they get,* Proverbs 6:33.   Is it a besotting sin?   Yes.   *It takes away the heart,* Hosea 4:11.   And an impoverishing sin?   Yes. *By means of a whorish woman a man is brought to a piece of bread,* Proverbs 6:26.   Is it a kind of sacrilege? Yes.   *Shall I take the members of Christ and make them the members of a harlot,* 1 Corinthians 6:15.   Doth it unfit for the fellowship of the saints?   Yes.   *I have written unto you not to keep company if any man that is called a brother be a fornicator,* 1 Corinthians 5:11.   And will it be severely punished both in this world and in that which is to come?   Yes.   *For whoremongers and adulterers God will judge,* Hebrews 13:4.

Is fornication as well as adultery a sin?   Yes. *Mortify your members which are upon earth, fornication,* Colossians 3:5.   And incest?   Yes.   *None of you shall approach to any that is near of kin to him,* Leviticus 18:6.   And polygamy?   Yes.   *Did not he make one, yet he had the residue of the spirit,* Malachi 2:15.   And all manner of uncleanness?

Yes. *But fornication and uncleanness, let it not be once named amongst you,* Ephesians 5:3.

Are unclean desires sinful? Yes. We must mortify *inordinate affection and evil concupiscence,* Colossians 3:5. And unclean reflections? Yes. *She multiplied her whoredoms by calling to remembrance the days of her youth,* Ezekiel 23:19. And unchaste looks? Yes. *Having eyes full of adultery,* 2 Peter 2:14. And immodest apparel? Yes. *There met him a woman with the attire of a harlot,* Proverbs 7:10. And obscene words? Yes. *Neither filthiness nor foolish talking,* Ephesians 5:4. And lascivious actions? Yes. Such as *chambering and wantonness,* Romans 13:13. And that intemperance and idleness which lead hereto? Yes. *This was the iniquity of Sodom, pride, idleness, and fullness of bread, and she committed abomination before me,* Ezekiel 16:49,50.

Q 78. Which is the eighth commandment?
A. The eighth commandment is, *Thou shalt not steal.*

Hath God a supreme and sovereign right over all things? Yes. *He is Lord of all,* Acts 10:36. But have men a delegated right over their lawful possessions? Yes. *The earth God hath given to the children of* men, Psalm 115:16. Is it a sin therefore to deprive any of this their right? Yes. *Ye shall not steal nor deal falsely,* Leviticus 19:11. And was such prohibition necessary? Yes. *For every brother will utterly supplant,* Jeremiah 9:4.

Q 79. What is required in the eighth commandment?
A. The eighth commandment requireth the lawful procuring and furthering the wealth and outward estate of ourselves and others.

Is it lawful for us to seek our own temporal advantage? Yes. *And now when shall I provide for my own house?*, Genesis 30:30. Should we do this by an application to some lawful calling? Yes. *Study to be quiet and to do your own business*, 1 Thessalonians 4:11. And by diligence in that calling? Yes. *Not slothful in business*, Romans 12:11. And by frugality? Yes. *He that gathereth in the summer is a wise son*, Proverbs 10:5. And by a discreet conduct? Yes. *For by understanding is a house established*, Proverbs 24:3. And to all this should we join fervent prayer? Yes. *I will for this be enquired of by the house of Israel*, Ezekiel 36:37.

Must we be just to all that we deal with? Yes. *Render to all their due*, Romans 13:7. Must we not over-reach the ignorant? No. *Let no man defraud or go beyond his brother*, 1 Thessalonians 4:6. Nor oppress the indigent? No. *We must not buy the poor for silver, and the needy for a pair of shoes*, Amos 8:6. But should we rather relieve them? Yes. *If thy brother be waxen poor and fallen into decay, thou shalt relieve him*, Leviticus 25:35. And be forward so to do? Yes. *We must be ready to distribute, willing to communicate*, 1 Timothy 6:18.

Must we faithfully fulfill our promise? Yes. *I took an oath of them that they should do according to this promise*, Nehemiah 5:12. And be true to our trusts? Yes. *It is required in stewards that a man be found faithful*, 1 Corinthians 4:2. And return what we have borrowed? Yes. *For the wicked borroweth and payeth not again*, Psalm 37:21. And discharge our just debts? Yes. *Owe no man any thing*, Romans 13:8. And make restitution where wrong has been done? Yes. *He shall restore that which he took violently away, or the thing which he hath deceitfully gotten*, Leviticus 6:4. And is such honesty the best policy? Yes. *For a little that a righteous man hath is better than the riches of many wicked*, Psalm 37:16.

Q 80. What is forbidden in the eighth commandment?
A. The eighth commandment forbiddeth whatsoever doth or may unjustly hinder our own or our neighbour's wealth or outward estate.

Doth this commandment forbid the foolish and extravagant wasting of our own substance? Yes. *The prodigal went into a far country, and wasted his substance,* Luke 15:13. Is this done by luxury and intemperance? Yes. *The glutton and the drunkard shall come to poverty,* Proverbs 23:21. And by sloth and idleness? Yes. *A little more sleep, a little more slumber, so shall thy poverty come, like one that travelleth,* Proverbs 24:33. And by keeping loose company? Yes. *He that followeth after vain persons shall have poverty enough,* Proverbs 28:19. And by an excessive love of pleasure? Yes. *He that loveth pleasure shall be a poor man,* Proverbs 21:17. And by rash and imprudent engagements for others? Yes. *Be not a surety for debts, for why should he take away thy bed from under thee,* Proverbs 22:26,27. And doth that which tends to poverty tend to injustice too? Yes. *Lest I be poor and steal,* Proverbs 30:9.

Is this commandment broken by covetousness? Yes. *Woe to him that coveteth an evil covetousness,* Habakkuk 2:9. And by cruelty and uncharitableness? Yes. *Whoso stoppeth his ears at the cry of the poor, shall cry himself, and shall not be heard,* Proverbs 21:13. And by unlawful contracts? Yes. *Thy money perish with thee, because thou hast thought that the gift of God may be purchased with money,* Acts 8:20. And by all unwarrantable arts for the increase of our substance? Yes. *There shall not be found among you one that useth divination or an observer of times, or an enchanter, or a witch,* Deuteronomy 18:10.

Doth this commandment forbid all exaction and oppression? Yes. *Ye shall not oppress one another,* Leviticus 25:14. And cozening and cheating? Yes. *Shall I count them pure with the wicked balances, and with the bag of deceitful weights,* Micah 6:11. And vexatious law suits? Yes. *Now therefore there is utterly a fault among you, because you go to law, one with another,* 1 Corinthians 6:7.

Is theft particularly forbidden in this commandment? Yes. *Do not steal,* Mark 10:19. Is it a sin for servants to defraud their masters? Yes. *A certain rich man had a steward, and the same was accused to him, that he had wasted his goods,* Luke 16:1. Or for children to steal from their parents? Yes. *Whoso robbeth his father or mother, and saith it is no transgression, is the companion of a destroyer,* Proverbs 28:24. Is it a sin to steal even the necessaries of life? Yes. For such *shall restore seven fold,* Proverbs 6:31. And is it equally so to receive or conceal stolen goods? Yes. *Whoso is partner with a thief, hateth his own soul,* Proverbs 29:24.

Q 81. Which is the ninth commandment?
A. The ninth commandment is, *Thou shalt not bear false witness against thy neighbour.*

Is a good name a great privilege? Yes. *'Tis better than precious ointment,* Ecclesiastes 7:1. Is there a law then made for the security of it? Yes. *The law is made for perjured persons,* 1 Timothy 1:10. And is it needful that there should? Yes. *For every neighbor will walk with slanders,* Jeremiah 9:4.

Q 82. What is required in the ninth commandment?
A. The ninth commandment requireth the maintaining and promoting of truth between man and man, and of our own neighbour's good name, especially in witness-bearing.

Should we endeavour to get a good name? Yes. *If there be any virtue, if there be any praise, think on these things,* Philippians 4:8. And to keep it? Yes. *For a little folly disgraceth him that is in reputation for wisdom and honor,* Ecclesiastes 10:1. May we for this purpose vindicate our character when aspersed [or slandered]? Yes. *My righteousness I hold fast, and will not let it go,* Job 27:6. And speak modestly in our own commendation? Yes. *In nothing am I behind the very chiefest apostles, though I am nothing,* 2 Corinthians 12:11.

Is a good name an honor to God? Yes. *On your part he is glorified,* 1 Peter 4:14. And a credit to religion? Yes. *We will go with you for we have heard that God is with you,* Zechariah 8:23. And a comfort to ourselves? Yes. *For a good report maketh the bones fat,* Proverbs 15:30. But do all enjoy this blessing who deserve it? No. *For I heard the defaming of many,* Jeremiah 20:10.

Should we be tender of other's good name as well as our own? Yes. *We also bear record,* 3 John ver. 12. Should we for this purpose cover their faults? Yes. *He that covereth transgression seeketh love,* Proverbs 17:9. And be secret in our reproofs? Yes. *Tell him between him and thee alone,* Matthew 18:15. Should we put the best construction on their actions? Yes. *Charity thinketh no evil,* 1 Corinthians 13:5. And discourage backbiting and detraction? Yes. *We must with an angry countenance drive away a backbiting tongue,* Proverbs 25:23. Should we also vindicate them from unjust aspersions? Yes. *Let not the King sin against David, because his works have been to thee-ward very good,* 1 Samuel 19:4. And joyfully receive all reports to their advantage? Yes. *I rejoiced greatly when the brethren came and testified of the truth that is in thee*, 3 John ver. 3. And will a regard to others good name be the best security to our own? Yes. *For with what measure you meet, it shall be measured to you again*, Matthew 7:2.

Is it our duty to speak the truth? Yes. *Speak ye every man the truth to his neighbor*, Zechariah 8:16. And when called thereto the whole truth? Yes. *Samuel told Eli every wit, and hid nothing from him*, 1 Samuel 3:18. And nothing but the truth? Yes. *Surely they are my people, children that will not lie*, Isaiah 63:8. Should truth be observed in our common conversation? Yes. *Lie not one to another*, Colossians 3:9. And in our promises and engagements? Yes. *Better it is that thou shouldst not vow, than vow and not pay*, Ecclesiastes 5:5. But especially in witness-bearing? Yes. *For a true witness delivereth souls*, Proverbs 14:25.

In order to speak the truth should we think before we speak? Yes. *Whatsoever things are true, think on these things*, Philippians 4:8. And avoid loquacity? Yes. *For in the multitude of words there wanteth not sin*, Proverbs 10:19. And accustom ourselves to a sober way of speaking? Yes. *I speak the words of truth and soberness*, Acts 26:25. And be careful of rash promises? Yes. *Suffer not thy mouth to cause thy flesh to sin, neither say thou before the angel, it was an error*, Ecclesiastes 5:6. And endeavor to overcome the fear of man? Yes. *Whom hast thou feared that thou hast lied*, Isaiah 57:11. And not do any thing that we should be ashamed to own? No. *As Sarah, who first laughed, and then denied it, saying, I laughed not*, Genesis 18:15.

Q 83. What is forbidden in the ninth commandment?
A. The ninth commandment forbiddeth whatsoever is prejudicial to the truth, or injurious to our own or our neighbour's good name.

Is lying a great sin? Yes. *Lying lips are an abomination to the Lord,* Proverbs 12:22. Is it a sin that makes us like the devil? Yes. *For when he speaketh a lie he speaketh of his own,* John 8:44. Is it an unprofitable sin? Yes. *The getting of treasures by a lying tongue is vanity tossed to and fro of them that seek death,* Proverbs 21:6. Is it a sin that will be detected? Yes. *For a lying tongue is but for a moment,* Proverbs 12:19. And severely punished? Yes. *For without are dogs, and whoso loveth and maketh a lie,* Revelation 22:15. Should we therefore hate it? Yes. *I abhor lying,* Psalm 119:163. And pray against it? Yes. *Remove from me the way of lying,* Psalm 119:29.

May we tell lies to make sport? No. *They make the King glad with their wickedness, and the Princes with their lies,* Hosea 7:3. Or to excuse a fault? No. *As Gehazi, who said, 'thy servant went no whither,'* 2 Kings 5:25. Or with an intention to do good? No. *We must not do evil that good may come,* Romans 3:8.

Is detraction and slander a sin? Yes. *Thou sittest and slandereth thine own mother's son,* Psalm 50:20. But may we not return slander for slander? No. *Render not railing for railing,* 1 Peter 3:9. Is flattery also a sin? Yes. *They spake vanity every one with his neighbor, with flattering lips and a double heart do they speak,* Psalm 12:2. Is self-detraction a sin? Yes. *There is that maketh himself poor and yet hath great riches,* Proverbs 13:7. And self-flattery? Yes. *There is that maketh himself rich, and yet hath nothing,* ibid.

Doth this commandment forbid perjury? Yes. *I will be a swift witness against false swearers*, Malachi 3:5. And subornation? Yes. *Thus the Jews set up false witnesses against Stephen*, Acts 6:11,13. And backbiting and tale-bearing? Yes. *Thou shalt not go up and down as a talebearer among thy people*, Leviticus 19:16. And all censorious and uncharitable reflections? Yes. *For he that speaketh evil of his brother, and judgeth his brother, speaks evil of the law, and judgeth the law*, James 4:11.

Q 84. Which is the tenth commandment?

A. The tenth commandment is *Thou shalt not covet thy neighbour's house, thou shalt not covet thy neighbour's wife, nor his man-servant, nor his maid-servant, nor his ox, nor his ass, nor anything that is thy neighbour's.*

Does the heart need a restraint? Yes. *For it is desperately wicked*, Jeremiah 17:9. And does the law of God lay a restraint upon the heart? Yes. *For the law is spiritual*, Romans 7:14. And will a restraint upon the sins of the heart be the most effectual preservative from all other sins? Yes. *Cleanse first that which is within the cup and platter, that the outside may be clean also*, Matthew 23:26.

Are we forbidden to covet another man's house? Yes. *As they that covet houses and take them away*, Micah 2:2. Or another man's wife? Yes. As David did, who seeing Bathsheba, the wife of Uriah, *sent and enquired after her*, 2 Samuel 11:3. Or another man's goods? Yes. *I have coveted no man's silver, or gold, or apparel*, Acts 20:33.

Q 85. What is required in the tenth commandment?

A. The tenth commandment requireth full contentment with our own condition, with a right and charitable frame of spirit toward our neighbour, and all that is his.

Have wicked men a civil property in their goods? Yes. *Was it not thine own,* Acts 5:4. Should they therefore be suffered quietly to enjoy them? Yes. *David's heart smote him, because he had cut off Saul's skirt,* 1 Samuel 24:5.

Is the good man's condition settled by God? Yes. *He performeth the thing that is appointed for me,* Job 23:14. And is it that which is best for him? Yes. *For God giveth to a man that is good in his sight,* Ecclesiastes 2:26. And infinitely better than he deserves? Yes. *For it is of the Lord's mercies that we are not consumed,* Lamentations 3:22. Should he therefore be contented in it? Yes. *I have learned in whatsoever state I am therewith to be content,* Philippians 4:11. And is contentment a powerful antidote against covetousness? Yes. *Let your conversation be without covetousness, and be content with such things as ye have,* Hebrews 13:5.

Should we not seek great things for ourselves? No. *Seekest thou great things for thyself, seek them not,* Jeremiah 45:5. Nor grieve at the more prosperous circumstances of others? No. *Fret not thyself because of him who prospereth in his way,* Psalm 37:7. But rather rejoice in their prosperity and endeavor to promote it? Yes. Thus Mordecai sought *the wealth of his people, and spoke peace to all his seed,* Esther 10:3.

In order to obtain this happy temper of mind, should we resign up our wills to the will of God? Yes. *He shall choose our inheritance for us,* Psalm 47:4. And be much in contemplating the vanity of the creature? Yes. *Wilt thou set thine eyes upon that which is not,* Proverbs 23:5. And make a due estimate of the blessings which we possess? Yes. *For better is the sight of the eyes than the wandering of the desire,* Ecclesiastes 6:9.   And frequently transfer our thoughts to the other world? Yes. *We look not at the things that are seen, which are temporal, but at the things which are not seen, which are eternal,* 2 Corinthians 4:18.   And if after all we find some risings of discontent should we check them in their first appearances? Yes.   *O my soul why art thou disquieted within me,* Psalm 42:5.

Q 86. What is forbidden in the tenth commandment?
A. The tenth commandment forbiddeth all discontentment with our own estate, envying or grieving at the good of our neighbour, and all inordinate motions and affections to anything that is his.

Is discontent a sin? Yes.   *The foolishness of man perverteth his way, and his heart fretteth against the Lord,* Proverbs 19:3.   Can it make our condition better? No.   *For which of you by taking thought can add one cubit to his stature,* Matthew 6:27.   And will it certainly make it worse? Yes.   *All this availeth me nothing so long as I see Mordecai the Jew sitting in the King's gate,* Esther 5:13.   Is it a sin to undervalue present mercies? Yes.   As those did, who *despisest the pleasant land,* Psalm 106:24. Or to aggravate present afflictions? Yes.   As Hezekiah, who said, *I reckoned till morning that as a lion, so will he break all my bones,* Isaiah 38:13.   Is a discontented spirit from Satan? Yes.   *Yea hath God said, ye shall not eat of every tree of the garden?,* Genesis 3:1.   Is a brand of ignominy affixed to it? Yes.   *These are murmurers, complainers,* Jude ver. 16. And is a curse entailed upon it? Yes.   *Let them wander up and down for meat, and grudge if they be not satisfied,* Psalm 59:15.

Is envy a sin? Yes. *Let us walk honestly as in the day, not in strife and envying*, Romans 13:13. Is it a sin for the wicked to envy the just? Yes. *They shall see and be ashamed, for their envy at thy people*, Isaiah 26:11. Or for the just to envy the wicked? Yes. *Envy not the oppressor*, Proverbs 3:31. And is it a sin to envy for the sake of others? Yes. *Envyest thou for my sake*, Numbers 11:29.

Is covetousness a great sin? Yes. *Covetousness let it not be once named among you, as becometh saints*, Ephesians 5:3. And a great vexation? Yes. *For he that loveth silver shall not be satisfied with silver*, Ecclesiastes 5:10. Is it a hurt to our families? Yes. *He that is greedy of gain troubleth his own house*, Proverbs 15:27. And an injury to our neighbors? Yes. Thus Ahab's covetousness caused Naboth's murder, 1 Kings 21:1-4. And above all an affront to God? Yes. For it is he that *maketh poor and maketh rich*, 1 Samuel 2:7. Is it a sin that rarely goes unpunished in this world? Yes. *For the iniquity of his covetousness I was wroth and smote him*, Isaiah 57:17. But will it be severely punished in the world to come? Yes. *For the covetous shall not inherit the kingdom of God*, 1 Corinthians 6:9. Should we therefore strive against it? Yes. *Thou O man of God flee these things*, 1 Timothy 6:11. And pray against it? Yes. *Incline my heart unto thy testimonies and not to covetousness*, Psalm 119:36.

May we desire unlawful enjoyments? No. *We must not lust after evil things*, 1 Corinthians 10:6. Or lawful enjoyments inordinately? No. *Labor not for the meat that perisheth*, John 6:27. Doth all sin begin in the desires of the heart? Yes. For sinners *walk in the way of their heart*, Ecclesiastes 11:9. Should we therefore keep a constant watch over it? Yes. *Keep thine heart with all diligence, for out of it are the issues of life*, Proverbs 4:23.

Q 87. Is any man able perfectly to keep the commandments of God?

A. No mere man since the fall is able in this life perfectly to keep the commandments of God, but doth daily break them in thought, word, or deed.

Was Adam before the fall perfect? Yes. For *in the image of God created he him,* Genesis 1:27. Was Christ, who was not a mere man, perfect? Yes. *He knew no sin,* 2 Corinthians 5:21. And are the saints in heaven perfect? Yes. *In their mouth is found no guile,* Revelation 14:5. But is any mere man since the fall in this life perfect? No. *For there is not a just man on earth, that doth good and sinneth not,* Ecclesiastes 7:20. And have the best of men acknowledged this? Yes. *We are all as an unclean thing; and our iniquities like the wind have taken us away,* Isaiah 64:6.

Did the Father of the faithful sin through unbelief? Yes. For he denied his wife, lest the Egyptians should have slain him, Genesis 12:12,19. Was Jacob a plain man guilty of deceit? Yes. For *Isaac said, 'Art thou my very son Esau,' and he said, 'I am,'* Genesis 27:24. Did the meekest man offend by passion? Yes. *For they provoked his Spirit so that he spoke unadvisedly with his lips,* Psalm 106:33. And the most patient man by impatience? Yes. For he *cursed his day,* Job 3:1. And was the wisest man guilty of the greatest folly? Yes. *For when Solomon was old, his wives turned away his heart after other gods,* 1 Kings 11:4. Did the most resolute of Christ's disciples sin through weakness and fear? Yes. For *he began to curse and to swear, saying, 'I know not the man,'* Mark 14:71. And did the apostle Paul who so earnestly breathed after perfection yet fall short of it? Yes. *I am carnal, sold under sin,* Romans 7:14.

Do the best of saints sin in thought? Yes. *Why think ye evil in your hearts,* Matthew 9:4. And in word? Yes. *Ye have not spoken of me the thing that is right,* Job 42:7. And in deed? Yes. *By this deed thou hast given great occasion to the enemies of the Lord to blaspheme,* 2 Samuel 12:14. Are they guilty of many sins which they know? Yes. *My sin is ever before me,* Psalm 51:3. And of many more which they do not know? Yes. *For who can understand his errors?* Psalm 19:12.

Are the saints sanctified in every part? Yes. *In soul, body and spirit,* 1 Thessalonians 5:23. And yet are they sanctified but in part? Yes. *For God will perfect that which is lacking,* 1 Thessalonians 3:10. Are they sincerely obedient? Yes. *Remember, I have walked before thee in truth,* Isaiah 38:3. But are they perfectly obedient? No. *For we cannot do the things that we would,* Galatians 5:17. Have they a relative perfection in Christ? Yes. *We are complete in him,* Colossians 2:10. But have they a personal perfection in themselves? No. *Look not upon me because I am black,* Song of Solomon 1:6. Is justification then by our own works impossible? Yes. *For if thou Lord shouldst mark iniquity, who shall stand?* Psalm 130:3.

Q 88. Are all transgressions of the law equally heinous?
A. Some sins in themselves, and by reason of several aggravations, are more heinous in the sight of God than others.

Are all our sins known to God? Yes. *They are before his face,* Hosea 7:2. And are all sins heinous in the sight of God? Yes. *They provoke him to anger*, Deuteronomy 9:18. But are they all equally so? No. *Turn thee yet again and thou shalt see greater abominations*, Ezekiel 8:15. And will the punishment of sin be proportioned to the aggravations of it? Yes. *These shall receive greater damnation*, Mark 12:40.

Do sins receive their aggravations from the persons offending? Yes. *My people is risen up as an enemy*, Micah 2:8. Are the sins of old persons more heinous than those of others? Yes. *See what the ancients of the house of Israel do in the dark*, Ezekiel 8:12. And of ministers? Yes. *Both the prophet and the priest are profane*, Jeremiah 23:11. And of magistrates? Yes. *He shall give Israel up because of Jeroboam who did sin*, 1 Kings 14:16. And of eminent professors? Yes. *Of whom is Hymeneus and Alexander*, 1 Timothy 1:20.

Do sins also receive their aggravations from the persons offended? Yes. *Against whom do ye sport yourselves*, Isaiah 57:4. Are those sins peculiarly aggravated which are immediately committed against God? Yes. *If a man sin against the Lord who shall entreat for him*, 1 Samuel 2:25. And against Christ? Yes. *When the husbandman saw the son, they said among themselves, 'this is the heir come let us kill him,'* Matthew 21:38. And against the person of the Holy Ghost? Yes. *The blasphemy against the Holy Ghost shall not be forgiven unto men*, Matthew 12:31. And against superiors? Yes. *Were ye not afraid to speak against my servant Moses?* Numbers 12:8. And against whole bodies and communities? Yes. *And Joshua said, 'why hast thou troubled us, the Lord shall trouble thee this day,'* Joshua 7:25. And against the souls of men? Yes. *To slay the souls that should not die, and to save the souls alive that should not live*, Ezekiel 13:19.

Doth presumption aggravate sin? Yes. *The soul that doth aught presumptuously reproacheth the Lord,* Numbers 15:30. And knowledge? Yes. *To him that knoweth to do good, and doth it not, to him it is sin,* James 4:17. And reproof? Yes. *He that being often reproved hardeneth his neck shall be suddenly destroyed,* Proverbs 29:1. And perseverance in sin? Yes. *He went on frowardly in the way of his heart,* Isaiah 57:17.

Are sins against the light of nature aggravated sin? Yes. *There is such fornication among you as is not so much as named among the Gentiles,* 1 Corinthians 5:1. And deliberate sins? Yes. *He deviseth mischief upon his bed,* Psalm 36:4. And public sins? Yes. Absalom *went into his father's concubines in the sight of all Israel,* 2 Samuel 16:22. And sins against mercies greatly aggravated? Yes. *Thus Solomon turned from the Lord who had appeared unto him twice,* 1 Kings 11:9. And sins against judgments? Yes. *For all this they sinned still,* Psalm 78:32. And sins against express commands? Yes. *We have forsaken thy command-ments which thou hast commanded by thy servants the prophets,* Ezra 9:10,11. And sins against our own covenants and engagements? Yes. *Thou saidst, 'I will not transgress',* Jeremiah 2:20.

Is it an aggravation of sin to commit it without shame? Yes. *Were they ashamed, nay, they were not at all ashamed,* Jeremiah 6:15. And with delight? Yes. *Their soul delighteth in their abominations,* Isaiah 66:3. And to boast of it? Yes. *Whose glory is in their shame,* Philippians 3:19. May the place also be an aggravation of sin? Yes. *In the land of uprightness he will deal unjustly,* Isaiah 26:10. And the time? Yes. *Is it a time to receive money and garments and olive-yards and vineyards?* 2 Kings 5:26.

Should we take notice of the aggravations of sin in our confessions? Yes. *Aaron shall confess the iniquity of the children of Israel, and all their transgressions in all their sins*, Leviticus 16:21. But though aggravated may we hope that it will be pardoned? Yes. *Thou hast wearied me with thine iniquities; I, even I, am he that blotteth out thy transgressions for mine own sake*, Isaiah 43:24,25.

Q 89. What doth every sin deserve?
A. Every sin deserveth God's wrath and curse, both in this life and that which is to come.

Is sin against the body of man? Yes. *There is no rest in my bones because of my sin*, Psalm 38:3. And against the soul of man? Yes. *He that sinneth against me wrongeth his own soul*, Proverbs 8:36. Is it against his temporal interest? Yes. *If ye will walk contrary to me, then I will walk contrary to you, and will bring a sword upon you*, Leviticus 26:24,25. And against his eternal welfare? Yes. *Depart from me ye that work iniquity*, Matthew 7:23. And are all sins though not alike heinous, alike destructive? Yes. *For he that said, 'do not commit adultery,' said also, 'do not kill,'* James 2:11.

Doth sin subject one to the wrath of God? Yes. *Behold thou art wroth, for we have sinned*, Isaiah 64:5. Is the wrath of a common man dreadful? Yes. *Cursed be their wrath for it was cruel*, Genesis 49:7. But may this wrath be appeased? Yes. *A soft answer turneth away wrath*, Proverbs 15:1. Is the wrath of a king more dreadful? Yes. *The king's wrath is as the roaring of a lion*, Proverbs 19:12. But may this wrath be pacified? Yes. *Then was the king's wrath pacified*, Esther 7:10. Is the wrath of devils more terrible than either? Yes. *Woe to the inhabitants of the earth, for the devil is come down having great wrath,* Revelation 12:12. But may this wrath be restrained? Yes. *He bound Satan a thousand years,* Revelation 20:2. Is God's wrath then infinitely more dreadful than all? Yes. *Who knoweth the power of thine anger,* Psalm 90:11.

Doth sin expose men to the curse? Yes. *Ye are cursed with a curse,* Malachi 3:9. Will this curse certainly come upon impenitent sinners? Yes. *All these curses shall come upon thee and overtake thee,* Deuteronomy 28:15. Are they cursed whilst they live? Yes. *Their portion is cursed in the earth,* Job 24:18. And cursed in death? Yes. *Ye shall leave your name for a curse to my chosen, for the Lord shall slay thee,* Isaiah 65:15. And cursed for ever? Yes. *They are nigh unto cursing whose end is to be burned,* Hebrews 6:8.

Is the wrath and curse of God the due desert of sin? Yes. *Whose damnation is just,* Romans 3:8. And of every sin? Yes. *Cursed is every one that continueth not in all things that are written in the book of the law to do them,* Galatians 3:10. But is there not a possibility of deliverance herefrom? Yes. For God that devised *means that his banished should not be expelled from him,* 2 Samuel 14:14.

Q 90. What doth God require of us that we may escape his wrath and curse, due to us for sin?
A. To escape the wrath and curse of God due to us for sin, God requireth of us faith in Jesus Christ, repentance unto life, with the diligent use of all the outward means whereby Christ communicateth to us the benefits of redemption.

Is salvation from wrath a great salvation? Yes. 'Tis called *so great salvation*, Hebrews 2:3. And is it a needful salvation? Yes. *Lord save, or else we perish*, Matthew 8:25. Should it therefore be enquired after? Yes. *If ye will enquire, enquire ye*, Isaiah 21:12.

Is faith in our Lord Jesus Christ requisite in order to salvation? Yes. *Believe on the Lord Jesus Christ, and thou shalt be saved*, Acts 16:31. Shall none be saved but those who believe? No. *He that believeth not is condemned already*, John 3:18. And shall all those be saved who do believe? Yes. *Whosoever believeth on me shall never die*, John 11:26. Is repentance also necessary unto salvation? Yes. *God now commandeth all men every where to repent*, Acts 17:30. And shall all those who do not repent as well as believe perish? Yes. *Except ye repent, ye shall all likewise perish*, Luke 13:3,5.

Did Christ preach up the necessity of faith and repentance? Yes. *Repent ye, and believe the gospel*, Mark 1:15. And did the apostles do the same? Yes. *Testifying both to the Jews and also to the Greeks, repentance towards God, and faith towards our Lord Jesus Christ*, Acts 20:21. But are these in our own power? No. *For without Christ we can do nothing*, John 15:5.

Doth God require of us the use of means? Yes. *Work out your own salvation with fear and trembling*, Philippians 2:12. And should we be diligent in the use of means? Yes. *For the kingdom of heaven suffereth violence*, Matthew 11:12. Is God then obliged to second our endeavors? No. For *it is not of him that willeth, nor of him that runneth*, Romans 9:16. But if grace excites them, will that crown them with success? Yes. *Those that seek me early shall find me*, Proverbs 8:17.

Q 91. What is faith in Jesus Christ?
A. Faith in Jesus Christ is a saving grace, whereby we receive and rest upon him alone for salvation, as he is offered to us in the gospel.

Is faith a free gift and therefore a grace? Yes. *Unto you it is given in the behalf of Christ to believe on him*, Philippians 1:29. Is it particularly a gift of the Spirit? Yes. Thus Barnabas is said to be *full of the Holy Ghost and of faith*, Acts 11:24. And a gift that distinguishes the elect of God from all others? Yes. *'Tis the faith of God's elect*, Titus 1:1. Is it a saving grace? Yes. For we *believe to the saving of the soul*, Hebrews 10:39. But is it so by any inherent merit or efficacy of its own? No. But as it *receives the gift of righteousness*, Romans 5:17.

Is God the ultimate object of faith? Yes. *Ye believe in God*, John 14:1. And is Christ the immediate object of it? Yes. *Believe also in me*, John 14:1. Is the heart the seat of it? Yes. *With the heart man believeth unto righteousness*, Romans 10:10. And are sensible convinced sinners the subject of it? Yes. *They shall come who were ready to perish*, Isaiah 27:13. Is faith imperfect in the present life? Yes. *Lord I believe, help thou mine unbelief*, Mark 9:24. But shall weak faith be supported? Yes. *A bruised reed shall he not break, and smoking flax shall he not quench*, Matthew 12:20. And strengthened? Yes. *I can do all things through Christ, who strengtheneth me*, Philippians 4:13.

Does true faith imply an assent of the understanding? Yes. *I believe that Jesus Christ is the Son of God*, Acts 8:37. And a consent of the will? Yes. *This is a faithful saying, and worthy of all acceptation, that Christ Jesus came into the world to save sinners*, 1 Timothy 1:15.

Doth it imply the soul's reception of Christ? Yes. *Ye have received the Lord Jesus Christ,* Colossians 2:6. And its reliance upon him? Yes. *In whom ye also trusted,* Ephesians 1:13. And its cleaving to him? Yes. *And exhorted them all that with purpose of heart, they would cleave unto the Lord,* Acts 11:23. And that to the utter exclusion of every thing else? Yes. *For whom I have suffered the loss of all things, and do count them but dung, that I may win Christ,* Philippians 3:8.

Is there something which the believing soul commits to Christ? Yes. *I know whom I have believed, and am persuaded that he is able to keep that which I have committed to him,* 2 Timothy 1:12. And something that he expects from him? Yes. *Looking for the mercy of our Lord Jesus Christ unto eternal life,* Jude ver. 21. Is true faith a vital principle? Yes. *The just shall live by faith,* Habakkuk 2:4. And an active principle? Yes. *It worketh by love,* Galatians 5:6. And a victorious principle? Yes. *This is the victory that overcometh the world, even our faith,* 1 John 5:4. And an establishing principle? Yes. *By faith ye stand,* 2 Corinthians 1:24. And a soul comforting principle? Yes. *I had fainted unless I had believed,* Psalm 27:13. And a God exalting principle? Yes. *Abraham was strong in faith, giving glory to God,* Romans 4:20. And is it on all these accounts a precious principle? Yes. *To them that have obtained like precious faith,* 2 Peter 1:1.

Q 92. What is repentance unto life?

A. Repentance unto life is a saving grace, whereby a sinner, out of a true sense of his sin, and apprehension of the mercy of God in Christ, doth, with grief and hatred of his sin, turn from it unto God, with full purpose of and endeavour after new obedience.

Is true repentance, repentance unto life? Yes. *God hath unto the Gentiles granted repentance unto life,* Acts 11:18. Is there then a repentance that is not so? Yes. *Judas repented and went and hanged himself,* Matthew 27:3,5. Is true repentance a grace? Yes. *Christ is exalted to give repentance,* Acts 5:31. Is it wrought by the word as an instrument? Yes. *Is not my word like a fire, and like a hammer that breaketh the rock in pieces,* Jeremiah 23:29. And by the Spirit as an agent? Yes. *I will pour upon the inhabitants of Jerusalem the Spirit of grace, and they shall mourn,* Zechariah 12:10. Is it a saving grace? Yes. *It is repentance unto salvation,* 2 Corinthians 7:10. And shall none be saved without it? No. *Thou, after thy hardness and impenitent heart treasureth up wrath,* Romans 2:5.

Is there such a thing as legal repentance? Yes. *See thou how Ahab humbleth himself,* 1 Kings 21:29. And may this be attended with great terror? Yes. It is *a spirit of bondage unto fear,* Romans 8:15. And with some external reformations? Yes. *Herod observed John and when he heard him, did many things,* Mark 6:20. But is gospel repentance quite of a different nature? Yes. *Ye sorrowed after a godly sort,* 2 Corinthians 7:11.

Does true repentance imply conviction of sin? Yes. *He is convinced of all,* 1 Corinthians 14:24. And is this conviction deep? Yes. *They were pricked in their heart,* Acts 2:37. And painful? Yes. *A wounded spirit who can bear?* Proverbs 18:14. And abiding? Yes. *Thine arrows stick fast in me,* Psalm 38:2. And in a sense mortal? Yes. *Sin revived and I died,* Romans 7:9. Doth this conviction extend to the sin of our nature? Yes. *In sin did my mother conceive me,* Psalm 51:5. And to the corruptions of the heart? Yes. *The whole heart is faint,* Isaiah 1:5. And to all actual sins? Yes. *Come see a man which told me all things that ever I did,* John 4:29. And to the filth of sin as well as the guilt of it? Yes. *Behold I am vile,* Job 40:4. Can those therefore be said to repent who are not so much as convinced of sin? No. *I hearkened and heard, but they spake not aright, no man repented of his wickedness, saying 'what have I done',* Jeremiah 8:6.

Does repentance imply sorrow for sin? Yes. *My sorrow is continually before me,* Psalm 38:17. But may there be a sorrow without repentance? Yes. *Now I rejoice, not that ye were made sorry, but that ye sorrowed to repentance,* 2 Corinthians 7:9. Is true sorrow for sin genuine and free? Yes. *Mine eyes pour out tears unto God,* Job 16:10. Is it upright and sincere? Yes. *They shall mourn for him as one mourneth for his only son,* Zechariah 12:10. Is it pungent and strong? Yes. *The people wept very sore,* Ezra 10:1. And does it love to be private and retired? Yes. *And the land shall mourn every family apart, and their wives apart,* Zechariah 12:12.

Doth repentance imply hatred of sin? Yes. *What I hate that do I,* Romans 7:15. And hatred of ourselves for sin? Yes. *I abhor myself,* Job 42:6. Is this hatred of sin universal? Yes. *I hate every false way,* Psalm 119:128. And irreconcilable? Yes. *How shall we that are dead to sin, live any longer therein,* Romans 6:2.

Is true repentance attended with a view of God's mercy? Yes. *There is forgiveness with thee,* Psalm 130:4. And a hope in that mercy? Yes. *There is hope in Israel concerning this thing,* Ezra 10:2. Is a hope in God's mercy a leading step to repentance?

Yes. *The goodness of God leadeth thee to repentance*, Romans 2:4. And therefore where there is no hope can there be no true repentance? No. *Thou saidst, 'there is no hope, I have loved strangers, and after them I will go,'* Jeremiah 2:25.

Is repentance attended with holy shame? Yes. *I am ashamed and blush*, Ezra 9:6. And anxious fear? Yes. *What carefuleness it wrought in you—yea what fear*, 2 Corinthians 7:21. And a clearing of God? Yes. *That thou mayest be clear when thou judgest*, Psalm 51:4. And a humble submissive demeanor towards men? Yes. *He giveth his cheek to him that smiteth him*, Lamentations 3:30. Will penitent sinners confess their sins? Yes. *I acknowledged my sin unto thee*, Psalm 32:5. And aggravate their sins? Yes. *We have sinned and committed iniquity and have done wickedly and have rebelled*, Daniel 9:5,6. And make reparation where it is possible? Yes. *If I have taken any thing from any by false accusation I restore him fourfold*, Luke 19:8.

Does repentance imply a turning from sin? Yes. *If I have done iniquity, I will do so no more*, Job 34:32. Doth the true penitent turn from his beloved sin? Yes. *I kept myself from mine iniquity*, Psalm 18:23. And from all sin? Yes. *Repent and turn yourselves from all your abominations*, Ezekiel 14:6. And so as never fully to return to it again? Yes. *Ephraim shall say, 'what have I to do any more with idols?'* Hosea 14:8.

Doth true repentance also imply a return to God? Yes. *If thou wilt return, O Israel, return unto me*, Jeremiah 4:1. And to Christ? Yes. *Ye are returned unto the Shepherd and Bishop of your souls*, 1 Peter 2:25. And a return to ourselves? Yes. *He came to himself*, Luke 15:17. And to duty? Yes. *I turned my feet unto thy testimonies*, Psalm 119:59. But can we thus turn ourselves? No. *Surely after that I was turned, I repented*, Jeremiah 31:19.

Do true penitents perform duty from a different principle than they did before? Yes. *For the love of Christ constraineth them*, 2 Corinthians 5:14. And in a different manner? Yes. *They serve God in newness of spirit, and not in oldness of the letter*, Romans 7:6. But do they perform it in a perfect manner? No. *For in many things we offend all*, James 3:2.

Q 93. What are the outward means whereby Christ communicateth to us the benefits of redemption? A. The outward and ordinary means whereby Christ communicateth to us the benefits of redemption are his ordinances, especially the word, baptism, the Lord's Supper, and prayer; all which means are made effectual to the elect for salvation.

Are there ordinances which are not of God's appointment? Yes. We read of the *statutes of Omri*, Micah 6:16. But are these unprofitable? Yes. For *those that observe lying vanities, forsake their own mercies*, Jonah 2:8. And should they therefore be rejected? Yes. *Why are we subject to ordinances after the commandments of men*, Colossians 2:20.

Are there ordinances of God's appointment? Yes. *Thou shalt teach them my ordinances*, Exodus 18:20. Are the word, sacraments and prayer the great gospel ordinances? Yes. *Then they that gladly received the word were baptized, and they continued steadfastly in the apostles doctrine and fellowship, and in breaking of bread, and in prayers*, Acts 2:41-42. Is singing of psalms also an ordinance? Yes. *O come let us sing unto the Lord, let us make a joyful noise to the rock of our salvation*, Psalm 95:1.   Is it an ordinance very pleasing to God? Yes. *This also shall please the Lord better than an ox or a bullock*, Psalm 69:31. And very useful and instructive to men? Yes. *Teaching and admonishing one another in psalms and hymns and spiritual songs*, Colossians 3:16. Should it therefore be attended to in a very serious manner? Yes. *Singing with grace in your hearts onto the Lord*, ibid. Are these ordinances made effectual to all God's elect? Yes. *For as many as were ordained to eternal life believed*, Acts 13:48. And to none but such?   No. *Ye believe not because ye are not my sheep*, John 10:26.

Have some been wrought upon by religious discourse? Yes. *He that walketh with wise men shall be wise*, Proverbs 13:20. And others by dreams? Yes. *In a dream, in a vision of the night he openeth the ears of men and sealeth their instruction*, Job 33:15,16. And others by afflictive providences? Yes. *When Manasseh was in afflictions he humbled himself greatly before the God of his fathers*, 2 Chronicles 33:12. And others in a yet more miraculous manner? Yes. *Thus Saul was called by a voice from heaven*, Acts 9:4. But are God's word and ordinances the ordinary means of salvation? Yes. *He hath given pastors and teachers for the edifying of the body of Christ*, Ephesians 4:11,12.   Should we therefore attend upon them? Yes. *Blessed is the man that heareth me*, Proverbs 8:34. And that diligently and constantly? Yes. *Watching daily at my gates, and waiting at the posts of my doors*, ibid.

Q 94. How is the word made effectual to salvation?

A. The Spirit of God maketh the reading, but especially the preaching of the word, an effectual means of convincing and converting sinners, and of building them up in holiness and comfort through faith unto salvation.

Is the word of God profitable for conviction? Yes. *It is quick and powerful, piercing even to the dividing asunder of soul and spirit*, Hebrews 4:12. And for conversion? Yes. *The law of the Lord is perfect converting the soul*, Psalm 19:7. But is it thus profitable to all that hear it? No. *For when they heard these things, some mocked, and others said, 'we will hear thee again of this matter,'* Acts 17:32.

Doth the word beget faith? Yes. *Faith comes by hearing*, Romans 10:17. And holiness? Yes. *That they also might be sanctified through the truth*, John 17:19. And comfort? Yes. *Thy word was unto me the joy and rejoicing of my heart*, Jeremiah 15:16. Is it a means of enlightening our understandings? Yes. *The commandment of the Lord is pure, enlightening the eyes*, Psalm 19:8. And of restraining our corruptions? Yes. *By the words of thy lips I have kept me from the paths of the destroyer*, Psalm 17:4. And of perfecting our graces? Yes. *It is able to build us up*, Acts 20:32. And of preparing us for heaven? Yes. *To give us an inheritance among them that are sanctified*, ibid. But is it so by any inherent virtue or efficacy of its own? No. *For it is the power of God unto salvation*, Romans 1:16.

Should the word of God be read for these purposes? Yes. *They read in the book of the law distinctly*, Nehemiah 8:8. And preached? Yes. *Then will I teach transgressors thy law*, Psalm 51:13. Should it be preached purely? Yes. *Teach thou the things which become sound doctrine*, Titus 2:1. And plainly? Yes. *Not with enticing words of man's wisdom*, 1 Corinthians 2:4. And prudently? Yes. *Rightly dividing the word of truth*, 2 Timothy 2:15. And affectionately? Yes. *I ceased not to warn every one with tears*, Acts 20:31. And boldly? Yes. *These things command and teach*, 1 Timothy 4:11. And diligently?

Yes. *Reprove, rebuke, exhort, with all long-suffering and doctrine,* 2 Timothy 4:2. And may we hope that the word thus preached will be crowned with success? Yes. When *the law of truth was in his mouth—he did turn many away from iniquity,* Malachi 2:6.

Q 95. How is the word to be read and heard, that it may become effectual to salvation?
A. That the word may become effectual to salvation, we must attend thereunto with diligence, preparation, and prayer; receive it with faith and love, lay it up in our hearts, and practice it in our lives.

That the word of God may profit, should we attend thereto with diligence? Yes. *All the people were attentive to hear him,* Luke 19:48. And be inquisitive into the meaning of it? Yes. *Of whom speaketh the prophet this, of himself, or of some other man?* Acts 8:34. And compare one Scripture with another? Yes. *Comparing spiritual things with spiritual,* 1 Corinthians 2:13.

Is preparation also necessary in order to our profiting by the word? Yes. *Ezra prepared his heart to seek the law of the Lord,* Ezra 7:10. Should we for this purpose lay aside worldly cares? Yes. *For the thorns choke the seed,* Matthew 13:7. And carnal passions? Yes. *All malice, and guile, and hypocrisies, and envies, and evil speakings,* 1 Peter 2:1. And all pre-imbibed prejudices? Yes. Not like those who cried, '*what will this babbler say?*' Acts 17:18. Should we pray for our ministers? Yes. *And for me that utterance may be given unto me,* Ephesians 6:19. And for ourselves? Yes. *Teach me thy judgments,* Psalm 119:103. Should we also come with desire? Yes. *As new born babes desire the sincere milk of the word,* 1 Peter 2:2. And with expectation? Yes. *My soul wait thou only on God, for my expectation is from him,* Psalm 62:5. And will such a preparation of the heart be greatly to our advantage? Yes. *Thou wilt prepare their heart, thou wilt cause thine ear to hear,* Psalm 10:17. But will a want of preparation excuse a neglect of duty? No. *For a multitude of the people had not cleansed themselves, yet did they eat of the passover,* 2 Chronicles 30:18.

Should the word be received in faith? Yes. Thus we read of *the hearing of faith,* Galatians 3:2. And in love? Yes. *Consider how I love thy precepts,* Psalm 119:159. And will a want of this be a hindrance to our profiting? Yes. *They received not the love of the truth that they might be saved,* 2 Thessalonians 2:10.

Should we hear the word with reverence? Yes. *When Ezra opened the book all the people stood up,* Nehemiah 8:5. And with judgment? Yes. *For the ear trieth words as the mouth tasteth meat,* Job 34:3. And with care? Yes. *Take heed how ye hear,* Luke 8:18. Must we keep from roving thoughts in hearing? Yes. *Their heart goeth after their covetousness,* Ezekiel 33:31. And from a wandering eye? Yes. *The eyes of all were fastened on him,* Luke 4:20. And from sleep and drowsiness? Yes. *Could not ye watch with me one hour?* Mathew 26:40.

Should we treasure up what we hear? Yes. *Remember, thertefore, how ye have received and heard and hold fast,* Revelation 3:3. Should we therefore meditate upon it? Yes. *And she pondered all these things in her heart,* Luke 2:19,51. And talk of it? Yes. *And shalt talk of them when thou sittest in thine house, and when thou walkest in the way,* Deuteronomy 6:7.

And is this necessary in order to our profiting by it? Yes. *By which also ye are saved, if ye keep in memory what I preached unto you,* 1 Corinthians 15:2.

Is it also requisite that we practice what we hear? Yes. *As thou hast said, so must we do,* Ezra 10:12. And is this the way to obtain the blessing? Yes. *This man shall be blessed in his deed,* James 1:25. And to avoid the curse? Yes. For some will *say, 'thou hast taught in our streets,'* but he will reply, *'I know not whence you are,'* Luke 13:26.

Q 96. How do baptism and the Lord's Supper become effectual means of salvation?

A. Baptism and the Lord's Supper become effectual means of salvation, not for any virtue in them, or in him that doth administer them, but only by the blessing of Christ, and the working of the Spirit in those that by faith receive them.

Are sacraments signs? Yes. Thus *Abraham received the sign of circumcision,* Romans 4:11. Are they outward signs of spiritual and invisible blessings? Yes. *Neither is that circumcision which is outward in the flesh but that of the heart,* Romans 2:28,29. Doth baptism signify the work of regeneration wrought in us? Yes. *Buried with him in baptism, wherein also ye are risen with him,* Colossians 2:12. And doth the Lord's Supper signify the work of redemption wrought for us? Yes. *This do in remembrance of me,* Luke 22:19. And are these outward signs useful to stir up inward affections? Yes. *Mine eye affecteth mine heart,* Lamentations 3:51.

Are the sacraments effectual means of salvation to all who partake of them? No. For *if thou be a breaker of the law, thy circumcision is made uncircumcision,* Romans 2:25. Do they save by an inherent virtue in themselves? No. For baptism doth not save as it is a *putting away the filth of the flesh,* 1 Peter 3:21. Or in those that administer them? No. *For neither is he that planteth any thing, neither he that watereth,* 1 Corinthians 3:7. Are they therefore the less effectual when administered by an ungodly person? No. *For Judas was numbered with us, and obtained a part of the ministry,* Acts 1:17. Or the more so when administered by one that is godly? No. *For Philip baptized Simon, who yet was in the gall of bitterness,* Acts 8:13,23. Should this then prevent a partial regard to one minister to the neglect of others? Yes. *Who then is Paul, and who is Apollos?* 1 Corinthians 3:5.

Doth the efficacy of sacraments depend upon the blessing and presence of Christ? Yes. *Lo I am with you always,* Matthew 28:20. And upon the cooperating influences of the Spirit? Yes. *By one Spirit we are all baptized,* 1 Corinthians 12:13. And are they only effectual to those who by faith receive them? Yes. *He that believeth and is baptized shall be saved, he that believeth not shall be damned,* Mark 16:16.

Q 97. What is baptism?

A. Baptism is an ordinance of the New Testament instituted by Jesus Christ, to be unto the party baptized a sign of his fellowship with him, in his death, burial, and resurrection; of his being ingrafted into him; of remission of sins; and of his giving up himself unto God through Jesus Christ, to live and walk in newness of life.

Doth the Scripture speak of a baptism with the Holy Ghost? Yes. *He shall baptize you with the Holy Ghost,* Matthew 3:11. And was this accomplished? Yes. *They were filled with the Holy Ghost,* Acts 2:4. Doth it also speak of a baptism of sufferings? Yes. *Are ye able to*

be baptized with the baptism that I am baptized with?
Matthew 20:22. And was Christ indeed eminently
baptized herewith? Yes. *I am come into the deep waters
where the floods overflow me*, Psalm 69:2. But is there
besides these a baptism with water? Yes. *I baptize you
with water*, Matthew 3:11.

Did the Jews baptize before John? No. For they ask,
'*why baptizeth thou, if thou be not the Christ, nor
Elias?*' John 1:25. Did John's baptism introduce the
gospel dispensation? Yes. *The beginning of the
gospel of Jesus Christ—John did baptize*, Mark 1:1,4.
And had it a reference to a Savior shortly to come?
Yes. He said, *that they should believe on him, which
should come after him, that is on Christ Jesus*, Acts
19:4. Was John sent of God, to baptize? Yes. *He
that sent me to baptize with water, the same said
unto me*, John 1:33. Did the people receive his
baptism as from God? Yes. *They justified God, being
baptized with the baptism of John*, Luke 7:29. And
was John's baptism the same for substance as that
of Christ? Yes. *For Jesus baptized, and John also
was baptizing*, John 3:22,23.

Was Christ himself baptized? Yes. *Then came Jesus
unto John to be baptized of him*, Matthew 3:13. Did
he thereby confer an honor upon his ordinance?
Yes. *For there came a voice from heaven, saying,
'This is my beloved Son, in whom I am well pleased'*,
Matthew 3:17. And is this a powerful engagement
upon us to submit to it? Yes. For thus *it becometh
us to fulfill all righteousness*, Matthew 3:15.
Is water baptism a sign of our fellowship with Christ?
Yes. *For as many as have been baptized into Christ
have put on Christ*, Galatians 3:27. Is it a sign of our
fellowship with him in his death? Yes. *We are
baptized into his death*, Romans 6:3. And in his

burial? Yes. *We are buried with him in baptism*, ver. 4. And in his resurrection? Yes. *For we are planted together in the likeness of his resurrection*, ver. 5. Is this fellowship by faith? Yes. *We are risen with him by faith of the operation of God*, Colossians 2:12.

Is baptism a sign of our engrafting into Christ? Yes. *We are baptized into Jesus Christ*, Romans 6:3. And of the crucifixion of the old man? Yes. *Knowing this, that our old man is crucified with him*, ver. 6. And of the destruction of sin? Yes. *That the body of sin might be destroyed*, ibid. Doth it signify the removal of the guilt of sin? Yes. *Be baptized for the remission of sins*, Acts 2:38. And the washing away the filth of it? Yes. *Be baptized and wash away thy sins*, Acts 22:16. But is baptism of itself sufficient for any of these purposes? No. *For it is the blood of Christ that cleanseth us from all sin*, 1 John 1:7.

Is baptism an engagement to yield ourselves unto God? Yes. *Yield selves unto God as those that are alive from the dead*, Romans 6:13. And to live in brotherly love? Yes. *For we are baptized into one body*, 1 Corinthians 12:13. And to walk in newness of life? Yes. *We also should walk in newness of life*, Romans 6:4. And was it designed to be a standing ordinance in the church of Christ? Yes. *To the end of the world*, Matthew 28:20.

Q 98. To whom is baptism to be administered?
A. Baptism is to be administered to all those who actually profess repentance towards God, faith in and obedience to our Lord Jesus Christ, and to none other.

Is baptism to be administered to such who repent? Yes. It is *the baptism of repentance*, Mark 1:4. And to all such? Yes. *Repent and be baptized every one of you*, Acts 2:37. And to none but such? No. *O generation of vipers, who hath warned you to flee from the wrath to come*, Matthew 3:7. Should this repentance be actually professed? Yes. *They were baptized in Jordan confessing their sins*, Matthew 3:6. And appear in its fruits? Yes. *Bring forth fruits meet for repentance*, Matthew 3:8. And have the worst of sinners upon their repentance a right to baptism? Yes. *Then came also Publicans to be baptized*, Luke 3:12.

Should faith be before baptism? Yes. The Corinthians *believed and were baptized*, Acts 18:8. Will a credible profession of faith justify the administration of this ordinance? Yes. For Simon Magus *believed and was baptized*, Acts 8:13. But will real faith only justify a submission to it? Yes. *If thou believest with all thine heart thou mayest*, Acts 8:37. And will the ordinance be unavailable where faith is wanting? Yes. For *whatsoever is not of faith is sin*, Romans 14:23.

Must persons first be taught before they are baptized? Yes. *Go teach all nations baptizing* them, Matthew 28:19. And appear to be partakers of the Holy Ghost? Yes. *Can any man forbid water that these should not be baptized, who have received the Holy Ghost as well as we*, Acts 10:47. And gladly receive the word? Yes. *They that gladly received the word were baptized*, Acts 2:41. And discover a disposition to obey? Yes. '*Men and brethren what shall we do?' And Peter said, 'Repent and be baptized*,' Acts 2:37.

Should baptism be a matter of choice in those that submit to it? Yes. *See here is water, what doth hinder me to be baptized?* Acts 8:36. And their own act and deed? Yes. *They went out to him and were baptized,* Mark 1:5.   And the answer of a good conscience?   Yes.   *For baptism saveth us, as it is the answer of a good conscience towards God,* 1 Peter 3:21.   And where these qualifications are wanting, should baptism be refused?   Yes.   *Give not that which is holy unto dogs,* Matthew 7:6.

Q 99. Are the infants of such as are professing believers to be baptized?
A. The infants of such as are professing believers are not to be baptized, because there is neither command nor example in the Holy Scriptures, or certain consequence from them to baptize such.

Are the subjects of baptism plainly set forth in the divine word?   Yes.   *They were baptized both men and women,* Acts 8:12.   And doth the silence of the Scripture   concerning   others   amount   to   a prohibition?   Yes.   *Who hath required this at your hand?* Isaiah 1:12.

Had children a right to circumcision under the law? Yes.   *Every man child among you shall be circumcised,* Genesis 17:10.   And had servants the same?   Yes.   *Abraham circumcised his son and all that were bought with his money the same day,* Genesis 17:23.   Was this in itself a privilege?   No. For it was a part of that *hand writing of ordinances that was against us,* Colossians 2:14.   And is it now abolished?   Yes.   For Christ hath *taken it out of the way, nailing it to his cross,* Colossians 2:14.

Doth   not   baptism   come   in   the   room   of circumcision?   No.   For Christ was both *circumcised and baptized,* Luke 2:21, 3:21.   Had the apostles a fair opportunity to mention such a substitution had it taken place? Yes. For some said, '*Except ye be circumcised after the manner of Moses ye cannot be saved,*' Acts 15:1. And did they mention it? No. They only made a decree, Acts 15:19,28.

Was not the covenant made with Abraham the covenant of grace? No. But a mixed covenant, consisting partly of temporal blessings, Genesis 17:2-14. But as far as it was a covenant of grace did it not belong to all Abraham's natural seed? No. *Not because they are the seed of Abraham are they all children,* Romans 9:7. But is it not said for an everlasting covenant to be a God to thee and to thy seed after thee? Yes. *But the children of the promise are counted for the seed,* ver. 8. Are all others then, whether infants or adults excluded? Yes. For they are *aliens from the commonwealth of Israel,* Ephesians 2:12.

Was not circumcision a seal of the covenant? No. But *a token of it,* Genesis 17:11. Was it a seal to Abraham? Yes. And to him only a *seal of the righteousness of the faith which he had yet being uncircumcised,* Romans 4:11. Are not the children of believers included in the covenant? No. *They which are the children of the flesh, are not the seed of God,* Romans 9:8. Must they therefore be Christ's in order to be the right seed? Yes. *If ye be Christ's then are ye Abraham's seed, and heirs according to the promise,* Galatians 3:29.

Were not children brought to Christ to be baptized? No. But *that he should put his hands on them and pray,* Matthew 19:13. And does even this appear to have been an unusual thing? Yes. For *the disciples rebuked them,* ibid.   But does not the apostle say, the promise is to you and to your children?   Yes. But he adds *even to as many as the Lord our God shall call,* Acts 2:39.

Might not infants be included in the household of Crispus which was baptized?   No.   For we read that he *believed with all his house,* Acts 18:8.   Or in that of the jailor?   No.   For *he rejoiced, believing in God, with all his house,* Acts 16:34.   Or in that of Stephanas? No.   For *they had addicted themselves to the ministry of the saints,* 1 Corinthians 16:15.   Or in that of Lydia?   No.   For the apostles *entered into the house of Lydia, and when they had seen the brethren, they comforted them and departed,* Acts 16:40.

Are not infants members of the gospel church as they were once of the Jewish?   No.   For it consists of such as *are sanctified in Christ Jesus and called to be saints,* 1 Corinthians 1:2.   May they not be disciples?   No.   For we are *made* and not born *disciples,* John 4:1.[10]   But are they not said to be holy?   Yes.   In the same sense as *the unbelieving husband or wife,* 1 Corinthians 7:14.

Does not that passage of *such is the kingdom of heaven,* favor infant baptism?   No.   For Christ explains it, by adding, *Whosoever shall not receive the Kingdom of God as a little child shall not enter therein,* Mark 10:15.   Nor the passage *if the root is holy so also are the branches?*   No.   For *that which is born of the flesh is flesh,* John 3:6.   Should we in this and all other controversies be guided by the word of God?   Yes.   *In*

---

[10] Christ did not make them disciples by baptizing them, but first made them disciples and then baptized them.

all things I have said unto thee, be thou circumspect, Exodus 23:13. And not pay an undue regard to the customs or opinions of men? No. *Walk ye not in the statutes of your fathers, nor observe their judgments, I am the Lord your God,* Ezekiel 20:18,19.

Q 100. How is Baptism rightly administered?

A. Baptism is rightly administered by immersion, or dipping the whole body of the party in water, into the name of the Father, and of the Son, and of the Holy Spirit, according to Christ's institution, and the practice of the apostles, and not by sprinkling or pouring of water, or dipping some part of the body, after the tradition of men.

Should we be concerned about the mode or manner of religious worship? Yes. *Let one of the priests teach them the manner of the God of the land,* 2 Kings 17:27. And will God be displeased if we are negligent herein? Yes. *The Lord our God made a breach upon us, for that we sought him not after the due order,* 1 Chronicles 15:13.

Is water requisite in baptism? Yes. *See here is water,* Acts 8:36. And much water? Yes. *John was also baptizing in Enon, near to Salim, because there was much water there,* John 3:23. And is this used to signify an internal washing? Yes. *And our bodies washed with pure water,* Hebrews 10:22.

Does baptism appear to be by immersion from the action of the person administering? Yes. For *Philip went down into the water,* and baptized the eunuch, Acts 8:38. And the action of the person to whom it was administered? Yes. *And Jesus when he was baptized, went strait way up out of the water,* Matthew 3:16. And from the place where it was administered? Yes. *They were baptized of him in Jordan,* Matthew 3:6. And from the thing signified thereby? Yes. *Being buried with him in baptism, wherein also ye are risen with him,* Colossians 2:12. But may not sprinkling or pouring of water do as well? No. For there is but *one baptism,* Ephesians 4:5.

Was water brought or carried to the persons that were to be baptized? No. *The same baptizeth and all men come unto him,* John 3:26. Might not water be applied to the persons when they came? No. *For Jesus was baptized of John* into Jordan[11] Mark 1:9. But may not another method be used in cold countries? No. *Go ye into all the world, and teach all nations, baptizing* (or dipping) *them,* Matthew 28:19, Mark 16:15.

Was the children of Israel's passage through the Red Sea a figure of baptism? Yes. *They were all baptized unto Moses in the cloud and in the sea,* 1 Corinthians 10:1,2. May we not suppose then that they were sprinkled by the cloud No. For *it was a cloud of darkness to the Egyptians but gave light to the Israelites,* Exodus 14:20. Or that they were washed by the sea? No. For *the waters were a wall to them on their right hand, and on their left,* Exodus 14:22.

Q 101. What is the duty of such who are rightly baptized?
A. It is the duty of such who are rightly baptized to give up themselves to some particular and orderly church of Jesus Christ, that they may walk in all the commandments and ordinances of the Lord blameless.

Is there an invisible church of Christ? Yes. *Unto the general assembly and church of the first-born,* Hebrews 12:23. Doth this consist of all the elect? Yes. *Which are written in heaven,* ibid. Is there a visible church of Christ upon earth? Yes. For we read

---

[11] ἐις Ιορδάνην

that *Saul made havoc of the church*, Acts 8:3. Doth this consist of professing believers? Yes. *They that gladly received the word were added to the church*, Acts 2:41. Is this church divided into separate assemblies which are also called churches? Yes. *Then had the churches rest*, Acts 9:31. Were these churches national or provincial? No. For we read of *the churches in Galatia*, Galatians 1:2.

Doth a particular gospel church consist of as many as may comfortably meet together in one place? Yes. *When they had gathered the church together they rehearsed all that God had done*, Acts 14:27. Is it a voluntary society? Yes. *They first gave their own selves unto the Lord, and unto us by the will of God*, 2 Corinthians 8:5. And an authoritative one? Yes. *When ye are gathered together with the power of our Lord Jesus Christ to deliver such an one to Satan*, 1 Corinthians 5:5. And should it be an orderly one? Yes. *Joying and beholding your order*, Colossians 2:5. And doth Christ own such churches as his own? Yes. *What thou seest write in a book, and send it to the seven churches, which are in Asia*, Revelation 1:11.

Is it the duty of baptized believers to separate themselves from the world? Yes. *Come out from among them and be ye separate*, 2 Corinthians 6:17. And to join themselves to some particular church of Christ? Yes. *Paul essayed to join himself to the disciples*, Acts 9:26. And should they do this soon after their baptism? Yes. *They were baptized, and the same day there were added to them about three thousand souls*, Acts 2:41.

Is Christian fellowship necessary for the glory of God? Yes. *That we may with one mind and with one mouth glorify God*, Romans 15:6. And for the celebration of gospel ordinances? Yes. The church of Corinth *came together into one place—to eat the Lord's supper,* 1 Corinthians 11:20. And for mutual edification? Yes. *Woe to him that is alone when he falleth, for he hath not another to help him up,* Ecclesiastes 4:10. Should those therefore that enter into church fellowship endeavor to answer the ends of it? Yes. *Let us consider one another, to provoke unto love and to good works,* Hebrews 10:24.

Q 102. What is the Lord's Supper?

A. The Lord's Supper is an ordinance of the New Testament, instituted by Jesus Christ; wherein by giving and receiving bread and wine, according to his appointment, his death is shown forth, and the worthy receivers are, not after a corporal and carnal manner, but by faith, made partakers of his body and blood, with all his benefits, to their spiritual nourishment and growth in grace.

Is the Lord's Supper of divine appointment? Yes. It was *received of Lord,* 1 Corinthians 11:23. Did Christ institute it a little before his death? Yes. *The same night wherein he was betrayed,* 1 Corinthians 11:23. And doth this add force to the command? Yes. *Thy Father did command before he died,* Genesis 50:16. Are all true Christians invited hereto? Yes. *Come for all things are now ready,* Luke 14:17. And shall they be welcome if they come? Yes. *Eat O friends, drink, yea drink abundantly, O beloved,* Song of Solomon 5:1.

Is bread to be used in this ordinance? Yes. *For he took bread,* Matthew 26:26. And wine? Yes. *He took the cup when he had supped,* 1 Corinthians 11:25. Are bread and wine significative of all the necessaries of life? Yes. *Eat thy bread with joy and drink thy wine with a merry heart,* Ecclesiastes 9:7. And do they herein aptly represent Christ? Yes.

For it hath pleased the Father that in him should all fullness dwell, Colossians 1:19.

Must the elements be blessed? Yes. *The cup of blessing which we bless,* 1 Corinthians 10:16. And when blessed be given and received? Yes. *Jesus took bread and gave it to them, he also took the cup and gave it to them,* Mark 14:22,23. And may all partake of the latter as well as the former? Yes. *Drink ye all of it,* Matthew 26:27.

Doth the bread signify the body of Christ? Yes. *This is my body,* 1 Corinthians 11:24. Doth the wine signify the blood of Christ? Yes. *This cup is the New Testament in my blood,* Luke 22:20. Is the doctrine then of Christ crucified meat and drink to a believing soul? Yes. *My flesh is meat indeed, and my blood is drink indeed,* John 6:55. And are we to feed upon that doctrine? Yes. *He that eateth me, even he shall live by me,* John 6:57.

Is this a commemorative ordinance? Yes. *Do this in remembrance of me,* 1 Corinthians 11:24. Doth it shew forth the death of Christ? Yes. *As oft as ye eat of this bread and drink of this cup, ye do show forth the Lord's death,* 1 Corinthians 11:26. Doth it show forth the painfulness of his death? Yes. *This is my body which is broken,* 1 Corinthians 11:24. And the end of it? Yes. *This is my blood which is shed for many, for the remission of sins,* Matthew 26:28. Should we therefore be careful how we attend upon it? Yes. *Lest we crucify to ourselves the Son of God afresh,* Hebrews 6:6.

Is this ordinance a public testimony of our communion with Christ? Yes. *The cup of blessing which we bless, is it not the communion of the blood of Christ?* 1 Corinthians 10:16. And of our love to and fellowship with the saints? Yes. *We are all partakers of that one bread*, 1 Corinthians 10:17. Is it designed to promote spiritual joy and thankfulness? Yes. *A feast is made for laughter*, Ecclesiastes 10:19. And as an earnest of better provisions above? Yes. *I will not drink henceforth of the fruit of the vine till I drink it new with you in my Father's kingdom*, Matthew 26:29. Is it therefore to be a standing ordinance in the church of Christ? Yes. *Till he come*, 1 Corinthians 11:26.

Q 103. Who are the proper subjects of this ordinance?
A. They who have been baptized upon a personal profession of their faith in Jesus Christ, and repentance from dead works.

May all come to the Lord's Supper? No. *It is not meet to take the children's bread and cast it to dogs*, Matthew 15:26. May those come who are prepared? Yes. *Sanctify yourselves and come with me to the sacrifice*, 1 Samuel 16:5. But after all our care will there be some intruders? Yes. *Friend, how camest thou in hither*, Matthew 22:12.

Are baptized believers proper subjects of this ordinance? Yes. *They that were baptized— continued in the apostle's fellowship, and in breaking of bread*, Acts 2:41. Should this their faith be professed? Yes. *For with the heart man believeth unto righteousness, and with the mouth confession is made unto salvation*, Romans 10:10. And be joined with repentance? Yes. For we read of *the foundation of repentance from dead works, and of faith towards God*, Hebrews 6:1. And be exemplified in a good conversation? Yes. *If any man that is called a brother, be a drunkard, or an extortioner, with such an one, no not to eat*, 1 Corinthians 5:11.

May weak believers be admitted? Yes. *Him that is weak in the faith receive ye*, Romans 14:1. And returning backsliders? Yes. *Restore such an one in the spirit of meekness*, Galatians 6:1. And in all difficult cases should we rather err on the charitable side? Yes. For *Charity believeth all things, hopeth all things*, 1 Corinthians 13:7.

Q 104. What is required to the worthy receiving of the Lord's Supper?

A. It is required of them that would worthily partake of the Lord's Supper, that they examine themselves of their knowledge to discern the Lord's body, of their faith to feed upon him, of their repentance, love, and new obedience, lest coming unworthily they eat and drink judgment to themselves.

Is previous examination necessary to a right participation of this ordinance? Yes. *Let a man examine himself, and so let him eat*, 1 Corinthians 11:28. Should we examine our hearts? Yes. *I commune with mine own heart*, Psalm 77:6. And our ways? Yes. *I thought on my ways*, Psalm 119:59. Should we do this impartially? Yes. *Thus saith the Lord, 'deceive not yourselves,'* Jeremiah 37:9. And diligently? Yes. *My spirit made diligent search*, Psalm 77:6. And sedately? Yes. *They sat down to examine the matter*, Ezra 10:16. And when scruples arise should we desire God's assistance? Yes. *Examine me, O Lord, and prove me*, Psalm 26:2.

Should we examine concerning our knowledge? Yes. *Know ye what I have done unto you*, John 13:12. And without this do we partake unworthily? Yes. *Not discerning the Lord's body*, 1 Corinthians 11:29. Should we also enquire into our faith in

Jesus Christ? Yes. *Examine yourselves whether ye be in the faith*, 2 Corinthians 13:5. And our love to God and one another? Yes. *For without charity we are nothing*, 1 Corinthians 13:2. And our repentance? Yes. *For the sacrifices of God are a broken spirit*, Psalm 51:17. And our new obedience? Yes. *Let us keep the feast, not with the leaven of malice and wickedness*, 1 Corinthians 5:8.

Must this sacrament be received with great reverence? Yes. *In thy fear will I worship towards thy holy temple*, Psalm 5:7. And with warm affections? Yes. *We will remember thy love more than wine*, Song of Solomon 1:4. And with godly sorrow? Yes. The Passover was to be eaten *with bitter herbs*, Exodus 12:8. And with an holy indifference to the world? Yes. *Ye shall eat with your loins girded, your shoes on your feet, and your staff in your hand*, Exodus 12:11. And with spiritual joy and gladness? Yes. *They did eat their meat with gladness praising God*, Acts 2:46,47. Should we now renew our engagements to God? Yes. *Thy vows are upon me*, Psalm 56:12. And should we afterwards remember and discharge them? Yes. *Pay that which thou hast vowed*, Ecclesiastes 5:4.

Do the carnal and unregenerate receive this ordinance unworthily? Yes. *What hast thou to do, to take my covenant into thy mouth, seeing thou hatest instruction*, Psalm 50:16,17. And the wrathful and uncharitable? Yes. *When ye come together in the church I hear that there be divisions among you, this is not to eat the Lord's Supper*, 1 Corinthians 11:18,20. And those who partake of it as a common meal? Yes. *Have ye not houses to eat and to drink in*, 1 Corinthians 11:22. And who use it as a qualification for civil offices? Yes. For they say that *the table of the Lord is contemptible*,

Malachi 1:7. Do such offer a great affront to Christ? Yes. *They are guilty of the body and blood of the Lord,* 1 Corinthians 11:27. And a great injury to themselves? Yes. *For this cause many are weak and sickly among you, and many sleep,* 1 Corinthians 11:30. And do all these things make self-examination the more necessary? Yes. *For if we would judge ourselves we should not be judged,* 1 Corinthians 11:31.

Q 105. What is prayer?
A. Prayer is an offering up our desires to God, by the assistance of the Holy Spirit, for things agreeable to his will, in the name of Christ, believing, with confession of our sins, and thankful acknowledgments of his mercies.

Is prayer the duty of all men? Yes. *Men ought always to pray,* Luke 18:1. Is it the duty of the carnal? Yes. *Pray to God if perhaps the thought of thine heart may be forgiven thee,* Acts 8:22. And of the gracious? Yes. *Unto thee will I pray,* Psalm 5:2. Is it in a particular manner the duty of the afflicted? Yes. *Is any afflicted let him pray,* James 5:13. But do all men pray? No. *For some restrain prayer before God,* Job 15:4.

Is ejaculatory prayer a duty? Yes. *So I prayed to the God of heaven,* Nehemiah 2:4. And secret prayer? Yes. *When thou prayest enter into thy closet,* Matthew 6:6. And family prayer? Yes. *As for me and my house, we will serve the Lord,* Joshua 24:15. And public prayer? Yes. *My house is the house of prayer,* Luke 19:46. And should we conscientiously attend to prayer of every kind? Yes. *Praying always with all prayer,* Ephesians 6:18.

Is God the object of prayer? Yes. *O thou that hearest prayer, unto thee shall all flesh come,* Psalm 65:2.

And is the offering up of our desires to him the essence of prayer? Yes. *Unto thee do I lift up my soul,* Psalm 25:1. Must these desires be presented through Christ? Yes. *Whatsoever ye shall ask the Father in my name he will give it unto you,* John 16:23. And by the assistance of the Holy Spirit? Yes. *I will pray with the Spirit,* 1 Corinthians 14:15. And be in all things regulated by his revealed will? Yes. For *this is the confidence that we have in him, that if we ask anything according to his will he heareth us,* 1 John 5:14.

Is invocation a part of prayer? Yes. *O God thou art my God, early will I seek thee,* Psalm 63:1. And adoration? Yes. *O Lord my God, thou art very great, thou art clothed with honor and majesty,* Psalm 104:1. And confession? Yes. *Father I have sinned against heaven and in thy sight,* Luke 15:21. And supplication? Yes. *Lord if thou wilt thou canst make me clean,* Matthew 8:2. And pleading? Yes. *Remember thy word unto thy servant,* Psalm 119:49. And intercession? Yes. *I exhort that supplication be made for all men,* 1 Timothy 2:1. And thanksgiving? Yes. *Unto thee, O God, do we give thanks,* Psalm 75:1.

Should we pray with judgment? Yes. *I will pray with understanding,* 1 Corinthians 14:15. And with humility? Yes. *Let not the Lord be angry and I will speak but this once,* Genesis 18:32. And with sincerity? Yes. *Ye shall seek me and find me when ye shall search for me with all your heart,* Jeremiah 29:13. And in faith? Yes. *Whatsoever ye shall ask in prayer, believing, ye shall receive,* Matthew 21:22.

Must our prayers be particular? Yes. *I would order my cause before him,* Job 23:4. And importunate? Yes. *I will not let thee go except thou bless me,* Genesis 32:26.

And submissive? Yes. *Not as I will but as thou wilt,* Matthew 26:39. And joined with suitable endeavors? Yes. *Wherefore criest thou unto me? speak unto the children of Israel, that they go forward,* Exodus 14:15. And constant? Yes. *Pray without ceasing,* 1 Thessalonians 5:17. And are such prayers likely to be effectual? Yes. For *God will fulfill the desire of them that fear* him, Psalm 145:19.

Do all that pray succeed in prayer? No. *When ye make many prayers, I will not hear,* Isaiah 1:15. Will a bad principle hinder the success of prayer? Yes. *If I regard iniquity in my heart, God will not hear me,* Psalm 66:18. And a bad intention? Yes. *Ye ask and receive not, because ye ask amiss, that ye may consume it upon your lusts,* James 4:3. And will a want of success in prayer soon lead to a neglect of it? Yes. For *what profit should we have, if we pray unto him?* Job 21:15.

Q 106. What rule hath God given for our direction in prayer?
A. The whole word of God is of use to direct us in prayer; but the special rule of direction is that prayer which Christ taught his disciples, commonly called the Lord's Prayer.

Do we need direction in prayer? Yes. *For we cannot order our speech by reason of darkness,* Job 37:19. Should we therefore seek direction of God? Yes. *Lord, teach us to pray,* Luke 11:1. Are there particular directions for prayer in the word of God? Yes. *Take with you words and turn unto the Lord, say unto him,* Hosea 14:2. And particular examples of prayer? Yes. *And Jabez called upon the God of Israel, saying,* 1 Chronicles 4:10. Is the Scripture then the best rule for our direction in prayer? Yes. For *the words of the Lord are pure words, as silver* tried in a furnace of earth, purified seven times, Psalm 12:6. And is it through a neglect hereof that we are guilty of so many mistakes in prayer? Yes. *Ye know not what ye ask,* Matthew 20:22.

Is the Lord's Prayer of singular use as a directory for prayer? Yes. *After this manner therefore pray ye,* Matthew 6:9. Doth this prayer consist of a preface? Yes. *Our Father which art in heaven,* ibid. And of petitions? Yes. *Hallowed be thy name, thy kingdom come,* ibid. And of a doxology or conclusion? Yes. *For thine is the kingdom, the power and the glory,* Matthew 6:13. Should we imitate this prayer in the brevity and comprehensiveness of it? Yes. *When ye pray, use not vain repetitions,* Matthew 6:7. And in making the glory of God the top and chief of our desires? Yes. For *what wilt thou do unto thy great name?* Joshua 7:9. And in preferring spiritual to temporal good? Yes. *Seek first the kingdom of God and his righteousness,* Matthew 6:33. Should those that are teachers of others like Christ instruct them to pray? Yes. We should *be like minded after the example of Christ Jesus,* Romans 15:5.

Q 107. What doth the preface of the Lord's Prayer teach us?

A. The preface of the Lord's prayer, which is *Our Father which art in heaven,* teacheth us to draw near to God with all holy reverence and confidence, as children to a father, able and ready to help us; and that we should pray with and for others.

Is God a Father? Yes. *O Lord thou art our Father,* Isaiah 64:8. Is he the Father of all the saints? Yes. *There is one God and Father of all,* Ephesians 4:6. Should they then plead this relation? Yes. *Wilt thou not from this time cry unto me, 'My Father',* Jeremiah 3:4.

And continually acknowledge his fatherly kindness and care? Yes. *I was cast upon thee from the womb, thou art my God from my mother's belly*, Psalm 22:10. Doth this title peculiarly belong to the first person of the ever blessed Trinity? Yes. *I will pray the Father*, John 14:16. But is it confined to him? No. For Christ is called *the everlasting Father*, Isaiah 9:6.

Should we take occasion from hence to approach God with reverence? Yes. *If ye call on the Father, pass the time of your sojourning here in fear*, 1 Peter 1:17. And with delight? Yes. *I will go unto God my exceeding joy*, Psalm 43:4. And with boldness? Yes. *Doubtless thou art our Father, though Abraham be ignorant of us, and Israel acknowledge us not*, Isaiah 63:16. And with frequency? Yes. *Morning, and evening, and at noon, will I pray*, Psalm 55:17. And is such a temper peculiarly suited to the gospel dispensation? Yes. *For ye have not received the Spirit of bondage again unto fear, but the Spirit of adoption, whereby ye cry, 'Abba Father'*, Romans 8:15.

Is God our Father in heaven? Yes. *O Lord God of our fathers, art not thou God in heaven*, 2 Chronicles 20:6. Doth this set forth the greatness of God? Yes. *Is not God in the height of heaven? And behold the height of the stars, how high they are*, Job 22:12. And his omniscience? Yes. *The Lord's throne is in heaven, his eyes behold, his eyelids try the children of men*, Psalm 11:4. And his power? Yes. *God is in the heavens, he hath done whatsoever he pleased*, Psalm 115:3. And his holiness? Yes. *Thus saith he whose name is holy, 'I dwell in the high and holy place'*, Isaiah 57:15. And his absolute dominion? Yes. *For the Lord hath prepared his throne in the heavens*, Psalm 103:19. Doth this title distinguish the great God from dumb idols? Yes. For the *most high dwelleth not in temples made with hands*, Acts 7:48. And from frail men?

Yes. For we *dwell in houses of clay, and our foundation is in the dust,* Job 4:19.

Is this a ground for humility in prayer? Yes. *God is in heaven and thou upon earth, therefore let thy words be few,* Ecclesiastes 5:2. And for confidence? Yes. *Hear thou in heaven and do,* 1 Kings 8:32. And for heavenly-mindedness? Yes. *Let us lift up our heart with our hands unto God in the heavens,* Lamentations 3:41.

Must we pray with others? Yes. *There were many gathered together praying,* Acts 12:12. And for others? Yes. We must make *supplication for all saints,* Ephesians 6:18. And shall prayers put up on earth find acceptance in heaven? Yes. *I will cry unto God most high, he shall send from heaven and save me,* Psalm 57:2,3.

Q 108. What do we pray for in the first petition?
A. In the first petition, which is, *Hallowed be thy name,* we pray that God would enable us and others to glorify him in all that whereby he maketh himself known, and that he would dispose all things to his own glory.

Should God's name be remembered? Yes. *I have remembered thy name in the night,* Psalm 119:55. And be loved? Yes. *Let them that love thy name be joyful in thee,* Psalm 5:11. And be feared? Yes. *Unite my heart to fear thy name,* Psalm 86:11. And be adored? Yes. *I will bless thy name for ever and ever,* Psalm 145:1. And is God's name worthy of all this? Yes. For *holy and reverend is his name,* Psalm 111:9.

Should we glorify God in our words? Yes. *If any man speak, let him speak as the oracles of God, that God in all things may be glorified,* 1 Peter 4:11. And in our actions? Yes. *Being filled with the fruits of righteousness, which are by Jesus Christ unto the glory of God,* Philippians 1:11. Should we do this in the most common actions of life? Yes. *Whether ye eat or drink, or whatsoever ye do, do all to the glory of God,* 1 Corinthians 10:31. And at all times and in all circumstances? Yes. *That Christ might be magnified in us, whether it be by life or by death,* Philippians 1:20. And should it be our constant prayer and desire that we might thus glorify God? Yes. *Open thou my lips, and my mouth shall shew forth thy praise,* Psalm 51:15.

Should we pray that others might glorify God? Yes. *Let them give glory unto the Lord,* Isaiah 42:12. And use our utmost endeavors to excite them so to do? Yes. *Let your light so shine before men, that they may see your good works, and glorify your Father which is in heaven,* Matthew 5:16. Should we particularly pray that God's enemies might glorify his name? Yes. *Fill their faces with shame, that they may seek thy name,* Psalm 83:16. And grieve when they dishonor and reproach it? Yes. *The reproaches of them that reproached thee are fallen upon me,* Psalm 69:9.

Should we pray that God would glorify himself? Yes. *Father, glorify thy name,* John 12:28. And that by all events? Yes. *That the wrath of man might praise him,* Psalm 76:10. And is it certain that he will do it? Yes. *I have both glorified it, and I will glorify it again,* John 12:28. Is God's own glory his end in all that he does? Yes. *I do not this for your sakes, O house of Israel, but for mine holy name's sake,* Ezekiel 36:22. Should it therefore be our end in all that we ask? Yes. *Help us, O God of our salvation, for the glory of thy name,* Psalm 79:9.

Q 109. What do we pray for in the second petition?
A. In the second petition, which is, *Thy kingdom come,* we pray that Satan's kingdom may be destroyed, and that the kingdom of grace may be advanced, ourselves and others brought into it and kept in it, and that the kingdom of glory may be hastened.

Hath God a peculiar kingdom in this world? Yes. *For the kingdom of God is within you,* Luke 17:21. Is this a spiritual kingdom? Yes. *For the kingdom of God is not meat and drink, but righteousness, and peace and joy in the Holy Ghost,* Romans 14:17. And a powerful kingdom? Yes. *For the kingdom of God is not in word but in power,* 1 Corinthians 4:20. Is Christ the administrator of this kingdom? Yes. *He therefore died and rose, and revived that he might be Lord both of the dead and living,* Romans 14:9. And are the saints the subjects of it? Yes. They are *translated into the kingdom of God's dear Son,* Colossians 1:13. And is the written word the law of it? Yes. *Out of Zion shall go forth the law, and the word of the Lord from Jerusalem,* Isaiah 2:3.

Hath Satan set up a kingdom in opposition to that of Christ? Yes. *He is the Prince of this world,* John 16:11. And doth he rule in this kingdom? Yes. He *now worketh in the children of disobedience,* Ephesians 2:2. Doth he do all that he can to hinder the progress of Christ's kingdom? Yes. *We would have come to you once and again, but Satan hindered us,* 1 Thessalonians 2:18. But is his power limited? Yes. *Behold he is in thine hand, but save his life,* Job 2:6. And should we pray that it might be more and more restrained? Yes. *The Lord rebuke thee, O Satan,* Zechariah 3:2. And have we reason to hope that our prayer shall be answered?

Yes. *The God of peace shall bruise Satan under your feet shortly*, Romans 16:20.

Doth antichrist receive his power from Satan? Yes. *And the dragon gave his power, his seat, and his authority*, to the beast, Revelation 13:2. And doth he imitate him in malice, cunning and cruelty? Yes. *His coming is after the working of Satan*, 2 Thessalonians 2:9. And join with him in his opposition to the kingdom of Christ? Yes. *He opposeth and exalteth himself above all that is called God*, 2 Thessalonians 2:4. Should we therefore pray for his downfall? Yes. *How long, O Lord, dost thou not judge and avenge our blood on them that dwell on the earth*, Revelation 6:10. And will our prayer be answered? Yes. *Babylon the great is fallen, is fallen*, Revelation 18:2.

Should we pray for sinners? Yes. *God forbid that I should cease praying for you*, 1 Samuel 12:23. Should we pray that wicked principles might be exploded? Yes. *O send out thy light and thy truth*, Psalm 43:3. And wicked practices restrained? Yes. *O let the wickedness of the wicked come to an end*, Psalm 7:9. And that wicked persons might be converted and changed? Yes. *I would to God that all that hear me this day were both almost and altogether such as I am*, Acts 26:29. And should we not only pray for others, but for ourselves? Yes. *Turn thou me, and I shall be turned*, Jeremiah 31:18.

Should we pray for the church? Yes. *Do good in thy good pleasure unto Zion*, Psalm 51:18. Should we pray that the church might be established? Yes. *That the mountain of the Lord's house might be established upon the top of the mountains*, Isaiah 2:2. And united? Yes. *Peace be within thy walls*, Psalm 122:7. And increased? Yes. That *the kingdoms of this world* might become *the kingdoms of the Lord, and of his Christ,* Revelation 11:15. And reformed? Yes. That *judgment might return unto righteousness and all the upright in heart might follow it,* Psalm 94:15. And delivered from the fury of all its oppressors? Yes. *That the rod of the wicked might not rest upon the lot of the righteous,* Psalm 125:3.

Should we pray for the farther calling of the Gentiles? Yes. *That thy way may be known upon earth, and thy saving health among all nations,* Psalm 67:2. And for the conversion of the Jews? Yes. *My heart's desire and prayer to God for Israel is, that they may be saved,* Romans 10:1. Should we pray that magistrates might be raised up to favor the gospel? Yes. That *Kings* might *be nursing fathers and Queens nursing mothers* to the Israel of God, Isaiah 49:23. And that ministers might be raised up to preach the gospel? Yes. *Pray ye the Lord of the harvest that he will send forth more laborers into his harvest,* Matthew 9:38. And that the gospel wherever it is preached might be followed with success? Yes. *That the word of the Lord might have free course, and be glorified,* 2 Thessalonians 3:1.

Should we pray that particular Christians might be comforted? Yes. *Now our Lord Jesus—comfort your hearts,* 2 Thessalonians 2:17. And sanctified? Yes. *The very God of peace sanctify you wholly,* 1 Thessalonians 5:23. And preserved? Yes. *I pray God that your whole spirit and soul and body be preserved blameless unto the coming of our Lord Jesus Christ,* ibid.

Is the state of blessedness above called a kingdom? Yes. *This I say that flesh and blood cannot inherit the kingdom of God,* 1 Corinthians 15:50. Is this kingdom yet to come? Yes. It is *glory that shall be revealed,* 1 Peter 5:1. Should we be fully persuaded that it will come? Yes. *Looking for the blessed hope and glorious appearance of the great God and our Savior,* Titus 2:13. And should we pray that it might come? Yes. *Even so come Lord Jesus,* Revelation 22:20. And that we and others might be prepared for it? Yes. That we might *be sincere and without offence till the day of Christ,* Philippians 1:10. And admitted into it? Yes. *Desiring to be clothed upon with our house which is from heaven,* 2 Corinthians 5:2.

Q 110. What do we pray for in the third petition?

A. In the third petition, which is, *Thy will be done on earth as it is in heaven,* we pray that God by his grace would make us able and willing to know, obey, and submit to his will in all things, as the angels do in heaven.

Is God's purpose his will? Yes. *He doth according to his will in the army of heaven and among the inhabitants of the earth,* Daniel 4:35. Should all our actions be referred to this determining will of God? Yes. *Ye ought to say if the Lord will, we will do this or that,* James 4:15. And should we submit to it in all dispensations? Yes. *When he would not be persuaded they ceased, saying, 'the will of the Lord be done',* Acts 21:14.

Doth this submission consist with a due sense of the evil of affliction? Yes. For we must not *despise the chastening of the Lord,* Hebrews 12:5. And with a moderate grief and sorrow, on account of it? Yes. *Hezekiah wept sore,* Isaiah 38:3. And with an earnest prayer for deliverance? Yes. *Why hidest thou thy face and forgettest our affliction,* Psalm 44:24. And with the use of all lawful means to obtain it? Yes. *Then the disciples took Saul by night and let him down by the wall in a basket,* Acts 9:25.

Should our understandings approve the severest dispensations of providence? Yes. *Good is the word of the Lord which thou hast spoken,* Isaiah 39:8. And our wills be resigned to them? Yes. *Wherefore doth a living man complain, a man for the punishment of his sin,* Lamentations 3:39. And our passions be composed under them? Yes. *Let him curse because the Lord hath said unto him, Curse David,' who then shall say, 'Wherefore hast thou done so?'* 2 Samuel 16:10. And should we pray that we and others might be enabled thus to submit to the will of God? Yes. That we may be *strengthened with all might unto all patience and long suffering with joyfulness,* Colossians 1:11.

Are God's precepts his will? Yes. *They are the good and perfect, and acceptable will of God,* Romans 12:2. Are we by nature unwilling to do this will of God? Yes. We are *to every good work reprobate,* Titus 1:16. Should we therefore pray that we might be made willing? Yes. *Incline my heart to thy testimonies,* Psalm 119:36. But when we are willing are we always able? No. *What I would that I do not,* Romans 7:15. Should we therefore pray that God would make us able as well as willing? Yes. *Strengthen thou me according to thy word,* Psalm 119:28. And should we desire this for others as well as ourselves? Yes. That they might be *perfect in every good work to do his will,* Hebrews 13:21.

Do the angels in heaven obey God's will? Yes. *They do his commandments,* Psalm 103:20. Do they do it cheerfully? Yes. *Bless the Lord all ye his hosts, ye ministers of his that do his pleasure,* Psalm 103:21.

And zealously? Yes. *Who maketh his angels spirits, and his ministers a flaming fire*, Psalm 104:4. And humbly? Yes. *They cover their faces, and their feet with their wings*, Isaiah 6:2. And universally? Yes. *They go strait forward: whithersoever the Spirit goes*, Ezekiel 1:9,12. And constantly? Yes. *They always behold the face of our Father*, Matthew 18:10. Do saints in the other world resemble the angels in their obedience? Yes. *They are as the angels of God in heaven*, Matthew 22:30. Should saints in this world therefore seek after such a resemblance? Yes. That *he that is feeble* might *be as David, and the house of David might be as the angel of the Lord*, Zechariah 12:8.

Q 111. What do we pray for in the fourth petition?
A. In the fourth petition, which is, *Give us this day our daily bread*, we pray that of God's free gift we may receive a competent portion of the good things of this life, and enjoy his blessing with them.

Are temporal blessings forfeited? Yes. *Cursed is the ground for thy sake*, Genesis 3:17. But are they promised? Yes. *My God shall supply all your need*, Philippians 4:19. Should we therefore pray for them? Yes. *O that thou wouldst bless me indeed, and enlarge my coast*, 1 Chronicles 4:10.

Should we pray for temporal blessings with religious views? Yes. That we *may give to him that needeth*. Ephesians 4:28. And should we only pray for a competency of them? Yes. *Feed me with food convenient for me*, Proverbs 30:8. But above all should we entreat God's blessing upon them? Yes. *And it came to pass as he sat at meat with them, he took bread and blessed it, and gave to them*, Luke 24:30. And are they then like to be most comfortable to us? Yes. *For every creature is sanctified by the word of God and prayer*, 1 Timothy 4:5.

Should we pray for the comforts of life believingly? Yes. *Thou saidst, 'I will surely do thee good,'* Genesis 32:12. And yet submissively? Yes. *If ye say I have no delight in him, behold here I am, let him do to me as seemeth him good*, 2 Samuel 15:26. Should our prayers be attended with suitable endeavors? Yes. *For thou shalt eat the labor of thine hands*, Psalm 128:2. And should we pray for others as well as ourselves? Yes. *Forget not the congregation of thy poor*, Psalm 74:19.

Should the bread that we pray for be our own bread? Yes. That we may *eat our own bread*, 2 Thessalonians 3:12. And not the bread of deceit? No. For though the *bread of deceit is sweet to a man, yet afterwards his mouth shall be filled with gravel*, Proverbs 20:17. Nor the bread of oppression? No. For *God shall break in pieces the oppressor*, Psalm 72:4. Nor the bread of idleness? No. For 'tis said of the virtuous woman, *that she eateth not the bread of idleness*, Proverbs 31:27. But above all must we pray for the bread of our souls? Yes. *Lord evermore give us this bread*, John 6:34.

Doth this petition exclude an anxious thoughtfulness for futurity? Yes. *Take no thought for the morrow*, Matthew 6:34. But doth it forbid a prudent thoughtfulness? No. *Go to the ant, thou sluggard, consider her ways—she provideth her meat in the summer*, Proverbs 6:6,8. Doth it teach us to cast all our care upon God? Yes. *For he careth for us*, 1 Peter 5:7. And to look to him for success in our several callings? Yes. *Establish thou the work of our hands upon us*, Psalm 90:17. And to ascribe all our prosperity to him? Yes. *Thou shalt remember the Lord thy God, for it is he that giveth thee power to get wealth,* Deuteronomy 8:18.

Q 112. What do we pray for in the fifth petition?
A. In the fifth petition, which is, *And forgive us our debts as we forgive our debtors,* we pray that God, for Christ's sake, would freely pardon all our sins; which we are rather encouraged to ask because of his grace we are enabled from the heart to forgive others.

Is sin a debt? Yes. *There was a certain creditor that had two debtors,* Luke 7:41. Is it a great debt? Yes. It is *ten thousand talents,* Matthew 18:24. Is it an increasing debt? Yes. For we *add sin to sin,* Isaiah 30:1. Does God keep an exact account of this debt? Yes. For our *transgression is sealed up in a bag and he soweth up our iniquity,* Job 14:17. And will he require it? Yes. *Whosoever will not hearken I will require it of him,* Deuteronomy 18:19.

Are we apt to think that we can pay this debt? Yes. *Have patience with me, and I will pay thee all,* Matthew 18:29. But can we really pay it? No. *They had nothing to pay,* Luke 7:42. Have we any friend upon earth that can pay it for us? No. *Call thou if there be any that will answer thee, and to which of the saints wilt thou turn?* Job 5:1. But is there such a friend in heaven? Yes. *Jesus Christ, who is the propitiation for our sins,* 1 John 2:2.

Doth God forgive debts? Yes. *There is forgiveness with thee,* Psalm 130:4. Doth he forgive them freely? Yes. The remission of sins is *according to the riches of his grace,* Ephesians 1:7. And fully? Yes. *Having forgiven all our trespasses* Colossians 2:13. And finally? Yes. *I will remember their sin no more,* Jeremiah 31:34.

Should we therefore pray for the forgiveness of our debts? Yes. *Enter not into judgment with thy servant,* Psalm 143:2. Should we pray that God would remit the present punishment of sin? Yes. *Pardon I beseech thee the iniquity of this people as thou hast forgiven them from Egypt even until now,* Numbers 14:19. And that he would deliver us from his everlasting wrath due to sin? Yes. *I will say unto God, do not condemn me,* Job 10:2. And that he would restore to us divine comfort forfeited by sin? Yes. *Restore unto me the joy of thy salvation, and uphold me by thy free Spirit,* Psalm 51:12.

Should we pray for the pardon of sin sensibly? Yes. As the publican who *smote upon his breast, saying, 'God be merciful to me a sinner,'* Luke 18:13. And sincerely? Yes. *Give ear unto my prayer that goeth not out of feigned lips,* Psalm 17:1. And importunately? Yes. *O Lord hear, O Lord forgive,* Daniel 9:19. And argumentatively? Yes. *Why dost thou not pardon my transgression, and take away mine iniquity?* Job 7:21. May we here plead the goodness of God's nature? Yes. *For thou Lord art good and ready to forgive,* Psalm 86:5. And the greatness of our transgressions? Yes. *Pardon mine iniquity; for it is great,* Psalm 25:11. And the glory of his name? Yes. *Purge away our sins, for thy name's sake,* Psalm 79:9. But above all, should we plead the merit and atonement of Christ? Yes. *Behold, O God our shield, and look upon the face of thine anointed,* Psalm 84:9.

Should we forgive those that have offended us? Yes. *Forbearing one another, and forgiving one another,* Colossians 3:13. Must we do this freely? Yes. *Thou shouldst have had compassion, even as I had pity on thee,* Matthew 18:33. And heartily? Yes. We must *from the heart forgive every one his brother's trespasses,* Matthew 18:35. And fully? Yes. *Ye have not injured me at all,* Galatians 4:12.   And immediately? Yes. *Go, and be reconciled to thy brother,* Matthew 5:24. And repeatedly? Yes. *Not only till seven times, but till seventy times seven,* Matthew 18:22. And must we not only forgive, but forget? Yes. *Grudge not one against another,* James 5:9.

Is this prudent? Yes. *The discretion of a man deferreth his anger,* Proverbs 19:11. And honorable? Yes. *And it is his glory to pass over a transgression,* ibid. And profitable? Yes. *For if ye forgive men their trespasses, your heavenly Father will also forgive you,* Matthew 6:14.   And cannot we hope for forgiveness without it? No. *But if ye forgive not men their trespasses, neither will your Father forgive yours,* Matthew 6:15.

Q 113. What do we pray for in the sixth petition?

A. In the sixth petition, which is, *And lead us not into temptation but deliver us from evil,* we pray that God would either keep us from being tempted to sin, or support and deliver us when we are tempted.

May God be said to lead into temptation? Yes. *It came to pass after these things, that God tempted Abraham,* Genesis 22:1. Doth he sometimes do this by withdrawing his assisting grace? Yes. *God left Hezekiah, to try him,* 2 Chronicles 32:31. And by letting loose our spiritual enemies? Yes. *And the Lord said, 'who shall persuade Ahab that he may go up and fall at Ramoth-Gilead?'* 1 Kings 22:20. And by providentially administering occasions of sin? Yes. *Thou shalt not hearken to the words of that prophet, or that dreamer of dreams, for the Lord your God proveth you,* Deuteronomy 13:3.

Do many temptations proceed from our own lusts? Yes. *Every man is tempted when he is drawn away of his own lusts and enticed*, James 1:14. And from the world? Yes. *For all that is in the world, the lust of the flesh, the lust of the eyes, and the pride of life, is not of the Father, but is of the world*, 1 John 2:16. And from wicked men? Yes. *They that lead thee, cause thee to err*, Isaiah 3:12. And from Satan? Yes. *Then was Jesus led into the wilderness to be tempted of the devil*, Matthew 4:1. And have these temptations their particular seasons of strength and prevalency? Yes. *In time of temptation they fall away*, Luke 8:13.

Doth Satan tempt to mental errors? Yes. *I fear lest as the serpent beguiled Eve, so your minds should be corrupted from the simplicity that is in Christ*, 2 Corinthians 11:3. And to criminal practices? Yes. Thus *the devil put it into the heart of Judas to betray Christ*, John 13:2. And to presumption? Yes. *If thou be the Son of God, cast thyself down*, Matthew 4:6. And to despair? Yes. *Lest such a one should be swallowed up with overmuch sorrow, and Satan should get an advantage of us*, 2 Corinthians 2:11.

Is Satan a powerful enemy? Yes. He is a *roaring lion*, 1 Peter 5:8. And a crafty enemy? Yes. We read of *the depths of Satan*, Revelation 2:24. And an industrious enemy? Yes. *He goeth to and fro in the earth, and walketh up and down in it*, Job 1:7. Should we therefore pray that we might be kept from his temptations? Yes. *Watch and pray that ye enter not into temptation*, Matthew 26:41. And supported under them? Yes. That we might not *be tempted above that which we are able to bear*, 1 Corinthians 10:13. And delivered out of them? Yes. That *the God of all grace after we have suffered a while* would *make us perfect, establish, strengthen, settle* us, 1 Peter 5:10. Should our prayers for this purpose be fervent? Yes. *Being in an agony he prayed more earnestly*, Luke 22:44. And frequent? Yes. *For this I besought the Lord thrice*, 2 Corinthians 12:8. And sometimes joined with fasting? Yes. *This kind goeth not out but by prayer and fasting*, Matthew 17:21.

May we pray to be delivered from afflictions? Yes. *Remove thy stroke away from me*, Psalm 39:10. But are not afflictions sometimes needful? Yes. *If need be we are in heaviness through manifold temptations*, 1 Peter 1:6. And useful? Yes. The good figs were *sent into the land of Chaldea for their good*, Jeremiah 24:5. Should we therefore absolutely pray against them? No. *Lord correct me but with judgment, not in thine anger, lest thou bring me to nothing*, Jeremiah 10:24. Should we under afflictions have recourse only to God? Yes. *We know not what to do, but our eyes are upon thee*, 2 Chronicles 20:12. And trust in him? Yes. *At what time I am afraid, I will trust in thee*, Psalm 56:3. And have we reason so to do? Yes. For he that hath *delivered doth deliver, in whom we trust that he will yet deliver*, 2 Corinthians 1:10.

Should we especially desire to be delivered from the evil of sin? Yes. That we might be delivered *from every evil work*, 2 Timothy 4:18. Should we pray to be kept from the practice of sin? Yes. *Hold me up that my footsteps slip not*, Psalm 17:5. And from the dominion of sin? Yes. *Let no iniquity have dominion over me*, Psalm 119:133. Should we pray to be kept from heart sins? Yes. *Incline not my heart to any evil thing*, Psalm 141:4. And from tongue sins? Yes. *Keep the door of my lips*, Psalm 141:3. And from sins of life? Yes. That we might not *practice wicked works with men that work iniquity*, Psalm 141:4.

But are we not sufficient thus to keep ourselves? No. For *it is not in man that walketh to direct his steps,* Jeremiah 10:23.

Q 114. What doth the conclusion of the Lord's Prayer teach?

A. The conclusion of the Lord's Prayer, which is, *For Thine is the kingdom, and the power, and the glory, forever. Amen,* teacheth us to take our encouragement in prayer from God only, and in our prayers to praise Him, ascribing kingdom, power, and glory, to Him. And in testimony of our desire and assurance to be heard, we say, 'Amen'.

Must all our encouragement in prayer be taken from God? Yes. *Do not abhor us for thy name's sake,* Jeremiah 14:21. And not from ourselves? No. *We do not present our supplications before thee for our righteousness,* Daniel 9:18. Must we in prayer bless God? Yes. *Thy saints shall bless thee,* Psalm 145:10. And will this be an acceptable service to him? Yes. *Whoso offereth praise glorifieth me,* Psalm 50:23.

Is the kingdom the Lord's? Yes. *The Lord reigneth, he is clothed with majesty,* Psalm 93:1. Is his kingdom an ancient one? Yes. *Thy throne is established of old,* Psalm 93:2. And an enduring one? Yes. *His kingdom is an ever-lasting kingdom,* Daniel 7:27. Does this afford matter for praise? Yes. *I will extol thee my God, O King,* Psalm 145:1. And matter for trust? Yes. *Say among the heathen, that the Lord reigneth; the world also shall be established, that it shall not be moved,* Psalm 96:10. And may we make use of it as a plea in prayer? Yes. *Art not thou God in heaven, and rulest not thou over all the kingdoms of the heathen?* 2 Chronicles 20:6.

Does power belong unto God? Yes. *If we speak of strength, lo he is strong,* Job 9:19. And is all power from him? Yes. *The God of Israel is he that giveth strength and power unto his people*, Psalm 68:35. Should we therefore take to ourselves the comfort of this attribute? Yes. *If it be so, our God whom we serve is able to deliver us out of the burning fiery furnace*, Daniel 3:17. And give him the glory of it? Yes. *Give unto the Lord glory and strength O ye mighty, give unto the Lord glory and strength*, Psalm 29:1. And plead it in prayer? Yes. *Now let the power of my Lord be great according as thou hast spoken*, Numbers 14:17.

Is God's glory manifested in all his works? Yes. *The whole earth is full of his glory*, Isaiah 6:3. Should he then be glorified by all his works? Yes. *All nations shall glorify thy name*, Psalm 86:9. Is his glory particularly displayed in the church? Yes. *The Lord shall arise upon thee, and his glory shall be seen upon thee*, Isaiah 60:2. Should it therefore be particularly displayed by the church? Yes. *To him be glory in the church throughout all ages*, Ephesians 3:21. May we not then glory in ourselves? No. *He that glorieth, let him glory in the Lord*, 2 Corinthians 10:17.

Doth 'Amen' signify our desire to be heard? Yes. *So be it, O Lord*, Jeremiah 11:5. And our assurance that we shall be heard? Yes. *And the four beasts said, 'Amen;' and the four and twenty elders fell down and worshipped him that liveth for ever and ever*, Revelation 5:14. When used in public prayer by the people, does it express their approbation? Yes. *And all the people said, 'Amen,' and praised the Lord*, 1 Chronicles 16:36. Should such prayers then be made in a known tongue? Yes. *Else how shall he who occupieth the place of the unlearned, say, 'Amen'*, 1 Corinthians 14:16.

FINIS.

GENESIS

1:1	23
1:3	25
1:5	113
1:14	25
1:25	25
1:26	19
1:27	26,144
1:28	29
1:31	25
2:2	25,112,113
2:16	29,30
2:17	29,30
3:1	32,142
3:4	33
3:5	33
3:6	32 (3x)
3:8	30
3:10	3
3:11	32
3:13	30,32
3:15	55
3:17	189
3:19	38
3:20	33
3:24	30
4:4	69
4:10	129
4:13	35
4:26	3
5:2	26
5:3	34
6:3	64
8:25	30
9:5	126
9:6	90
12:12,19	144
15:15	80
17:1	14,15
17:2-14	167
17:10	166
17:11	167
17:23	166
18:15	138
18:19	90
18:25	30
18:27	107
19:17	17
20:9	131
22:1	193
23:4	80
27:24	144
28:7	122
30:30	134
31:30	96
32:12	190

GENESIS (cont'd)

32:26	178
37:26	127
39:9	100
39:10	131
39:11	131
42:18	97
45:8	27
48:16	95
49:7	148
49:8	102
50:16	172
50:20	27

EXODUS

1:1	94
3:13	106
3:14	13,106
4:23	72
8:10	5
12:8	176
12:11	176
12:41	94
12:42	94
14:15	179
14:20	170
14:22	170
15:11	2
16:23	113
16:25	112
16:26	116
16:29	118
17:7	20,99
18:20	156
18:24	122
20:1	90
20:2	94
20:5	36
20:8	112
20:10	112,115
20:11	25
20:18	91 (2x)
21:14	129
22:2	129
22:21	94
23:2	8
23:13	102,169
23:21	106
23:30	53
25:40	103
31:13	113
31:15	119
31:17	119
32:1f.	96 (2x)
32:16	90
33:19	106

EXODUS (cont'd)

34:7	106
34:21	116
35:31	28

LEVITICUS

5:1	110
6:4	134
10:1	104
16:21	148
18:3	103
18:5	95
18:6	132
18:20	131
18:21	107
19:3	121
19:4	105
19:11	133
19:12	109
19:16	140
19:17	93
19:32	124
19:37	102
23:3	116,117 (2x)
23:6	115
24:22	105
25:14	136
25:35	134
26:24,25	148

NUMBERS

11:29	143
12:8	146
14:17	197
14:19	192
15:30	147
15:39	103
20:15	94
30:2	108
32:14	106
35:31,32	130

DEUTERONOMY

1:36	97
4:12	90
4:13	90
4:15	101,104
4:16	104
4:17,18	101
4:19	103
5:2	89
5:3	89
5:12	116
5:13	111
5:14	112,119
5:15	113
5:32	13

DEUTERONOMY (cont'd)

6:4	19
6:7	160
6:15	105
8:18	191
9:18	146
10:1	91
10:12	87
11:1	95
11:12	27
13:3	193
15:15	94
16:3	94
17:10,12	129
17:19	9
18:10	135
18:15	46,47 (footnote)
18:19	191
19:4,5	129
22:8	128
27:15	103
27:16	124
28:15	149
28:22	38
28:37	39
28:58	106
28:59	110
29:2,3	94
29:17	99
29:19	35
29:29	23 (2x)
31:11	9
31:20	105
32:1	11
32:4	16,31
32:6	88
32:16	101
32:18	99
32:21	105
32:39	129
32:46	10
33:2	91
33:27	14
34:10	47

JOSHUA

7:9	180
7:19	98
7:25	146
8:31	102
10:13	28
21:45	126
23:11	92
24:15	97,177
24:18	105
24:21	97
24:22	95

JUDGES
2:1   94
5:18   129
6:31   104
18:25   127

1 SAMUEL
2:2   16
2:7   143
2:9   84
2:25   125,146
2:30   98
2:31   126
3:13   125
3:18   138
12:23   185
15:3   129
16:5   174
19:4   137
21:7   119
24:5   141

2 SAMUEL
6:20   122
11:3   140
12:9   130
12:14   145
14:14   149
15:26   97,190
16:10   188
16:22   147
17:23   128
21:7   108
23:3   6,123
23:5   41

1 KINGS
8:32   182
8:38   64
11:4   144
11:9   147
14:6   146
18:4   128
19:18   106
21:1-4 143
21:29   74,153
22:20   193
22:22   24
22:34   27

2 KINGS
2:11   82
5:13   121
5:25   139
5:26   147
17:27   169

1 CHRONICLES
4:10   180,189
15:13   169
16:36   197
28:9   96,101
29:11   28
29:14   97
29:19   122

2 CHRONICLES
2:6   14
14:11   95
20:6   181,196
20:12   195
20:20   10
30:8   97
30:18   160
32:31   193
33:12   157

EZRA
7:10   159
9:6   155
9:10,11 147
9:14   37
9:15   65
10:1   154
10:2   154
10:12   161
10:16   175

NEHEMIAH
2:4   177
5:12   134
8:5   160
8:8   158
9:33   17
13:15   112,116
13:19   116

ESTHER
3:7   109
5:13   142
7:11   148
10:3   141

JOB
1:5   122
1:7   194
2:4   127
2:6   185
3:1   144
4:19   182
5:1   191
5:7   39
5:13   84
6:14   93

JOB (cont'd)
7:15   127
7:16   78
7:21   192
9:3   69
9:19   196
10:2   192
10:4   13
12:7   4
12:9   5
12:16   16
13:15   66
13:26   64
14:5   27
14:13   80
14:17   191
15:4   177
15:14   33
15:16   36
16:20   154
18:11   84
18:21   3
19:25   42
19:26   81
20:12   36
21:7   125
21:15   179
21:30   85
22:12   181
22:21   12
22:22   102
22:28   24
23:4   179
23:13   23,29
23:14   141
24:18   149
24:19   85
24:20   85
27:6   137
27:20   38
29:13   128
29:23   124
31:1   131
31:16   93
31:27   104
31:29   130
33:4   21
33:13   29
33:15,16 157
34:3   160
34:32   155
36:13   109
37:19   179
38:4   15
38:7   72
38:31   27
39:27   28

JOB (cont'd)
40:4   154
41:11   25
42:5,6 64
42:6   154
42:7   145

PSALMS
2:6   46
2:9   53
5:2   177
5:5   39
5:7   176
5:11   182
7:9   185
8:5   26
8:6   26
9:16   5
9:17   86
10:1   92
10:13   99
10:17   160
11:4   181
11:6   86
11:7   69
12:2   139
12:4   99
12:6   180
14:1   2
15:4   108
16:10   57
16:11   59
17:1   192
17:4   158
17:5   195
17:15   79
18:23   155
19:1   4
19:3   64
19:7   7,158
19:8   158
19:12   145
21:9   83
22:6   44,54
22:10   28,181
22:15   57
22:16   55
22:22   107
22:27,28 88
22:28   51
25:1   178
25:2   97
25:5   87
25:11   192
25:14   70
26:2   175
26:3   76

PSALMS (cont'd)		PSALMS (cont'd)		PSALMS (cont'd)		PSALMS (cont'd)	
27:11	117	51:13	158	89:19	50	119:104	65
27:13	152	51:14	130	89:34	60	119:105	7
29:1	197	51:15	183	89:35	18	119:128	89,154
29:2	96	51:17	176	90:2	14	119:130	11
30:7	76	51:18	185	90:8	100	119:133	195
32:5	155	52:6	84	90:11	84,101,149	119:159	160
32:10	38	55:15	39	90:17	191	119:163	139
33:9	1	55:17	181	91:11	73	119:165	77
34:9	126	56:2	2	92	117	122:7	186
34:10	72	56:3	195	92:8	2	125:3	186
34:12,14	126	56:12	176	93:1	196	127:2	28
34:20	28	57:2,3	182	93:2	1,196	128:2	190
36:4	147	58:3	34	94:15	186	129:4	17
36:6	27	58:11	3	95:1	157	130:3	145
37:5	29	59:7	110	95:3	2	130:4	154,191
37:7	141	59:13	28	95:6	105	130:8	95
37:16	134	59:15	142	96:10	196	133:1	124
37:21	134	60:3	74	99:3	107	134:1	117
37:23	27	62:5	160	101:2	122	135:6	26
37:37	77	62:9	31	102:23	125	138:2	107
38:1	37	62:11	16	102:27	15	138:7	59
38:2	153	63:1	117,178	103:1	17,98	138:8	65
38:3	148	63:2	92	103:13	72	139:7	14,20
38:17	154	65:2	177	103:19	26,182	139:8	14
39:9	92	66:7	28	103:20	24,188	139:11	100
39:10	195	66:9	28	103:21	188	139:14	4
40:8	13	66:18	179	104:1	178	139:16	24
42:4	112	67:2	186	104:4	189	139:18	2
42:5	142	68:17	59	104:34	92	139:21	92
42:11	76	68:35	197	106:1	17	141:3	195
43:3	185	69:2	163	106:4	27	141:4	195 (2x)
43:4	181	69:9	183	106:5	17	143:2	192
44:20	101	69:31	157	106:24	142	144:15	2
44:24	188	72:4	190	106:33	144	145:1	182,196
45:7	45,60	73:11	99	107:22	108	145:2	111
46:10	29	73:24	79	109:18	37	145:9	17
47:2	95	73:25	2	110:1	20,59	145:10	196
47:4	141	74:18	109	111:2	24	145:17	29
49:1,2	87	74:19	190	111:9	60,182	145:19	179
49:7	42	75:1	178	115:1	67	147:5	15
49:8	50	76:10	183	115:3	181	147:19	87
49:12	26	76:11	98	115:8	19		
49:13	32	77:6	175 (2x)	115:16	133	PROVERBS	
49:14	84,85	78:32	147	116:15	78	2:1,5	12
49:17	85	78:37	99	116:16	96	2:4,5	10
50:4	86	79:9	183,192	116:17	107	2:10	66
50:5	82	80:18	97	117:2	18	3:1,2	126
50:9	14	82:5	10	118:24	113	3:6	97
50:16	109	83:16	183	119:18	10	3:31	143
50:16,17	176	83:18	20	119:28	188	3:33	38
50:20	139	84:9	192	119:29	139	4:1	121
50:22	35	84:11	67	119:36	143,188	4:3	122
50:23	196	86:5	17,192	119:49	178	4:18	75
51:3	145	86:9	98,197	119:55	182	4:23	143
51:4	155	86:11	182	119:59	156,175	5:8	131
51:5	34,153	89:6	2	119:96	7	5:11	132
51:12	192	89:7	108	119:103	159	6:6,8	190

PROVERBS (cont'd)

6:25	131
6:26	132
6:31	136
6:33	132
7:10	133
8:4	64
8:5	12
8:8,9	7
8:14	15
8:17	92,150
8:34	157
8:36	148
10:5	134
10:29	138
11:21	84
11:30	124
12:19	139
12:22	139
13:4	111
13:7	139 (2x)
13:13	10
13:20	157
13:21	35
14:25	138
14:26	72
14:30	128
14:32	83
15:1	148
15:27	143
15:30	157
16:4	23
16:9	27
16:33	22
17:9	137
18:10	107
18:14	153
18:24	124
19:3	142
19:11	193
19:12	148
19:26	125
20:17	190
20:27	4
21:6	139
21:13	135
21:17	135
21:30	16
22:6	122
22:15	36
22:26,27	135
23:1,2	127
23:5	141
23:21	111,135
23:24	122
23:26	97
23:32	128
24:3	134

PROVERBS (cont'd)

24:11	128
24:23	135
25:23	137
27:19	37
28:19	135
28:24	136
29:1	147
29:15	122
29:24	110,136
30:3	43
30:6	102
30:8	189
30:9	135
30:17	124
30:22	122
31:27	190

ECCLESIASTES

2:26	141
3:11	24
3:14	24
4:9,10	33
4:10	172
5:1	117
5:2	107,182
5:4	176
5:5	138
5:6	138
5:10	143
5:12	111
6:9	142
7:1	136
7:16	127
7:17	128
7:20	144
7:26	65
7:29	29,30
8:6	35
8:11	110
9:2	108
9:7	173
10:1	137
10:19	174
11:5	67
11:9	143
12:7	79,80
12:13	88
12:14	86

SONG OF SOLOMON

1:4	176
1:6	145
2:5	92
4:7	70
5:1	172

ISAIAH

1:2	72
1:3	7
1:5	34,154
1:12	166
1:15	179
1:18	69
1:19	67
1:27	16
2:2	185
2:3	184
3:5	125
3:12	194
6:2	189
6:3	197
6:5	65
6:9	5
6:10	10
7:14	44
7:18	24
8:17	76
8:19	18
8:20	5
9:6	51
11:3	50,60
13:8	84
14:24	23
21:12	150
25:1	22
26:4	14
26:10	147
26:11	35,143
26:13	52,97
27:13	151
28:7	8
28:10	102
28:29	15
30:1	191
30:33	84
31:5	52
32:1	51
33:24	79
34:16	8
37:29	52
38:3	145,187
38:13	142
39:8	188
40:14	15
40:15	16
40:18	13,104
41:21	16
42:4	46
42:8	95,101
42:12	183
42:17	104
42:21	56,70
43:1	67
43:22	99

ISAIAH (cont'd)

43:24,25	148
43:27	32
44:5	97
44:6	1,14
44:8	19
44:21	29,88
44:28	24
46:4	28
46:7	104
46:9,10	5
46:10	15,23 (2x)
46:12	36
48:5	104
48:8	31
48:11	107
49:23	186
49:25	52
49:26	95
50:4	48
50:11	70
51:6	71
52:13	46
53:2	53
53:3	54 (2x)
53:4	55
53:5	70
53:6	7,41
53:10	41,44
53:11	41,56
53:12	44
55:3	41
56:2	117
56:4,5	120
56:7	98
57:1	125
57:2	77,80
57:4	146
57:11	138
57:15	181
57:17	143,147
57:21	30,76
58:13	117,118 (2x)
58:14	120
59:1	16
59:2	37
60:2	197
61:10	71
63:1	42
63:5	24
63:8	138
63:10	20
63:16	181
64:5	115,148
64:6	36,70,144
64:8	180
65:3	101
65:15	149

ISAIAH (cont'd)
65:17   115
65:20   126
66:2   9
66:3   147
66:5   108
66:23   111

JEREMIAH
2:11   105
2:19   65
2:20   147
2:25   155
2:35   61
3:4   180
3:21   3
3:25   65
4:1   155
4:2   108
4:18   38
4:22   3
5:4   99
5:8   130
5:9   105
5:22   3
6:15   147
6:19   31
7:9,15   109
7:22,23   94
8:6   154
8:7   27
8:9   10
8:19   52
9:3   11
9:4   133,136
10:10   14,18
10:15   18
10:23   8,196
10:24   195
10:25   11
11:5   197
14:9   107
14:21   196
17:9   140
17:21   116
17:24,15   120
17:26   120
20:10   137
22:19   80
23:6   20
23:7   115
23:10   109
23:11   146
23:24   84
23:28   9
23:29   153
24:5   195
29:13   178

JEREMIAH (cont'd)
31:3   15
31:18   185
31:19   156
31:22   44
31:34   191
32:18   105
32:27   16
33:20   28
37:9   175
44:4   32
45:5   141
50:5   107
50:20   82
50:38   102

LAMENTATIONS
3:22   141
3:24   14
3:29   65
3:30   155
3:37   23
3:39   188
3:41   182
3:51   161
5:16   34

EZEKIEL
1:9,12   189
3:18   130
8:12   146
8:15   101,146
9:4   106
11:19   66
13:19   146
14:3   100
14:5   36
14:6   155
16:8   95
16:8,9   74
16:49,50   133
17:16   110
17:19   100
20:12   113
20:13   120
20:18,19   169
20:20   112
20:21   120
22:11   132
22:14   87
22:26   118
22:30   49
23:19   133
23:37,38   118
23:49   100
28:2   100
33:31   160
36:20   108

EZEKIEL (cont'd)
36:22   183
36:37   134
43:8   52
43:27   114
46:3   113

DANIEL
2:21   16,27
3:17   197
3:18   103
4:9   16
4:35   16,23,187
6:22   28
6:26   18
7:13   59
7:14   51
7:27   196
9:5   105
9:5,6   155
9:7   17
9:18   196
9:19   192
9:24   49
12:2   81,85

HOSEA
2:11   120
2:17   107
2:19   63
4:11   132
6:1   65
6:7   37
7:2   145
7:3   139
8:1   31
8:12   6
9:1   77,101
10:2   109
11:4   64
11:10   76
13:9   31
14:2   179
14:7   77
14:8   155

AMOS
3:3   37
3:10   11
8:5   119
8:6   134

JONAH
2:8   156
4:9   128

MICAH
2:2   140
2:8   146

MICAH (cont'd)
4:5   96,107
5:2   53
6:8   120
6:9   64
6:11   136
6:16   156
7:1   2
7:18   69
7:20   18

NAHUM
1:2   105
1:6   37

HABAKKUK
1:12   14
2:2   6,87
2:4   152
2:9   135
3:18   76

ZEPHANIAH
1:5   99
1:12   99

HAGGAI
1:9   38
2:4   14

ZECHARIAH
1:5   78
1:6   18
3:2   184
5:3   38
5:4   109
6:13   41
7:5   99
8:16   138
8:23   137
9:9   51
9:17   17,92
11:17   78
12:1   24
12:8   189
12:10   65,153,154
12:12   154
13:7   43
14:9   20

MALACHI
1:4   38
1:6   73,88
1:7   177
1:13   119
1:14   109
2:2   38
2:6   159

MALACHI (cont'd)		MATTHEW (cont'd)		MATTHEW (cont'd)		MARK (cont'd)	
2:9	103	9:6	69	22:38	91	11:10	121
2:10	73 (2x)	9:9	66	22:39	92	11:12	54
2:15	132	9:12	65	23:13	110	12:29	96
3:5	140	9:38	186	23:25	74	12:37	10
3:6	15 (2x)	10:23	127	23:26	140	12:40	146
3:8	96	10:28	2,79	23:33	84	13:32	60
3:9	149	10:29	28	24:15	10	14:22,23	173
3:17	69	10:32	82	24:20	113	14:71	144
		10:37	93	24:31	82	15:42	112
MATTHEW		11:12	150	25:10	83	16:9	114
1:18	34,45	11:29	47,51	25:23	82	16:15	170
1:23	43	12:1	118	25:32	82	16:16	162
2:6	52	12:8	114	25:35	82		
3:6	165,170	12:20	151	25:41	86 (2x)	LUKE	
3:7	165	12:24	54	25:42	86	1:17	66
3:8	165	12:26	6	25:46	86	1:33	59
3:11	162,163	12:31	146	26:26	172	1:35	34,44
3:13	163	12:36	110	26:27	173	1:46	43
3:15	163	12:37	86	26:28	44,173	1:70	45
3:16	169	12:40	57	26:29	174	1:74	95
3:17	46,163	13:7	159	26:39	179	1:76	46
4:1	194	13:42	84	26:41	194	2:7	53
4:2	44	15:6	7	26:56	56	2:10	41
4:6	194	15:8	119	26:59	56	2:11	45
4:10	102	15:9	98	26:64	59	2:13	45
4:23	48	15:19	126	27:3,5	153	2:19,51	160
5:8	83	15:26	174	27:4	130	2:21	53,166
5:16	183	16:16	42	27:26,29	56	2:49	46
5:21	129	16:25	127	27:33	55	2:52	44
5:22	130	17:5	48	27:34	55	3:12	165
5:24	193	17:21	195	27:39	55	3:21	166
5:28	31	18:8	75	27:52	81	3:38	25
5:29	87	18:10	189	27:59,60	57	4:16	9
5:37	108	18:15	137	28:1	113	4:20	160
5:45	17	18:16	58	28:2,3	58	4:22	44,48
5:48	73	18:20	20	28:6	57	7:29	163
6:4	100	18:22	193	28:11	57	7:34	54
6:6	21,177	18:24	191	28:18	51	7:41	191
6:7	180	18:29	191	28:19	21,165,170	7:42	191
6:9	180	18:33	192	28:20	52,162,164	7:47	69
6:13	180	18:35	193			8:13	194
6:14	193	19:6	121	MARK		8:18	78,160
6:15	193	19:13	167	1:1,4	163	9:58	54
6:25	126	19:19	93	1:4	164	10:25	90
6:27	142	19:28	82	1:5	166	10:26	9
6:33	180	20:16	40	1:9	170	10:27	2
6:34	190	20:22	18,163	1:15	150	10:42	78
7:2	138	20:23	62	2:27	116	11:1	179
7:6	166	21:5	51	3:5	54	11:13	5
7:9	122	21:22	178	4:33	48	12:1	109
7:12	93	21:38	146	5:36	62	13:3,5	150
7:16	6	22:3	64 (2x)	6:20	153	13:10	119
7:23	148	22:12	174	9:23	62	13:14	119
7:29	48	22:21	119	9:24	151	13:16	118
8:2	178	22:29	9	9:46	83	13:24	40
8:25	150	22:30	189	10:15	168	13:26	161
9:2	76	22:37	32	10:19	136	13:28	84
9:4	145						

LUKE (cont'd)		JOHN (cont'd)		JOHN (cont'd)		ACTS (cont'd)	
14:1	117	4:1	168	16:8	65	8:23	68
14:17	172	4:6	44	16:11	184	8:28	8
15:2	66	4:24	13	16:13	48	8:34	159
15:13	135	4:29	154	16:14,15	65	8:36	165
15:17	155	5:17	13	16:23	178	8:37	151
15:18	73	5:22	81	16:29	48	8:38	169
15:21	178	5:26	18	17:2	41	9:4	157
16:1	136	5:27	51	17:3	18	9:6	65
16:23	83	5:28	85	17:4	46 (2x)	9:15	40
16:25	84	5:29	85	17:6	41,106	9:25	188
16:26	82	5:36	47	17:8	47	9:26	171
16:31	13	5:37	13	17:9	50	9:31	171
17:5	77	5:39	9 (2x)	17:12	41	10:33	9
17:10	13	6:27	46,143	17:13	51,77	10:36	133
17:17	55	6:34	190	17:17	74	10:40	58
17:20	67	6:37	40,64	17:21	21	10:47	165
17:21	184	6:45	66	17:23	62	11:18	153
18:1	177	6:55	173	19:17	56	11:23	152
18:13	192	6:57	173	20:19	114 (2x)	11:24	151
19:8	155	6:63	61	20:26	114 (2x)	12:12	182
19:46	177	6:66	55	20:31	48	12:22	100
19:48	159	6:69	66	21:17	20	13:27	9,117
20:13	42	7:10	54			13:41	110
22:19	161	7:12	54	**ACTS**		13:42	10
22:20	173	7:18	36	1:2	58	13:44	117
22:24	125	8:34	30	1:3	57,58	13:46	10
22:32	51	8:44	129,139	1:9	58 (2x)	13:48	157
22:36	127	8:46	54	1:11	59	14:15	103
22:44	55,195	8:47	9	1:17	162	14:17	5,28
22:53	55	8:58	20	2:1	115	14:27	171
23:4	56	10:16	41	2:4	162	15:1	167
23:31	57	10:18	50	2:23	22,130	15:10	88
24:14	117	10:26	62,157	2:24	57	15:18	15
24:26	58	10:29	19	2:37	151,164,165	15:19,28	167
24:30	189	10:30	19	2:38	164	15:21	9
24:39	44,58	10:31	54	2:39	168	16:13	117
24:46	53	11:26	150	2:41	165,171,174	16:28	127
24:51	59	11:33	54	2:41,42	156	16:29	65
		11:42	50	2:46,47	176	16:31	150
JOHN		11:52	42	3:15	57	16:34	97,168
1:3	20	12:27	55	3:23	48	16:40	168
1:11	55	12:28	183 (2x)	4:12	42	17:7	51
1:12	61	13:2	55,194	4:19	88	17:11	8
1:14	42,43 (2x)	13:12	175	5:3,4	20	17:18	159
1:17	47,91	13:34	93	5:4	141	17:22	104
1:25	163	13:35	94	5:31	46,153	17:23	102
1:33	163	14:1	151 (2x)	6:11,13	140	17:24	24
1:41	45	14:2	83	7:38	91	17:26	25
2:19	58	14:16	181	7:48	181	17:27	4,14
3:2	47	14:19	63	7:53	91	17:28	1,27
3:6	168	14:26	20	7:59	21	17:29	104
3:18	62,150	14:27	76	8:3	171	17:30	150
3:22,23	163	14:30	45	8:12	166	17:31	60
3:23	169	15:5	150	8:13	165	17:32	158
3:26	170	15:8	98	8:13,23	162	18:8	165,168
3:27	61	15:15	47	8:20	135	19:4	163
3:34	46	15:16	40	8:21	61		
3:36	35,61			8:22	177		

ACTS (cont'd)

19:13	108
19:27	102
20:7	114
20:21	150
20:24	103
20:27	87
20:31	158
20:32	158
20:33	140
21:14	187
22:16	164
23:16	128
24:15	85
26:8	81
26:26	7
26:29	185

ROMANS

1:9	14
1:16	158
1:19	4
1:20	3,4
1:21	3
1:23	104
1:25	103
1:26	38
1:31	10,125
2:4	17,155
2:5	110,153
2:9	87
2:11	86
2:12	89
2:14	89
2:15	89
2:16	86
2:18	31
2:25	161
2:28,29	161
3:3	18
3:4	18
3:5	17
3:8	139,149
3:9	34
3:17	8
3:20	64
3:22	62
3:24	69
3:25	17,71
3:26	56
3:27	71
3:29	95
3:31	90
4:6	71
4:11	161,167
4:15	31
4:16	71

ROMANS (cont'd)

4:20	152
5:1	71
5:2	77
5:6	34
5:9	42
5:11	71
5:12	33,34(2x)
5:14	30,35
5:17	43,56,71,151
5:18	33
5:19	35,70
5:21	70
6:2	154
6:3	163,164
6:4	164
6:6	56,164
6:9	58
6:13	164
6:15	67,89
6:19	36
6:23	39
7:6	156
7:7	90
7:9	64,153
7:12	89
7:14	140,145
7:15	154,188
7:18	36 (2x)
7:24	35
8:1	68
8:3	56
8:7	36 (2x)
8:9	48
8:11	81
8:12	12
8:13	75
8:15	153,181
8:16	76
8:17	68
8:20	35
8:28	27
8:29	72 (2x)
8:30	64,68
8:33	69
8:38	80
9:1	6
9:5	20,43
9:7	167
9:8	167
9:11	39
9:14	17
9:15	40
9:20	22
9:23	22
9:27	39
10:1	186

ROMANS (cont'd)

10:3	70
10:10	151,174
10:12	68
10:14	3
10:17	158
10:18	7
10:21	48
11:6	69
11:7	40,61
11:8	38
11:29	15
11:33	15,29
11:34	22
11:35	1
12:1	88
12:2	188
12:11	75,134
12:16	124
12:18	128
12:19	128
13:7	121,134
13:8	134
13:10	92
13:13	133,143
14:1	175
14:4	78
14:8	127
14:9	184
14:17	184
14:22	118
15:2	124
15:4	76
15:5	180
15:6	171
15:13	76
16:20	185

1 CORINTHIANS

1:2	67,68,168
1:9	63
1:21	5
1:25	15
1:30	73
2:4	7,158
2:5	7
2:8	54
2:9	92
2:10	20
2:13	159
2:14	4
3:5	162
3:7	162
3:11	61
3:22	68
4:2	134
4:5	85

1 CORINTH. (cont'd)

4:15	121
4:16	114
4:20	184
5:1	147
5:5	171
5:8	176
5:11	132,174
6:7	136
6:9	100,109
6:15	62,132
6:17	62
6:18	128
6:19	96
6:20	87,98
7:9	132
7:14	168
7:16	123
7:33,34	123
8:4	19
8:5	19
8:6	1,19
9:21	89
9:27	131
10:1,2	170
10:6	143
10:7	99
10:12	31
10:13	194
10:15	12
10:16	104,173 (2x)
10:17	174
10:20	100
10:22	16
10:31	183
11:1	8
11:2	89
11:8	26
11:9	26
11:14	4
11:16	115
11:18,20	176
11:20	172
11:22	176
11:23	89,172 (2x)
11:24	173 (3x)
11:25	172
11:26	173,174
11:27	177
11:28	175
11:29	175
11:30	177
11:31	177
12:13	162,164
13:2	176
13:5	93,137
13:7	175

1 CORINTH. (cont'd)		2 CORINTH. (cont'd)		EPHESIANS (cont'd)		COLOSSIANS (cont'd)	
13:10	75	13:5	176	2:13	37	1:13	184
13:12	79	13:14	21	2:18	21	1:19	173
13:13	94			2:23	63	1:21	44
14:6	8	GALATIANS		3:10,11	22	1:27	61
14:15	178 (2x)	1:2	171	3:11	37	2:5	171
14:16	197	1:8	8	3:16	98	2:6	61,152
14:24	153	1:15	63	3:21	197	2:9	44
15:1	66	1:16	13	4:1	63	2:10	145
15:2	161	2:16	70	4:5	170	2:12	161,164,170
15:4	56,57	2:19	90	4:6	14,180	2:13	191
15:5	58	2:20	75	4:7	62	2:14	166 (2x)
15:20	58	3:2	160	4:8	42	2:15	52
15:25	53	3:10	149	4:10	58	2:18	5,103
15:34	3	3:12	29	4:11	52	2:20	156
15:37,38,42	81	3:13	42,54,55	4:11,12	157	2:21,22	104
15:43	81	3:19	89	4:15	77	3:1	59
15:44	81	3:24	90	4:18	4,30	3:5	100,132,133
15:45	25	3:26	68	4:23	74	3:9	138
15:49	34	3:27	163	4:24	26	3:10	26,74
15:50	186	3:29	167	4:28	189	3:11	46
15:51	82	4:3	11,88	4:29	31,131	3:13	192
15:53	81	4:4	45,53	5:1	119	3:16	157
15:55	80	4:5	41,72	5:3	133,143	3:21	122
15:56	39	4:6	72	5:4	133	3:22	122
16:1,2	115	4:7	72	5:22	123	3:25	86
16:15	168	4:8	19	6:1	121	4:1	123
		4:10,11	111	6:9	123	4:16	9
2 CORINTHIANS		4:12	193	6:18	177,182		
1:10	195	4:19	75			1 THESSALONIANS	
1:12	76	4:24	90	PHILIPPIANS		1:5	64
1:24	77,152	5:1	89	1:9	92	1:9	97
3:6	5	5:3	54	1:10	187	1:10	95
3:12	11	5:6	152	1:11	183	2:12	63
4:3	11	5:13	118	1:20	183	2:14	115
4:6	65	5:17	37,145	1:21	78	2:16	87
4:14	81	5:21	41	1:29	151	2:18	184
4:18	142	5:24	75	2:5	119	3:10	145
5:2	187	6:1	175	2:7	44,53 (2x)	4:3	73,131
5:8	79	6:9	13	2:8	55	4:4	131
5:14	49,156	6:14	57	2:8,9	51	4:6	134
5:17	74			2:12	150	4:7	67
5:18	1	EPHESIANS		2:13	66	4:11	134
5:21	144	1:3	14,41	3:8	66,152	4:14	80
6:10	68	1:4	22,40	3:9	70	4:16	81
6:14	37	1:5	72	3:12	75	4:17	83
6:17	171	1:5,6	72	3:16	8	4:18	83
7:1	36,131	1:6	22,69	3:19	100,147	5:2	60
7:9	154	1:7	69,191	3:21	81	5:3	83
7:10	129,153	1:8	15,71	4:7	77	5:9	40
7:11	153	1:9	40	4:8	137,138	5:15	120,124
7:21	155	1:11	22	4:11	141	5:16	77
8:5	2,171	1:13	152	4:13	151	5:17	179
10:5	66	1:19	61	4:19	189	5:23	145,186
10:17	197	2:2	38,184				
11:3	33,194	2:3	37	COLOSSIANS		2 THESSALONIANS	
12:8	95	2:10	22	1:6	66	1:3	77
12:20	125	2:12	12,167	1:11	188	1:6	39,86

2 THESS. (cont'd)
2:4   100,185
2:9   185
2:10   160
2:11   38
2:13   40 (2x),74
2:14   63
2:17   186
3:1   186
3:10   111

1 TIMOTHY
1:5   90
1:8   90
1:9   90
1:10   130,136
1:13   11,64
1:15   40,151
1:17   16
1:20   146
2:1   178
2:5   43,50
2:13   26
3:16   43
4:2   38
4:3   132
4:5   190
4:8   67 (2x)
4:10   7,27
4:11   158
4:13   11
5:4   122
5:13   111
5:23   127
6:1   122
6:2   123
6:3   71
6:11   143
6:12   97
6:13   18
6:16   13
6:18   134

2 TIMOTHY
1:9   63
1:10   47
1:12   152
1:13   21
1:14   103
2:15   158
2:19   40 (2x)
3:5   74
3:15   11 (2x)
3:16   5,6,12

TITUS
1:1   151
1:2   83
1:15   36

TITUS (cont'd)
1:16   99,188
2:1   158
2:9   123
2:10   122
2:12   121
2:13   60,187
2:14   42,74
3:3   42
3:5   62
3:7   69
3:8   12

HEBREWS
1:3   26,42
1:10   24
1:13   159
2:3   150
2:4   7
2:11   49
2:14   56
2:15   39
2:16   45
2:17   44,50
2:18   54
3:1   46
3:2   46
3:4   21
3:5   47
3:14   61
4:3   67
4:4   114
4:9   112
4:10   114
4:11   112
4:12   12,158
4:14   49 (2x)
4:16   51
5:1   47
5:4   49
6:1   174
6:6   173
6:8   149
6:11   76
6:16   108
7:12   88
7:15   49
7:20   49
7:21   49
7:24   43
7:25   50,66
7:26   45 (2x),49
8:1   59
8:6   30
8:12   69
9:10   88 (2x)
9:11   49
9:12   61

9:14   20,45
9:22   49
9:23   50
9:24   46
9:26   50
9:27   83
10:5   44
10:7   41
10:10   55
10:12   50,59
10:14   70
10:21   49
10:22   74,169
10:24   172
10:25   117
10:27   84
10:37   59
10:39   78,151
11:3   12,25
11:6   2
11:11   18
12:2   55
12:4   75
12:5   73,187
12:6   52,73
12:9   13,121
12:14   68
12:21   91
12:22,23   79
12:23   79,170
12:25   48
12:28   91
13:1   93
13:4   132
13:5   141
13:17   123
13:21   188

JAMES
1:5   16
1:14   194
1:15   40
1:17   15
1:18   67
1:21   10
1:25   161
2:3   125
2:7   109
2:11   148
2:19   3
3:2   156
3:10   109
4:3   179
4:7   32,97
4:11   140
4:12   16
4:15   187
4:17   147

JAMES (cont'd)
5:9   193
5:12   109
5:16   93
5:13   177

1 PETER
1:6   195
1:8   77
1:14   73
1:17   181
1:18,19   61
1:20   46
1:23   7
2:1   159
2:2   159
2:5   98
2:9   63
2:11   132
2:17   123
2:18   123
2:22   45,70
2:24   75
2:25   155
3:2   131
3:7   33
3:9   139
3:18   46
3:19   48
3:21   162,166
4:1   56
4:8   93
4:11   182
4:14   137
5:1   187
5:2   123
5:4   80
5:7   190
5:8   194
5:10   195

2 PETER
1:1   62,152
1:2   12
1:4   72
1:6   120
1:7   73
1:10   63
1:12   78
1:14   78
1:16   6
1:19   5,8
1:21   6 (2x)
2:1   99
2:9   85
2:14   133
3:12   60
3:16   10,11
3:18   77

1 JOHN
1:3	6
1:5	13
1:7	164
1:8	34
1:9	69
2:1	50 (2x)
2:2	191
2:7	66
2:16	194
2:25	126
3:1	68
3:2	83
3:4	31
3:9	78
3:15	129,130
3:16	93
3:18	93
3:21	77
4:3	43
4:10	71
4:16	76
4:19	1
4:21	93
5:3	92,119
5:4	152
5:7	19,20
5:10	7
5:14	178
5:17	32
5:19	36
5:20	18
5:21	19

3 JOHN
ver. 2	127
ver. 3	138
ver. 12	137

JUDE
ver. 1	52,63
ver. 4	22,99
ver. 10	89
ver. 14	82
ver, 15	85,86
ver. 16	142
ver. 21	93,152

REVELATION
1:1	6
1:3	9
1:4	21
1:7	60
1:10	115 (2x)
1:11	171
1:18	58
2:4	78,99
2:24	194

REVELATION (cont'd)
2:29	11
3:1	61
3:3	160
3:7	18
3:8	107
4:8	3,17
4:11	23
5:6	51
5:9	40,70
5:14	197
6:9	7
6:10	185
6:16	86
6:17	86
7:14	79
7:15	80
9:11	33
9:20	102
11:15	186
12:10	79
12:11	129
12:12	149
13:2	185
14:5	79,144
14:7	112
14:10	87
14:11	87
14:13	79
15:3	52
16:14	85
18:2	185
19:1,2	82
19:6	29
19:10	21,47
19:16	28
20:2	32,149
20:6	81
20:12	86
21:23	79
21:27	73
22:12	52
22:15	139
22:18	7
22:20	187

Other Solid Ground Titles

In addition to the volume which you hold in your hand, Solid Ground is honored to offer many other uncovered treasure, many for the first time in more than a century:

THE CHILD AT HOME by John S.C. Abbott

THE KING'S HIGHWAY: *The 10 Commandments for the Young* by Richard Newton

HEROES OF THE REFORMATION by Richard Newton

FEED MY LAMBS: *Lectures to Children on Vital Subjects* by John Todd

LET THE CANNON BLAZE AWAY by Joseph P. Thompson

THE STILL HOUR: *Communion with God in Prayer* by Austin Phelps

COLLECTED WORKS of James Henley Thornwell (4 vols.)

CALVINISM IN HISTORY *by Nathaniel S. McFetridge*

OPENING SCRIPTURE: *Hermeneutical Manual by Patrick Fairbairn*

THE ASSURANCE OF FAITH *by Louis Berkhof*

THE PASTOR IN THE SICK ROOM *by John D. Wells*

THE BUNYAN OF BROOKLYN: *Life & Sermons of I.S. Spencer*

THE NATIONAL PREACHER: *Sermons from 2nd Great Awakening*

FIRST THINGS: *First Lessons God Taught Mankind Gardiner Spring*

BIBLICAL & THEOLOGICAL STUDIES *by 1912 Faculty of Princeton*

THE POWER OF GOD UNTO SALVATION *by B.B. Warfield*

THE LORD OF GLORY *by B.B. Warfield*

A GENTLEMAN & A SCHOLAR: *Memoir of J.P. Boyce by J. Broadus*

SERMONS TO THE NATURAL MAN *by W.G.T. Shedd*

SERMONS TO THE SPIRITUAL MAN *by W.G.T. Shedd*

HOMILETICS AND PASTORAL THEOLOGY *by W.G.T. Shedd*

A PASTOR'S SKETCHES 1 & 2 *by Ichabod S. Spencer*

THE PREACHER AND HIS MODELS *by James Stalker*

IMAGO CHRISTI: *The Example of Jesus Christ by James Stalker*

A HISTORY OF PREACHING *by Edwin C. Dargan*

LECTURES ON THE HISTORY OF PREACHING *by J. A. Broadus*

THE SCOTTISH PULPIT *by William Taylor*

THE SHORTER CATECHISM ILLUSTRATED *by John Whitecross*

THE CHURCH MEMBER'S GUIDE *by John Angell James*

THE SUNDAY SCHOOL TEACHER'S GUIDE *by John A. James*

CHRIST IN SONG: *Hymns of Immanuel from All Ages by Philip Schaff*

COME YE APART: *Daily Words from the Four Gospels by J.R. Miller*

DEVOTIONAL LIFE OF THE S.S. TEACHER *by J.R. Miller*

Call us Toll Free at 1-877-666-9469

Send us an e-mail at sgcb@charter.net

Visit us on line at solid-ground-books.com

Uncovering Buried Treasure to the Glory of God